How Microsoft® Windows Vista™ Works

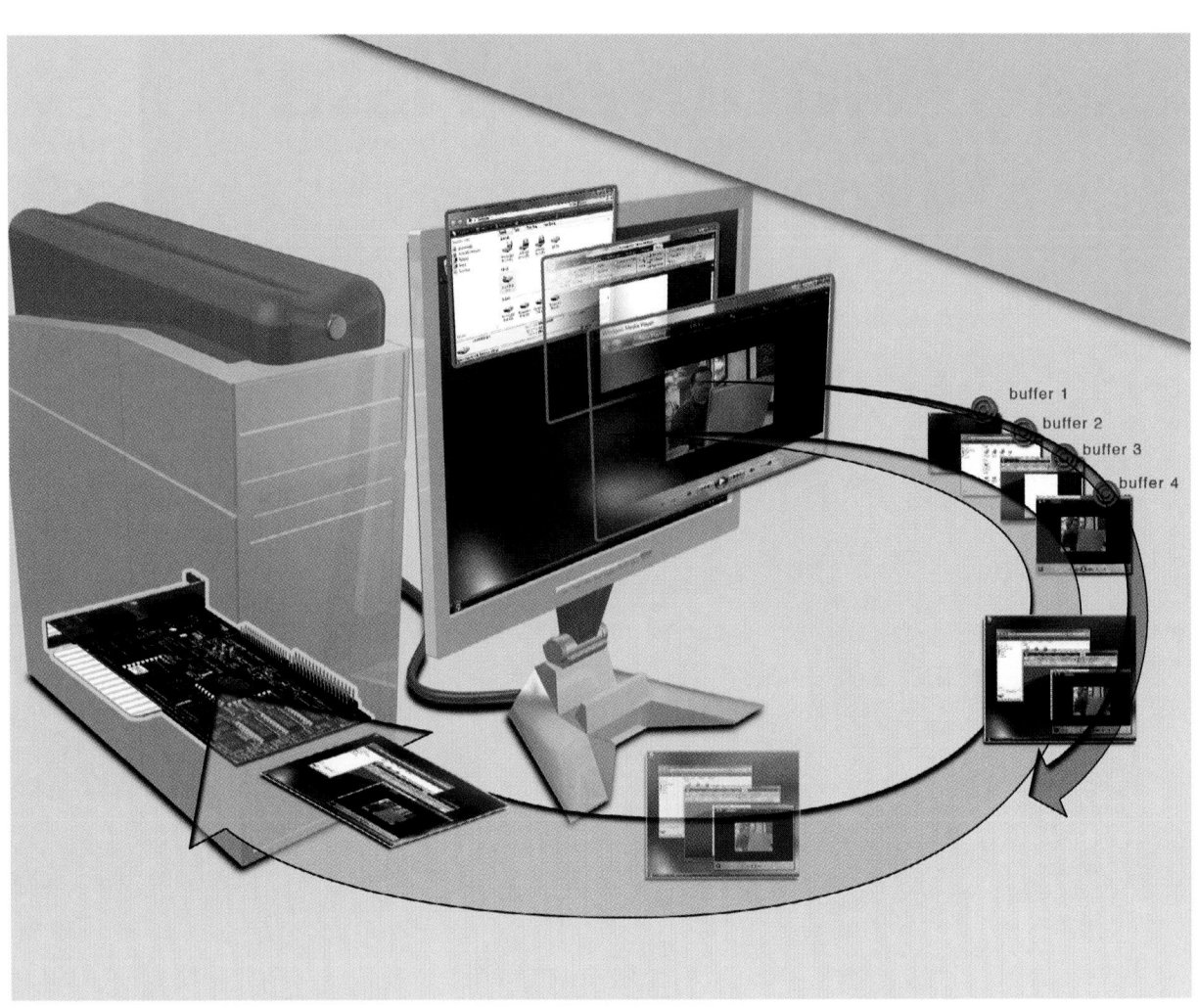

buffer 1
buffer 2
buffer 3
buffer 4

How Microsoft® Windows Vista™ Works

Michael Miller

Illustrations by Eric Lindley

800 East 96th Street
Indianapolis, IN 46240 USA

How Microsoft Windows Vista Works
Copyright © 2007 by Que Publishing

Associate Publisher	Greg Wiegand	Copy Editor	Rhonda Tinch-Mize
Executive Editor	Rick Kughen	Proofreader	Leslie Joseph
Development Editor	Todd Brakke	Senior Indexer	Cheryl Lenser
Technical Editor	Mark Edward Soper	Publishing Coordinator	Cindy Teeters
Illustrators	Eric Lindley, Seth Lindley	Interior Designer	Anne Jones
Managing Editor	Gina Kanouse	Cover Designers	Anne Jones
Project Editor	Lori Lyons	Page Layout	Nonie Ratcliff

International Standard Book Number 0-7897-3585-7

Printed in the United States of America

First Printing: December 2006

10   09   08   07   4   3   2   1

Trademarks

All terms mentioned in this book that are known to be trademarks or service marks have been appropriately capitalized. Que Publishing cannot attest to the accuracy of this information. Use of a term in this book should not be regarded as affecting the validity of any trademark or service mark.

Microsoft and Windows are registered trademarks and Vista is a trademark of Microsoft Corporation.

Warning and Disclaimer

Every effort has been made to make this book as complete and as accurate as possible, but no warranty or fitness is implied. The information provided is on an "as is" basis. The authors and the publisher shall have neither liability nor responsibility to any person or entity with respect to any loss or damages arising from the information contained in this book.

Bulk Sales

Que Publishing offers excellent discounts on this book when ordered in quantity for bulk purchases or special sales. For more information, please contact

U.S. Corporate and Government Sales
1-800-382-3419
corpsales@pearsontechgroup.com

For sales outside the United States, please contact

International Sales
international@pearsoned.com

 **This Book Is Safari Enabled**

The Safari® Enabled icon on the cover of your favorite technology book means the book is available through Safari Bookshelf. When you buy this book, you get free access to the online edition for 45 days.

Safari Bookshelf is an electronic reference library that lets you easily search thousands of technical books, find code samples, download chapters, and access technical information whenever and wherever you need it.

To gain 45-day Safari Enabled access to this book:
- Go to http://www.quepublishing.com/safarienabled
- Complete the brief registration form
- Enter the coupon code D1QF-P7NQ-EWM2-Q2P5-81CI

If you have difficulty registering on Safari Bookshelf or accessing the online edition, please e-mail customer-service@safaribooksonline.com.

Library of Congress Cataloging-in-Publication Data

Miller, Michael, 1958-
  How Windows Vista works / Michael Miller ; Illustrations by Eric Lindley.
     p. cm.
  ISBN 0-7897-3585-7
  1. Microsoft Windows (Computer file) 2. Operating systems (Computers) I. Title.
  QA76.76.O63M562165 2007
  005.4'46—dc22
                              2006038441

To Sherry, always and forever.
—Michael Miller

To my son, Seth, for being here and helping with the book. You have talent!
—Eric Lindley

About the Author and Illustrator

MICHAEL MILLER has authored more than 75 best-selling books over the past 15 years, including *Absolute Beginner's Guide to Computer Basics*, *Microsoft Windows XP for Home Users*, *Making a Living from Your eBay Business*, *Googlepedia: The Ultimate Google Resource*, and *How Home Theater and HDTV Work*. Mr. Miller has established a reputation for clearly explaining technical topics to non-technical readers and for offering useful, real-world advice about complicated topics. More information can be found at the author's website, located at www.molehillgroup.com.

ERIC LINDLEY is recognized as an innovative illustrator and photographer infusing realism into his distinctive style of digital imagery. His work has appeared in collateral for editorial, corporate, and publishing clients throughout the United States. With an inquisitive mind and an array of digital experiences, he continues to stay on the leading edge of technology and develop his vision for an ever expanding global market. His work has appeared in this series of "How To" books, including titles *How Personal & Internet Security Work* and *How Wireless Works*.

Acknowledgments

Michael Miller would like to thank the usual suspects at Que, including but not limited to Rick Kughen, Greg Wiegand, Todd Brakke, Lori Lyons, Daniel Knott, Rhonda Tinch-Mize, Nonie Ratcliff, and our technical editor, Mark Edward Soper. My special thanks go to my collaborator Eric Lindley, who supplied the amazingly detailed and beautiful illustrations that make this book what it is.

Eric Lindley would like to thank his wife Patty for her support and understanding during the months it took to complete a project as extensive as this. A special thanks goes out to Miranda and Sophia, who ran a small business catering snacks to their dad to keep the creative wheels moving. The apple peanut snack was the best. This book would not be the same without the skillful talent of Seth Lindley, who developed the majority of the detailed models. Keep pushing your ideas and let them take you to new experiences. They say that it takes a village to raise a child: I am convinced that it takes a family to illustrate a book. Thanks go to the author, Mike Miller, for making this book a challenging project that I am proud to be a part of.

We Want to Hear from You!

As the reader of this book, *you* are our most important critic and commentator. We value your opinion and want to know what we're doing right, what we could do better, what areas you'd like to see us publish in, and any other words of wisdom you're willing to pass our way.

As an executive editor for Que Publishing, I welcome your comments. You can email or write me directly to let me know what you did or didn't like about this book—as well as what we can do to make our books better.

Please note that I cannot help you with technical problems related to the topic of this book. We do have a User Services group, however, where I will forward specific technical questions related to the book.

When you write, please be sure to include this book's title and author as well as your name, email address, and phone number. I will carefully review your comments and share them with the author and editors who worked on the book.

Email: feedback@quepublishing.com

Mail: Rick Kughen
            Executive Editor
            Que Publishing
            800 East 96th Street
            Indianapolis, IN 46240 USA

For more information about this book or another Que Publishing title, visit our website at www.quepublishing.com. Type the ISBN (excluding hyphens) or the title of a book in the Search field to find the page you're looking for.

Introduction

Five years in the making, and here it is—another new version of Microsoft Windows.

Windows Vista is the latest in a long line of Windows operating systems, carrying the tradition first started in 1985 with the appropriately named Windows 1.0. That first version of Windows is only vaguely familiar to today's users, as Microsoft has made a lot of improvements since those humble beginnings. Of course, a lot besides Windows has changed in the past twenty years; the one constant is that a Microsoft operating system remains the face of personal computing.

It's that face users will first notice when they power on a PC running Windows Vista. Put simply, Vista looks different from previous versions of Windows. Oh, there are the expected windows and icons and taskbars and the ever-present Start menu, but they're a lot fancier in Vista than they were in Windows XP or prior operating systems. That's because Vista uses a totally new graphics engine—one that harnesses the massive graphics processing power of today's PCs to create a three-dimensional desktop with glass-like windows and sophisticated animation effects. It still looks like Windows, but it's more lifelike, if such a thing can be said.

The improvements in Vista don't stop with the interface. There are a lot of new or improved utilities to be found on the Start menu, including some fairly major changes in Internet Explorer and Windows Media Player. And then there are all the changes behind-the-scenes, where Vista has been beefed up, made faster and more dependable, and given increased security against viruses, spyware, and other forms of computer attack. You won't notice a lot of changes, except in the form of fewer crashes and less worry about malicious intrusions.

As is the case anytime Microsoft releases a new version of its core operating system, there is a lot of interest about the new features in Windows Vista—what they are and how they work. That is where this book comes in. *How Windows Vista Works* is a descriptive title for a book that both shows you what's new and improved in Vista and gets "under the hood" to illustrate what does what and how.

And I do mean "shows you." What's unique about this book is that it doesn't offer the typical text-based descriptions of the topics at hand; instead, it shows you what you want to know, via a series of detailed four-color illustrations. Want to know what the Aero interface looks like? Curious about how Internet Explorer protects against phishing scams? Well, this book answers all those questions and more, *visually*. It's the kind of sophisticated visual approach that is required to explain a sophisticated visual operating system.

To make it easier to find what you're interested in, this book is divided into 20 separate chapters, organized into 6 major sections. It's easy to go directly to any given topic; you can skip around as you like or read the book from front to back—whichever works best for you.

Part I, "What Vista Is—and What It Does," explains just what it is that an operating system does, as well as how Windows Vista is similar to—and differs from—previous versions of Windows and other operating systems. Turn here to discover all the new features of Windows Vista.

Part II, "Basic Operations," gets down to the nitty-gritty of how Windows Vista controls your computer hardware and software. You'll learn how Vista manages system resources, system settings, user accounts, data, and applications.

Part III, "Windows Vista Graphics," turns a sharp eye to what makes Vista look as good as it does. You'll learn all about the Vista Aero interface, Windows Flip3D task switching, the Sidebar and Sidebar gadgets, as well as how to personalize the Vista desktop.

Part IV, "Digital Media," is all about music, movies, and photos. As a bonus, you'll learn about Windows Media Center, the so-called "ten-foot interface" that's now built into Windows Vista.

Part V, "Networking and the Internet," shows you how Vista goes online and connects with other computers. A lot of new Internet-related features are included in Vista, and they're all covered here—including tabbed browsing in Internet Explorer, a new pop-up blocker and anti-phishing filter, an integrated RSS feed reader, browser-based search, and new Windows Mail and Windows Calendar applications.

Finally, Part VI, "Security and Maintenance," covers what makes Windows Vista more secure—and more reliable. You'll learn about Windows Service Hardening, the Windows Firewall, the new Windows Defender anti-spyware utility, and a lot more. And you'll rediscover the Windows Backup utility, back for all to use with a lot of useful new features.

By the time you're done reading this book, you'll be acquainted with all the new features of Windows Vista and have a much better understanding about how they all work. If you're already a Vista user, you'll have a greater appreciation of how the operating system does what it does. And if you're not yet a Vista user, I guarantee that you will be soon—there's a lot to like about Windows Vista, as you'll see in the pages of this book!

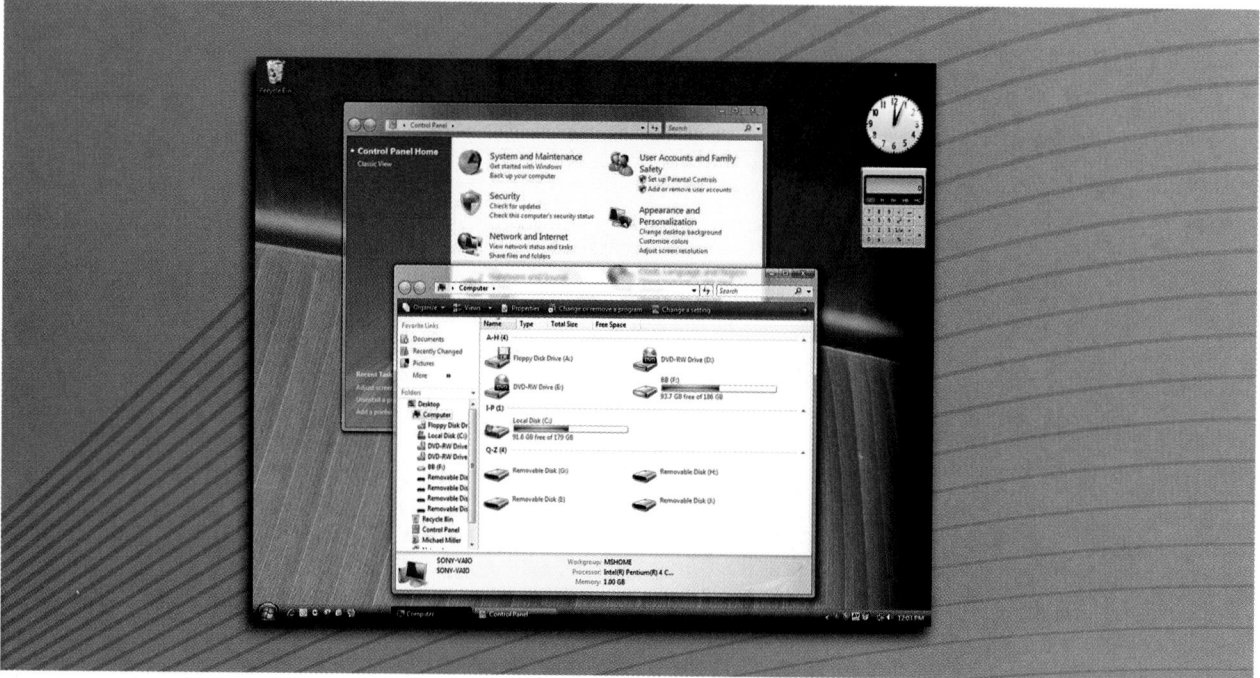

P A R T

WHAT WINDOWS VISTA IS—AND WHAT IT DOES

WHAT Is Windows Vista?

At its most basic, Windows Vista is an operating system for personal computers and servers. Like all operating systems, Vista serves as the interface between your computer software and hardware, and provides a means for you to control and manage basic computer operations, such as copying files and burning CDs.

That's not an adequate description, however, since practically any operating system—from DOS to Linux—performs those same functions. That is, after all, what an operating system does; it's a system that operates your computer.

It is more useful, perhaps, to compare Windows Vista with previous versions of Windows. That way, you can get a sense of what makes Vista unique and why you probably want to use it on your own PCs.

Chances are, you already have some version of Windows installed on your PC: Windows XP, perhaps, or maybe Windows 2000. A quick look at Windows Vista seems to suggest that there aren't a lot of differences between Vista and older versions of Windows. Windows is Windows, after all; it's an operating system that you use to run programs and control your computer. To that end, Vista does pretty much the same things that Windows XP or Windows 2000 did.

On closer inspection, however, there's a world of difference between Vista and all older versions of Windows. Even the most jaded user can see that Vista looks different; sure, there's still a taskbar and Start menu at the bottom of the screen, but these items simply look cooler in Vista. That's because of Vista's new Aero user interface, which displays true 3D elements with a see-through, glass-like look. And everything else in Vista looks a bit different, too—folder and file icons now show thumbnails of their contents, as do the program buttons on the Windows taskbar; the Start menu is a lot more streamlined, especially if you have a lot of programs installed; when you switch between open applications, the windows twist and turn to display in a three-dimensional stack; and the windows themselves are smoother and rounder and translucent, heightening the sense of depth when you view multiple windows onscreen.

These visual changes are just the surface of what's new in Windows Vista. Under the hood, Vista is designed to run more securely and more robustly. All sorts of new precautions are built into the operating system to protect your computer from spyware and other malicious code, and to protect you from falling victim to misleading phishing schemes. The new User Account Control function makes it more difficult for you to install dangerous programs on your PC, while Windows Service Hardening ensures that different internal services run isolated from each other, reducing the chances for system crash. And SuperFetch technology automatically pre-loads frequently used applications into your system's memory so that they start quicker.

Vista is also easier to use than past versions of Windows. Just about everywhere you turn, there's an Instant Search box to help you find files and data anywhere on your hard disk. The Address Bar in Windows Explorer (yes, Windows Explorer is back!) lets you leave "breadcrumbs" of past locations you've visited, to better find your way around your hard disk. And wireless networking—networking of any sort, in fact—is a lot easier to accomplish and manage than in the past.

There are also a lot of new applications that come bundled with Windows Vista. Internet Explorer 7 offers tabbed web pages in the browser; Windows Mail replaces Outlook Express; Windows Calendar helps you manage your schedule and appointments, and even share your calendars with other users; and Windows Movie Maker is now available in a high definition version. In addition, the new Windows Photo Gallery offers fairly robust digital photo editing, Windows Media Player 11 is a much improved version from what you're used to, and Vista now comes with Windows Media Center as an optional operating environment—great if you use your PC to drive your home theater system.

Of course, not all these features are available in all versions of Vista. That's right, Microsoft is marketing multiple versions of the new operating system, each with a slightly different feature set. For example, the Windows Vista Home Basic edition, which is included with many low-priced PCs, doesn't come with Windows DVD Maker, Windows Media Center, or the full Aero user interface. The Business and Enterprise editions also skip DVD Maker and Media Center, but include the Aero interface and some enterprise-oriented features, such as system image-based backup and BitLocker drive encryption. And the Vista Ultimate edition includes all the goodies from all the other versions—it's a complete superset of all Vista features.

If you start with a less-featured version of Windows Vista, Microsoft graciously and easily lets you upgrade to any higher-priced version. You don't even have to buy another software package; all the versions of Vista are included in the basic package, just waiting to be unlocked. The Windows Anytime Upgrade lets you purchase your upgrade online, and then immediately upgrade the version of Vista installed on your PC. So if you find yourself wanting more features than you initially have, there's more Vista available.

In short, there's a lot that's new about Windows Vista—both on and below the surface. If you're an experienced Windows user, you'll find Vista both familiar and sometimes frustratingly different; over time, however, you'll come to appreciate the new features and improved operation. But that's why you're reading this book—to learn all about what's new and different in this new version of your favorite operating system. So let's start with a look back, and see how Microsoft got from DOS to Vista, in just 20 short years.

CHAPTER

1

Understanding Windows and Other Operating Systems

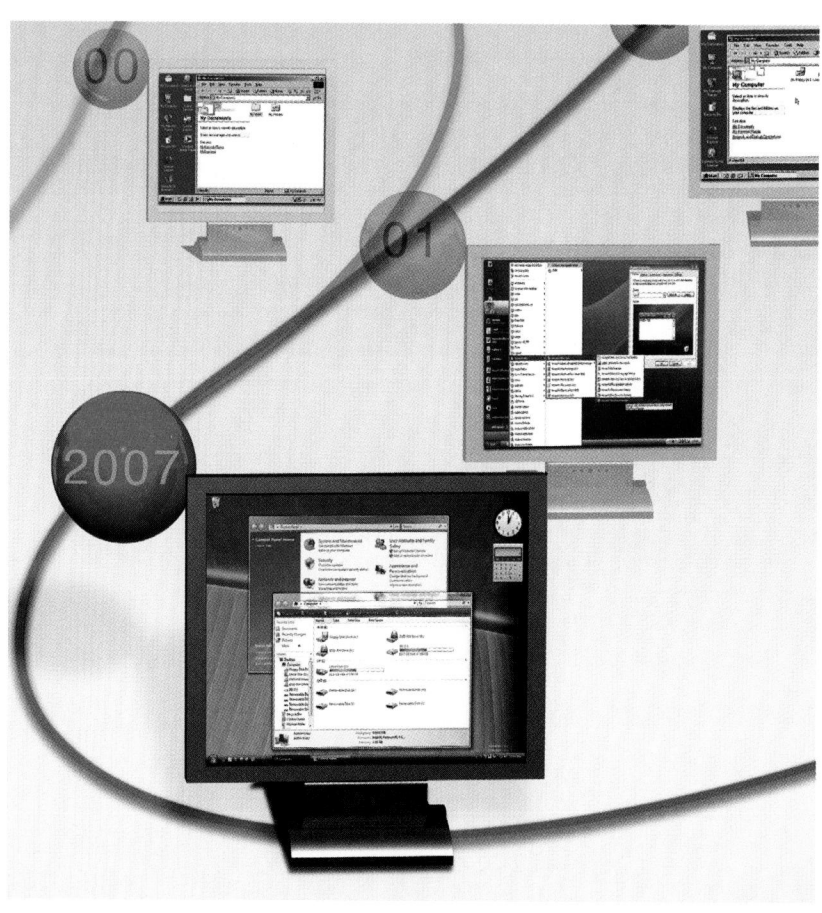

WINDOWS has a history.

It's been more than 20 years since Microsoft released the first version of Windows, and almost 15 years since Windows began to dominate the personal computer desktop. Of course, given all the technological changes that have occurred in the past 20 years, today's version of Windows bears only a passing resemblance to Windows 1.0. And that's a good thing.

That first version of Windows was pretty rudimentary. Yes, it was a tad easier on the eyes than the then-reigning DOS operating system, but it wasn't any easier to use. In fact, if you didn't have a mouse—which few users did back in 1985—it was actually harder to use than DOS's command-line interface.

DOS—the generic name for the almost-identical MS-DOS and PC DOS operating systems—was how most first-generation PC users learned to use their computers. DOS required users to memorize a series of obscure commands, and use those commands to perform most day-to-day operations, such as copying files, changing directories, and so forth. The chief advantage of DOS was its speed and small operating footprint; both important issues when most computers only had 640KB memory.

Windows was a step beyond the simple command-line interface. Building on work conducted at Xerox PARC labs and then adapted for the Apple Lisa and Macintosh computers, Windows was a graphical user interface that Microsoft grafted on top of its existing DOS operating system. It was a good idea, but the first versions of Windows were clunky and didn't have a lot of native applications; for several years, Microsoft Word and Excel were the only two applications that took full advantage of the Windows interface.

Fortunately, Windows got better—and more popular. Microsoft has upgraded Windows on a fairly consistent basis over the past two decades. The company has brought out a new version of Windows every few years or so: Sometimes the new version is a minor update; sometime it's a complete overhaul. For example, Windows 95 (released, unsurprisingly, in 1995) was a total rewrite of the previous 3.X version of Windows. Windows 98 (which followed in 1998) was a less-significant upgrade, and Windows 98 Second Edition (in 1999) was really no more than a minor bug fix.

Windows Vista, however, is the most significant upgrade since Windows 95. It has been five years since the last upgrade (Windows XP), and a lot of things have changed in the computer marketplace. Computer hardware is faster and more powerful, more users have broadband Internet connections, more users are using their PCs to listen to music and watch movies, and more viruses and security threats are out there. Windows Vista addresses all of these issues—and more. If you have the right computer hardware, it's definitely worth the upgrade.

The History of the Windows Operating System

1 **1981: DOS.** Microsoft developed the *disk operating system* to run the then-new IBM Personal Computer. Available in two variations (MS-DOS and PC DOS), it utilized a stark text-based interface and simple one-word user commands.

2 **1985: Windows 1.0.** The inaugural version of Windows was originally going to be called *Interface Manager*. It was nothing more than a graphical shell (with tiled—not overlapping—windows) that sat on top of the existing DOS operating system.

3 **1987: Windows 2.0.** The second version of Windows added overlapping windows and came bundled with Microsoft's Word and Excel applications. It received support from a Windows version of the Aldus PageMaker desktop publishing program.

4 **1990: Windows 3.0.** The third time was the charm. Windows 3.0 was the first commercially successful version of the operating system, selling 10 million copies before the 3.1 upgrade. Market acceptance was driven by its improved multitasking capabilities, as well as a wealth of new Windows-compatible applications.

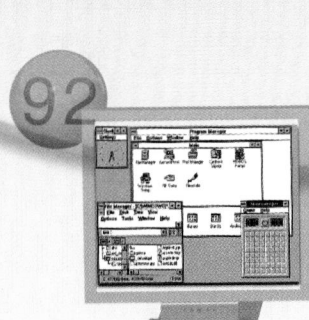

5 **1992: Windows 3.1.** This was more than a simple point upgrade; version 3.1 not only included the requisite bug fixes, but it was also the first version of Windows to display TrueType scalable fonts.

6 **1995: Windows 95.** This was the big one. The release of Windows 95 was a genuine media event, with customers lined up outside stores waiting for the midnight release of the product. Windows 95 dramatically improved the user interface and moved Windows to a 32-bit platform.

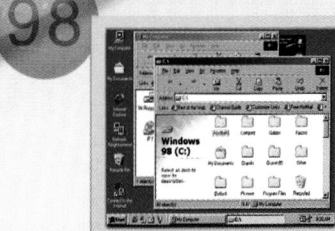

7 **1998: Windows 98.** This was an evolutionary change to the previous version, adding USB support, the FAT32 file system, and the Internet Explorer web browser. (Microsoft released an updated "Second Edition" version of Windows 98 in 1999; it contained mostly bug fixes.)

9 1992: Windows for Workgroups. Originally developed as an add-on for Windows 3.0, WFW added the necessary drivers and protocols for peer-to-peer networking.

10 1993: Windows NT. Windows NT wasn't a simple upgrade from Windows for Workgroups; instead, it was a true 32-bit operating system designed for networked organizations. With improved networking capability and near-bulletproof operation, NT (in its original and subsequent 3.0 and 4.0 versions) became the primary operating system for corporate servers and workstations worldwide.

8 2000: Windows Me. This "millennium edition" of Windows upgraded Windows 98's multimedia and Internet features, added the Windows Movie Maker application, and introduced the System Restore utility. Like Windows 95 and 98, it was positioned as an operating system for consumer—not corporate—desktops.

11 2000: Windows 2000. This was an evolution from the base Windows NT platform, still targeting the corporate market. It came in five different versions—Windows 2000 Professional, Server, Advanced Server, Datacenter Server, and Small Business Server.

12 2001: Windows XP. Windows XP was the first version of Windows to bring corporate reliability to the consumer market—and consumer friendliness to the corporate market. XP blended the best of the Windows 95/98/Me line with the bulletproof 32-bit operation of Windows NT/2000, and threw in a revamped user interface to boot. Microsoft also extended XP with segment-specific variations, such as Media Center Edition, Tablet PC Edition, and so on.

13 2007: Windows Vista. The newest version of Windows expands on XP's functionality and adds increased security and reliability, improved digital media functionality, and the dazzling Aero 3D user interface. With Vista, Media Center and Table PC versions are built into the operating system.

Other Computer Operating Systems

1 **DOS.** For IBM-compatible PCs, the original operating system was Microsoft's *disk operating system*, or DOS. IBM contracted with the then-startup Microsoft company to supply the operating system for the initial IBM PC; Microsoft purchased the existing QDOS (*Quick and Dirty Operating System*) from Seattle Computer Products and adapted it as necessary for the new computer system. The first version of DOS was released with the IBM PC in 1981 and became the dominant operating system of the decade. DOS utilized a command-line environment, which was eventually supplanted by Windows' graphical user interface. Microsoft halted DOS development in 2000—even though DOS itself remained a (buried) part of Windows until Windows Me.

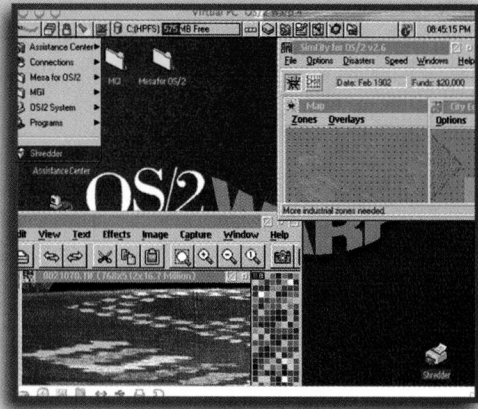

2 **OS/2.** Before Windows achieved dominance of the desktop, IBM developed its own GUI-based operating system. Initially released in 1987, it was dubbed OS/2 (for *operating system/2*) and was designed to complement IBM's new PS/2 series of computers. In fact, initial development of OS/2 was accomplished by IBM and Microsoft working in tandem, before Microsoft pulled out of the project in 1990 to concentrate its efforts on the next-generation version of its own Windows operating system. OS/2 shared operational similarities with the more robust Unix operating system, while adopting a similar interface to Windows. Competing manufacturers did not embrace it, and OS/2 eventually lost the OS war to Windows. The last release of OS/2 was in 1996 (OS/2 Warp 4).

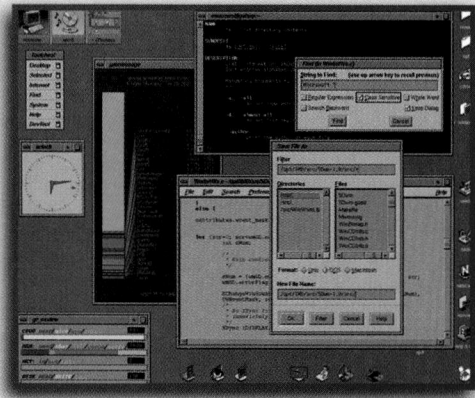

3 **Unix.** Originally developed in the 1960s and 1970s by AT&T, Unix (sometimes spelled UNIX, with all capital letters) was at one time the operating system of choice for large servers, especially in the academic environment. Originally a command-line system like DOS, Unix today is available in several variants—each with its own graphical desktop shell that runs on top of the core kernel. Unix's primary proponents include the SCO Group, Novell, and Sun Microsystems.

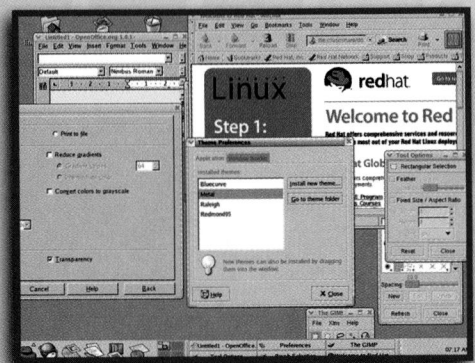

4 **Linux.** Developed by Finnish student Linus Torvalds, Linux is an open-source outgrowth of the Unix operating system. Linux is used in a variety of computer systems, from desktop PCs to web servers. Many users like the fact that Linux is a robust and relatively virus-free operating environment, as well as the fact that it's free (and not distributed by Microsoft). Several variations of Linux are available today, including Debian, Mandriva, and Red Hat—each with its own unique desktop interface.

Open Source
Open source software, like Linux, is free software, developed and distributed in the public domain. Unlike proprietary software, the source code for open source software is freely available for the public to use, modify, or redistribute as desired.

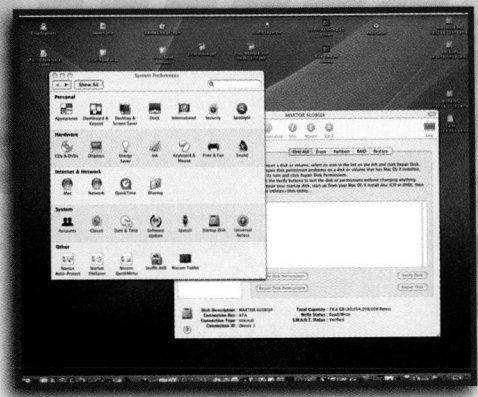

5 **Mac OS.** Apple has long been the ying to Microsoft's yang. Apple released its first graphical user interface (for the Apple Lisa) back in 1983, when DOS was the only operating system that Microsoft had. Apple revamped the Lisa interface for the original Macintosh computer, and has continued to update it over the years. The current version, Mac OS X Tiger, predated Windows with a glassy 3D interface—and is based on solid Unix underpinnings. Some critics decry Microsoft for continually copying Apple's OS efforts; others see the two companies following inevitably similar paths. There is no denying, however, that Vista bears more than a passing resemblance to the OS X interface.

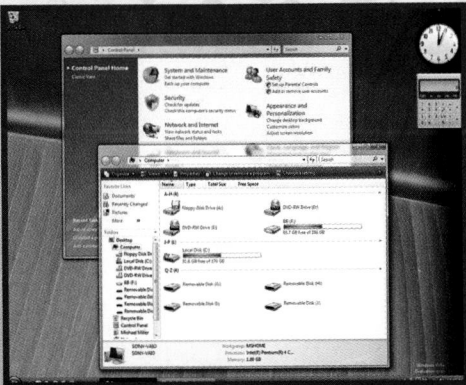

6 **Windows Vista.** And now we come to Windows Vista. Like Unix and Linux, Vista is a rock-solid interface designed for 32- and 64-bit computers. Like the Mac OS, it's visually stunning, taking the utmost advantage of today's high-performance graphics cards. And like past Microsoft operating systems, Vista is fully compatible with legacy Windows applications. For most users, it's the best of both worlds—operating stability and ease of use in one instantly familiar environment.

Different Versions of Windows Vista

Microsoft is distributing five different versions of Windows Vista—each targeted at a slightly different market. Home users can use either Windows Vista Home Basic or the more fully-featured Home Premium edition, either of which may also be distributed on new PCs. Windows Vista Business is targeted at small business users, whereas Windows Vista Enterprise is designed for large corporations and organizations. The final version, Windows Vista Ultimate, is a superset of all the best features of all the different editions, designed for power users in all environments. Which version you use should depend on your specific needs.

Windows Vista	Windows Vista Home Basic	Windows Vista Home Premium	Windows Vista Ultimate	Windows Vista Business	Windows Vista Enterprise
Target Market					
Home	✓	✓	✓		
Small business			✓	✓	
Corporate				✓	✓
Performance Features					
Dual Processor Support			✓	✓	✓
Maximum RAM (32-bit systems)	4GB	4GB	4GB	4GB	4GB
Maximum RAM (64-bit systems)	8GB	16GB	128+GB	128+GB	128+GB
Encrypting File System			✓	✓	✓
Network-Based Deployment and Management			✓	✓	✓
Interface Features					
Basic User Interface	✓	✓	✓	✓	✓
Aero User Interface		✓	✓	✓	✓
Windows Sidebar	✓	✓	✓	✓	✓
Internet Feature					
Internet Explorer 7 with Tabbed Browsing	✓	✓	✓	✓	✓
Windows Mail	✓	✓	✓	✓	✓

Digital Media Features					
Windows Media Player 11	✓	✓	✓	✓	✓
Windows Photo Gallery	✓	✓	✓	✓	✓
Themed Slide Shows		✓	✓		
Windows Movie Maker	✓	✓	✓		
Windows Movie Maker HD		✓	✓		
Windows DVD Maker		✓	✓		
Windows Media Center		✓	✓		
Productivity Features					
Windows Calendar	✓	✓	✓	✓	✓
Windows Fax and Scan			✓	✓	✓
Windows MeetingSpace	View only	✓	✓	✓	✓
Windows SideShow for Notebook PCs		✓	✓	✓	✓
Windows Tablet PC Support		✓	✓	✓	✓
Security Features					
Windows Defender	✓	✓	✓	✓	✓
Windows Firewall	✓	✓	✓	✓	✓
Microsoft Phishing Filter	✓	✓	✓	✓	✓
Parental Controls	✓	✓	✓		
Windows BitLocker Drive EncryptionX			✓		✓
Maintenance Features					
Manual File Backup	✓	✓	✓	✓	✓
Scheduled File Backup		✓	✓	✓	✓
System Image-Based Backup and Recovery			✓	✓	✓

CHAPTER

2

How Windows Vista Differs from Windows XP

IF you're a Windows XP user, you're probably asking the question, "So just how does Windows Vista differ from Windows XP?" Is it better, or just different? And is it worth the time and money to upgrade to?

You'll have to answer the last question yourself, but there's no denying that there are a lot of differences between XP and Vista—both superficial and substantive. The two versions of Windows look different, work different, and perform quite differently. It's easy enough to see how they're related, but it's also easy to see how they differ.

The most visible differences between XP and Vista are in the interface. XP's Luna interface was state-of-the-art at the time, but that time was more than five years ago. Vista pretties things up and takes advantage of today's more powerful video cards. Vista's Aero interface is smooth and sleek and provides a see-through 3D look to things. It also enables some slick three-dimensional program switching, which gives the illusion that you really have separate windows stacked on your virtual desktop.

Beneath the surface, Vista makes better use of the technology built into today's PCs, putting all that extra speed and memory to good work. A Vista-equipped PC starts up faster, loads programs faster, and crashes less frequently. It's also more secure, with built-in anti-spyware and anti-phishing utilities working alongside the established Windows Firewall.

You also get a lot more and better applications with Vista than you did with XP. Vista includes updated versions of Internet Explorer, Windows Media Player, and Windows Movie Maker, as well as new Windows Mail, Windows Calendar, Windows Photo Gallery, and Windows DVD Maker programs. It's safe to say that Vista is better for web browsing and for managing all digital media.

If all this sounds good to you, you now have to ask if your old PC is capable of running Windows Vista. The answer is a definite "maybe." Processor- and memory-wise, most mid- to high-end PCs sold in the past few years will probably do the job. But unless your PC has a modern 3D video card, it might not be capable of displaying the new Aero glass interface. If your video card isn't up to snuff, you'll be limited to the Aero basic interface—which looks better than Windows XP does, but doesn't offer all the neat translucent 3D effects.

The Aero interface might also be problematic if you have a notebook PC. That's because most current notebooks lack the high-end graphics processing necessary for the Aero display—and can't have their graphics upgraded. So even if you have a full-featured version of Vista, you may be limited to the Vista Basic interface on your notebook.

Hardware Requirements

1 **Microprocessor.** To run Windows Vista, Microsoft says that your PC must have a "modern CPU." (CPU is short for *central processing unit*, which is another word for microprocessor—the brains of your computer.) For the Home Basic edition, that translates into a 32-bit or 64-bit microprocessor running at a minimum of 800MHz; for all other editions, you'll need at least a 1GHz microprocessor.

2 **Memory.** The more memory your PC has, the better. To run the Home Basic edition, you'll need at least 512MB RAM; for all other editions, go with a minimum of 1GB of memory.

3 **Hard disk.** You need at least a 20GB hard drive with 15GB of free space to run Windows Vista Home Basic. For all other editions, Microsoft recommends a minimum 40GB hard drive. Obviously, you need a much larger hard disk if you want to install additional applications and store a fair number of files.

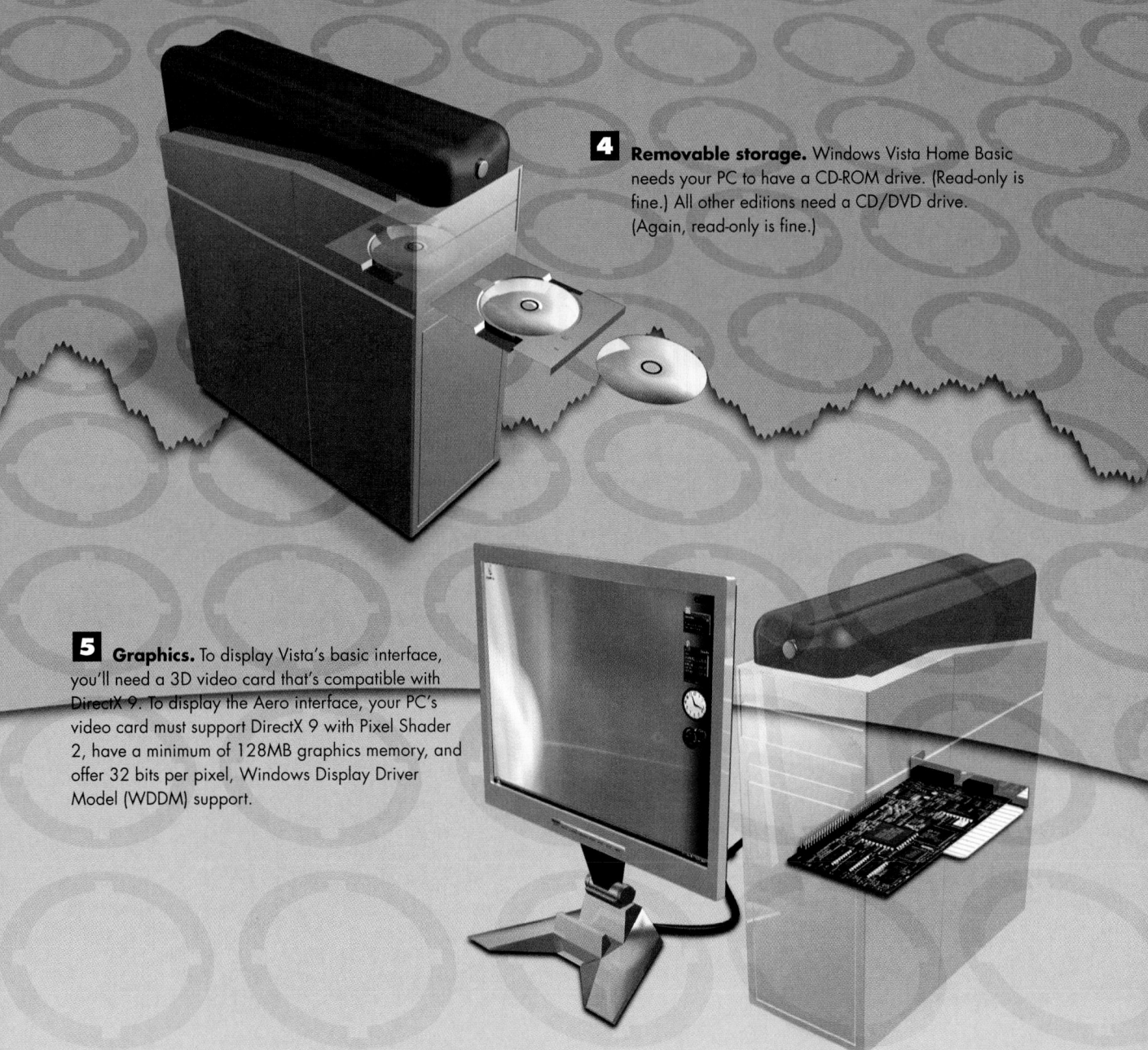

4 **Removable storage.** Windows Vista Home Basic needs your PC to have a CD-ROM drive. (Read-only is fine.) All other editions need a CD/DVD drive. (Again, read-only is fine.)

5 **Graphics.** To display Vista's basic interface, you'll need a 3D video card that's compatible with DirectX 9. To display the Aero interface, your PC's video card must support DirectX 9 with Pixel Shader 2, have a minimum of 128MB graphics memory, and offer 32 bits per pixel, Windows Display Driver Model (WDDM) support.

Displaying the Aero Interface

To display the Aero interface, your PC must be running Windows Vista Home Premium, Ultimate, Business, or Enterprise editions; you can't display the Aero interface if you're running Windows Vista Home Basic. While most new desktop PCs should meet Aero's advanced graphics requirements, many notebook PCs, which have more limited graphics capabilities, may not.

Interface Differences

1 **Aero interface.** Vista dramatically improves the user experience with the new Aero interface. Aero is a glass-like 3D interface; the translucent windows give a sense of depth when individual windows are stacked on top of each other.

Gadgets

2 **Windows Sidebar and Gadgets.** The Windows Sidebar is a pane on the side of the desktop that takes advantage of the extra screen real estate on widescreen computer displays. The Sidebar helps to organize new mini-applications that Microsoft calls Gadgets. Gadgets can deliver a variety of information and services, and can either be docked on the Sidebar or float above the desktop.

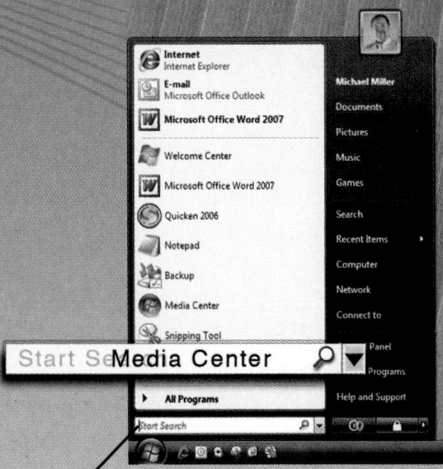

3 **Streamlined Start menu.** Vista's new Start menu is a lot less confusing than the one in Windows XP. The new Start menu expands and contracts in place if you have a lot of programs installed; just click to expand a folder and view its contents. To look for a specific program, enter the application name into the Instant Search box and Vista automatically displays a shortcut to that program.

Instant Search box

4 **Live taskbar thumbnails.** Say goodbye to generic icons. In Windows Vista, you see live thumbnails of all your documents and programs, even when they're minimized on the Windows taskbar. All you have to do is hover your cursor over a taskbar button, and you'll see the live contents of that item.

Thumbnail image

Flip3D

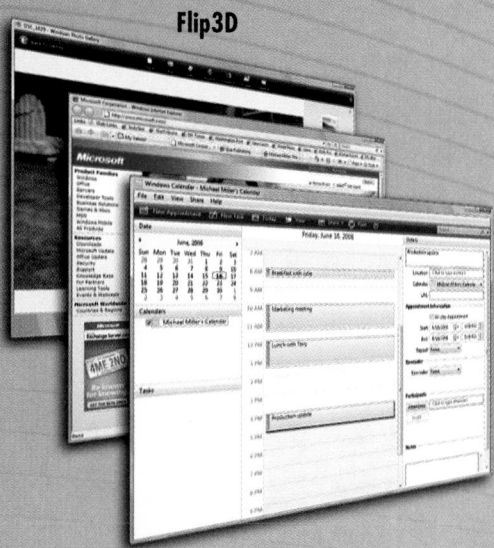

5 **Windows Flip and Flip3D.** Task switching is a lot more visual in Windows Vista. When you press Alt+Tab, the Windows Flip task switcher appears and shows live thumbnails of all active programs (instead of generic icons). Even better, press Start+Tab and Flip3D displays all open windows in a three-dimensional stack.

6 **Windows Media Center.** The Home Premium and Ultimate editions of Windows Vista come with Windows Media Center built-in. The Vista version of Media Center features a streamlined interface, improved music and video browsing, built-in support for HDTV, and support for CableCARD systems.

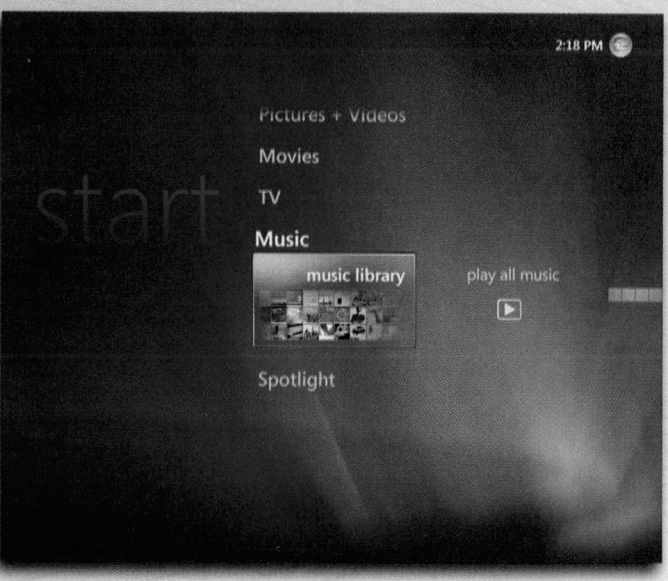

Operating Differences

Organize
button

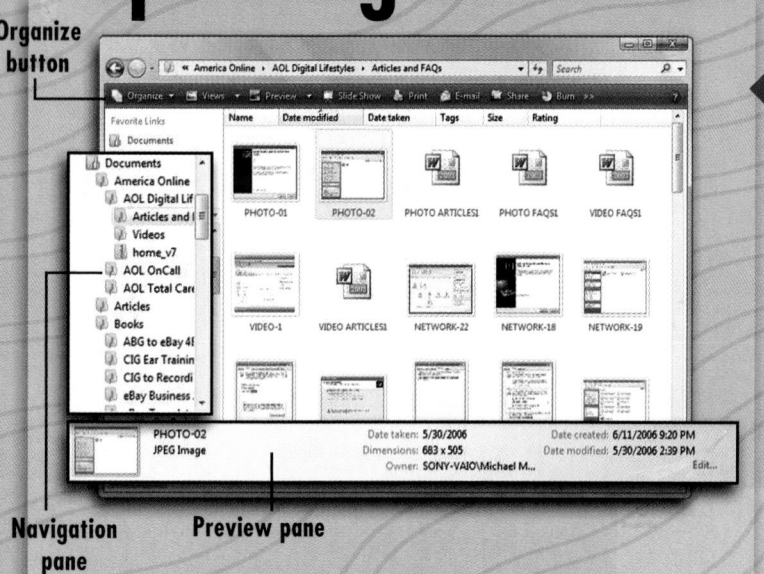

Navigation
pane

Preview pane

1 **Windows Explorer.** My Documents is gone, and Windows Explorer is back. Actually, Vista includes a lot of different Explorers—each of which displays scalable "live" document thumbnails, a Navigation Pane that contains a tree-like view of your folders, and a Preview Pane at the bottom of the window that contains metadata about the selected file. Instead of using the old Task Pane to perform various file functions, Vista groups all its commands (Copy, Move, Delete, and so on) on a new Organize pull-down menu.

2 **Instant Search.** Finding specific files has never been easier. Whatever you're doing in Vista, you're never far away from an Instant Search box. Just enter a word or part of a word, and Vista locates all matching files and folders.

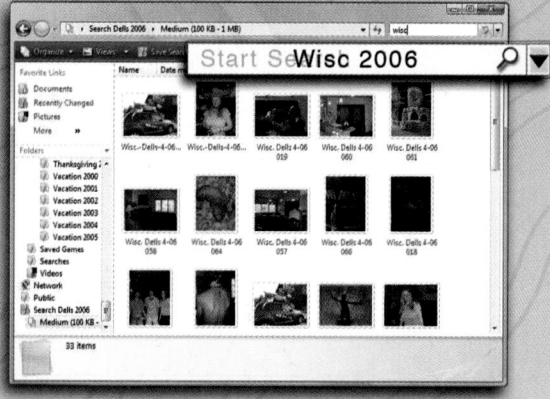

3 **SuperFetch.** Windows Vista knows how you use your PC. The new SuperFetch feature automatically preloads into memory your most frequently used applications—which helps them start up more quickly.

4 **Improved networking.** Whether you connect to a wired or a wireless network, Windows Vista does it better—both more quickly and with greater security. And you can monitor all your network connections from the new Network Center, which shows a visual map of your entire network.

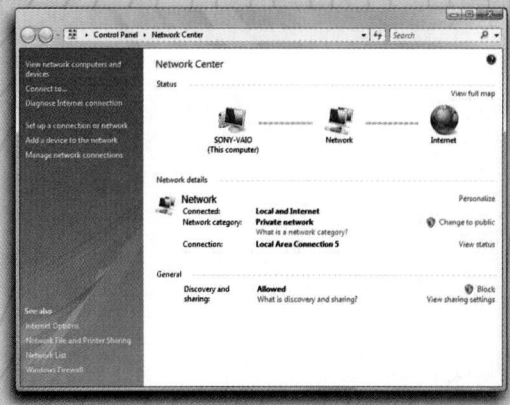

5 **Fast Boot and Resume—and new Sleep mode.** Let's face it; it took way too long to start up Windows XP. Windows Vista starts and stops a lot faster, thanks to the new Fast Boot and Resume feature, which performs many processing tasks in the background. You may not even need to shut down your computer; Vista has a new Sleep function that lets your PC rest without going through the entire shutdown procedure.

Security Differences

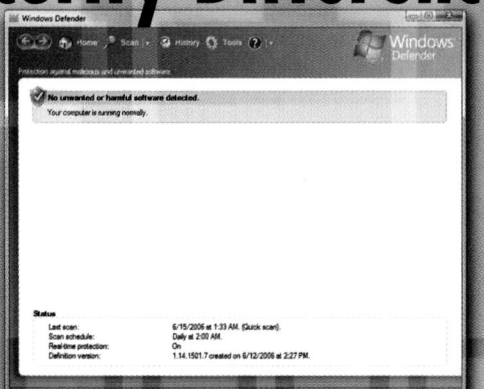

1 **Windows Defender.** Windows Vista is more secure than Windows XP in a number of ways—chief of which is the new Windows Defender anti-spyware utility. Defender runs in the background to protect your system against unwanted spyware programs—and deletes any spyware it finds.

2 **Microsoft Phishing Filter.** Have you ever been tricked into clicking to a fake website? Then you'll appreciate the new Microsoft Phishing Filter, which works with both Internet Explorer 7 and Windows Mail. The filter lets you know when it finds a link to a suspicious website, so you won't inadvertently disclose personal information.

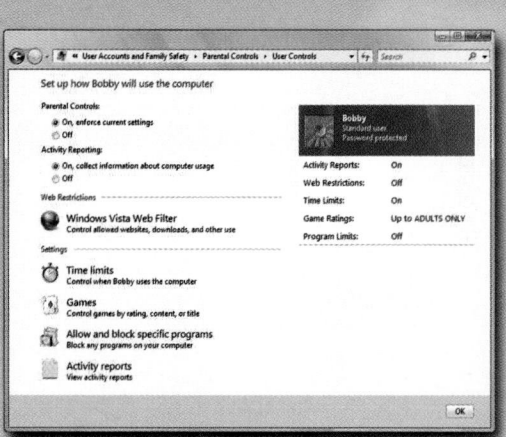

3 **Parental Controls.** Windows Vista makes it easier to keep track of your children's online activity. You limit when and how long your kids can use your PC, control which websites they can visit, restrict access to particular programs and games, and view detailed reports on your children's computer usage.

4 **User Account Control.** In previous versions of Windows, it was too easy for any user to inadvertently install dangerous software. Windows Vista makes it harder to do anything wrong by applying a new layer of User Account Control. You create a separate account for each member of your family and set which programs, games, and websites they can use and install.

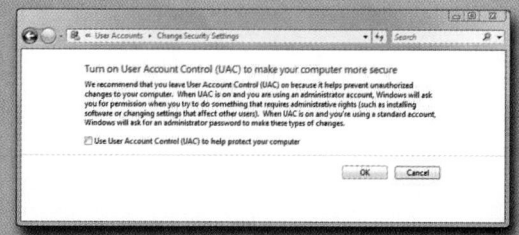

5 **Windows Service Hardening.** This new technology prevents critical Windows services from being misused in the file system, in the Windows registry, or on your network. With Service hardening, all background services are run in complete isolation from each other, and with the lowest-possible privileges. It's virtually impossible for one bad service to affect other legitimate ones—which makes your PC more secure than ever.

6 **Windows BitLocker Drive Encryption.** In large enterprises, even more security can be gained by employing Vista's new BitLocker Drive Encryption. Network administrators can encrypt the entire system drive, protecting data from physical theft. (It's also a great way to make sure that thieves can't access your personal data if your notebook PC is ever stolen.)

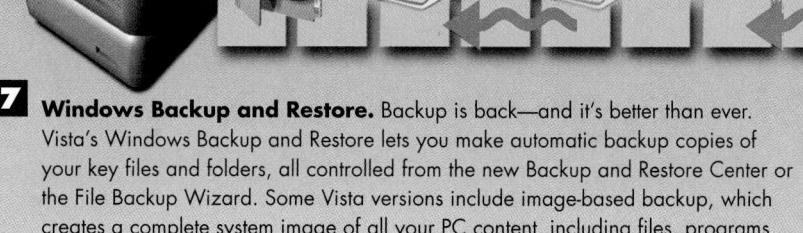

7 **Windows Backup and Restore.** Backup is back—and it's better than ever. Vista's Windows Backup and Restore lets you make automatic backup copies of your key files and folders, all controlled from the new Backup and Restore Center or the File Backup Wizard. Some Vista versions include image-based backup, which creates a complete system image of all your PC content, including files, programs, and settings.

Application Differences

1 **Internet Explorer 7.** Microsoft's web browser has been updated with a new streamlined interface and innovative tabbed browsing, where each new page appears as a new tab within the same browser window. A Quick Tabs feature lets you view thumbnails of all tabbed pages on a single page.

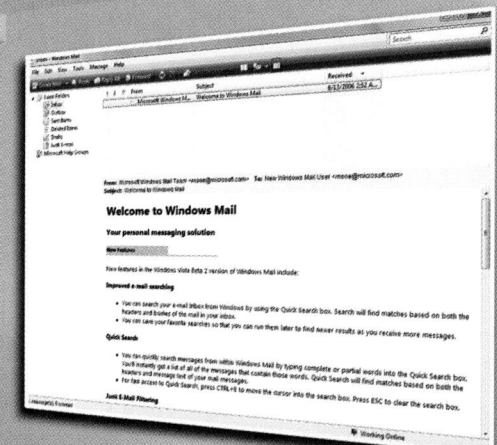

2 **Windows Mail.** This is the new name for the old Outlook Express email program. Windows Mail has been updated with an Instant Search field that lets you search all your archived email messages for specific information. It also includes a junk mail filter to reduce spam and a phishing filter to protect you from scam emails.

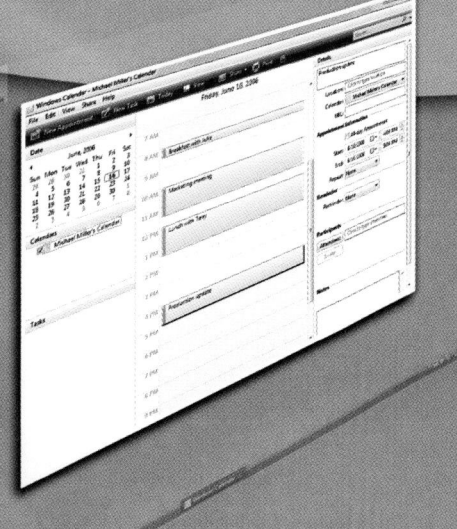

3 **Windows Calendar.** Windows Calendar is a full-featured calendar and scheduling program, similar to those features offered in Microsoft Outlook. You can schedule appointments, create tasks, and share your calendars with family members and colleagues.

4 **Windows Media Player 11.** The latest version of Microsoft's media player software features a totally revamped and easier to use interface. Just click a tab to access a function—and then view your entire music library sorted by album art. Instant search helps you find songs or albums, and its easier than ever to sync music between your PC and a portable music player.

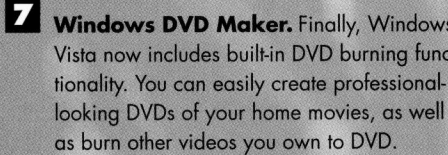

5 **Windows Photo Gallery.** This new application helps you organize and edit all your digital photos. It's easy to display your photos in variable-size thumbnail view, launch an automated slideshow, burn your photos to CD or DVD, or create photo prints. Fix and enhance your photos by adjusting exposure or color, cropping, removing red-eye, and more.

6 **Windows Movie Maker HD.** This popular video editing program sports a revamped interface and a batch of new tools to help you make professional-quality home movies. The HD version adds editing for high definition movies—in both normal and widescreen versions.

7 **Windows DVD Maker.** Finally, Windows Vista now includes built-in DVD burning functionality. You can easily create professional-looking DVDs of your home movies, as well as burn other videos you own to DVD.

CHAPTER

3

What Windows Vista Does

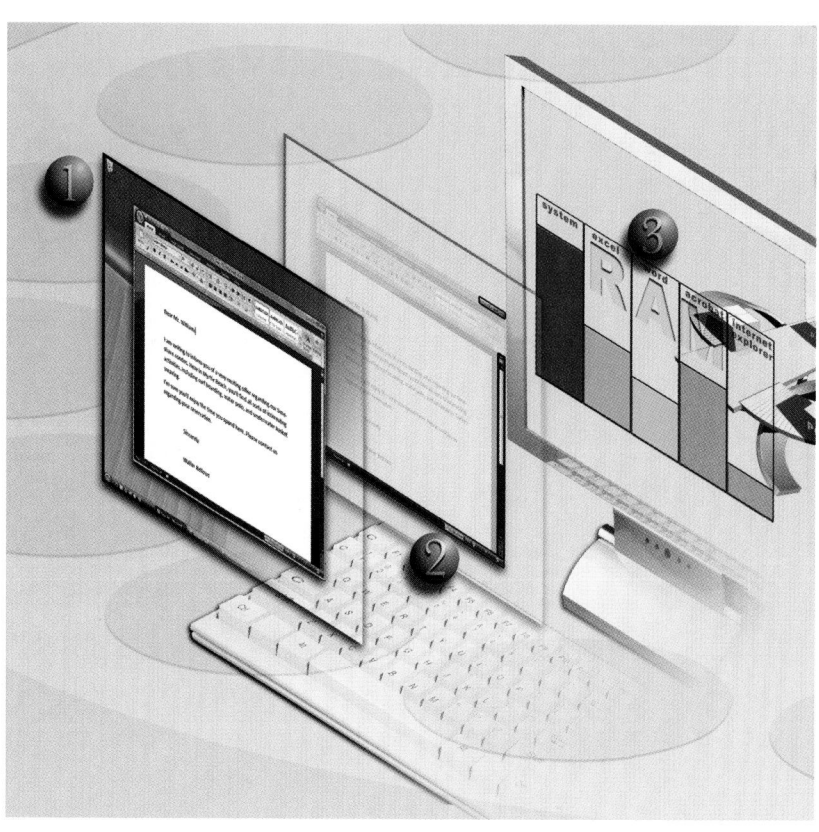

AN operating system is defined not just by how it looks, but by what it does. But just what does an operating system do?

Like all operating systems, Windows Vista operates all aspects of your computer system. Vista controls what you see onscreen and what happens behind the scenes. Everything your computer does, Vista has a hand in controlling.

When you see a program on your computer screen, Windows Vista puts it there. When you click a button in that program, Vista sends your instruction to your computer. When a program needs to open a file, print a document, or display a picture, Vista issues the instructions necessary to accomplish that task. Windows manages all the data flow between the desktop you see, the programs you use, and the internal components that make your computer run. Every single piece of your computer, from the microprocessor to the system memory to the hard disk storage to the monitor screen, is controlled by Windows.

Think of Windows as the director on a movie set. Like a movie director, Windows doesn't do every task itself; it directs others to do what needs to be done, and then lets them do their thing. Just as a movie's actors, camera operators, and lighting technicians need a director to tell them precisely what to do, your computers' microprocessor, hard disk drive, memory controller, and video card need Windows to tell them what to process, store, and display. Without Windows there to direct the action, nothing would get done.

Windows also controls what you see onscreen when you turn on your computer. The unified look of Windows Vista and all Windows applications is the result of the common resources used by the operating system. All Windows programs look and act similarly because Windows supplies them with common interface and operational elements. Each program doesn't have to invent a unique way to save its files, for example: Windows provides a common file saving operation that all programs use. These common elements make it easy for users to learn new Windows applications, as basic operations are going to be the same, no matter which program you use.

Without a well-designed operating system, all your programs would be fighting for control of your computer's scarce resources, and each program would work differently from the others. That's why what Windows does is so important. It makes sure that everything looks good and runs smoothly—which makes life easier for you, the user.

How Windows Controls Your Computer

1 User interface. Windows' user interface is the part of Windows that you, the user, sees and with which you interact. When you click an onscreen button or press a key on the keyboard, Windows translates that action and sends the appropriate instructions to the computer's memory and microprocessor. Windows Vista presents a *graphical user interface* (GUI), as it uses icons, buttons, and other graphical elements—instead of plaintext—to represent important operations.

3 Memory management. Windows is a multitasking operating system, which means that multiple operations take place simultaneously; this is how more than one program can run at once. Since each application or process needs to temporarily store some degree of information in system memory, Windows has to manage the use of that memory. Each process is assigned a specific memory location; Windows ensures that each process has enough memory to operate and that the memory space devoted to one process doesn't run into the memory space used by another process.

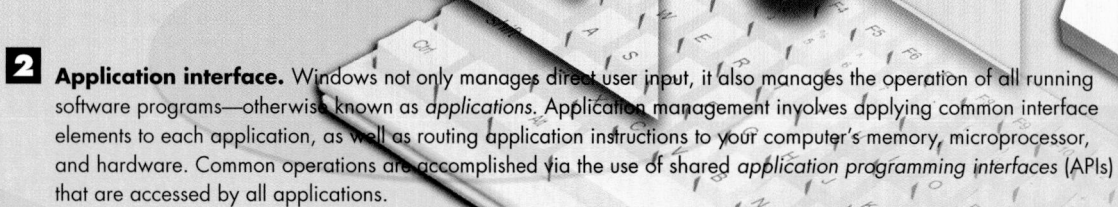

2 Application interface. Windows not only manages direct user input, it also manages the operation of all running software programs—otherwise known as *applications*. Application management involves applying common interface elements to each application, as well as routing application instructions to your computer's memory, microprocessor, and hardware. Common operations are accomplished via the use of shared *application programming interfaces* (APIs) that are accessed by all applications.

4 Processor management. When it comes to managing the use of your computer's microprocessor (CPU), Windows functions a little like a traffic cop. Each application and process is assigned a priority, and lower-priority operations are sometimes interrupted so that higher-priority operations can be completed. Before reaching the CPU, information about each process is packed into a data package called a *process control block* (PCB); each PCB contains a unique ID number, pointers to the process' memory location, a list of files the process opened, the status of all input/output devices the process needs, and so on. The CPU uses the information in the PCB to manage all ongoing processes.

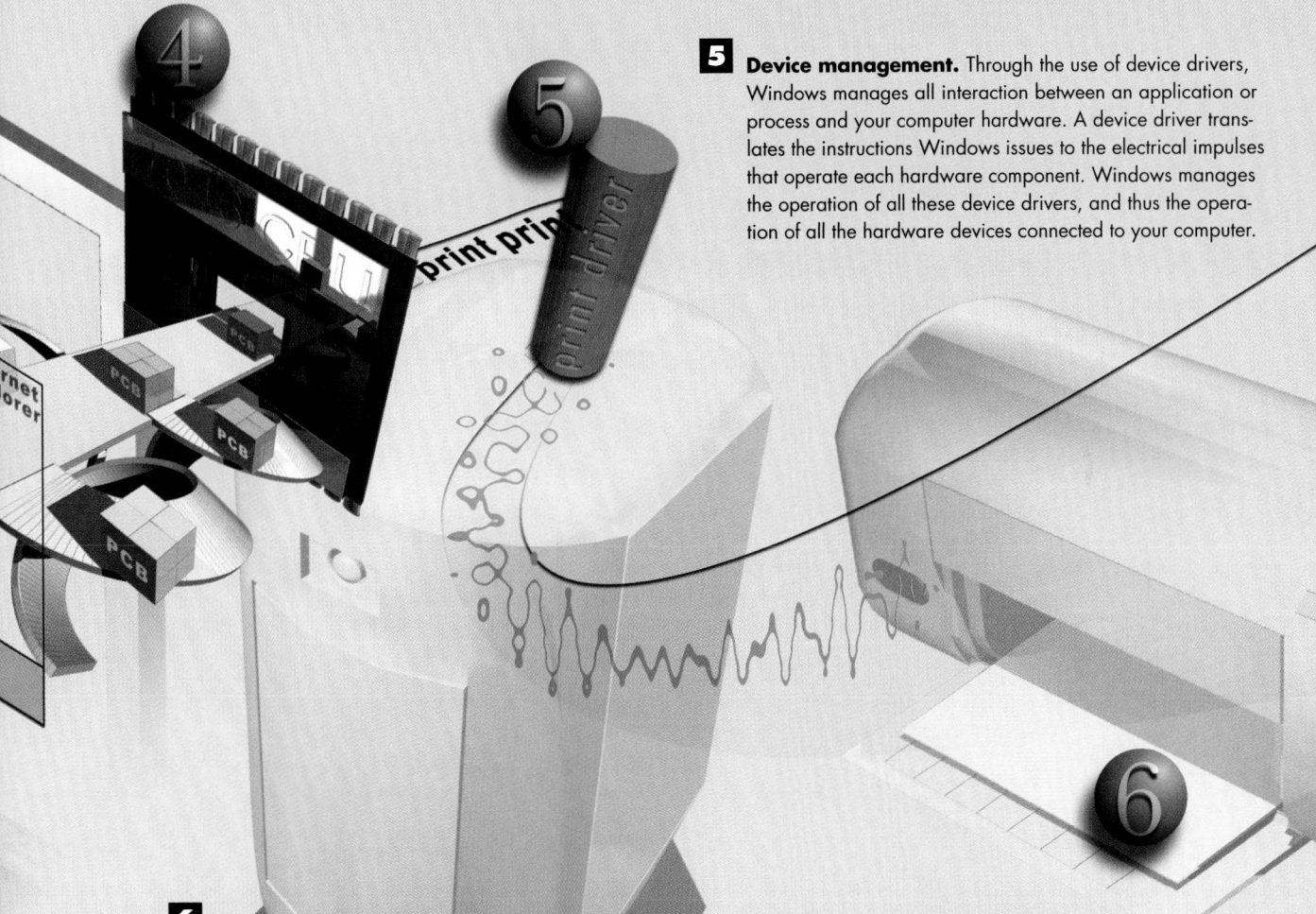

5 Device management. Through the use of device drivers, Windows manages all interaction between an application or process and your computer hardware. A device driver translates the instructions Windows issues to the electrical impulses that operate each hardware component. Windows manages the operation of all these device drivers, and thus the operation of all the hardware devices connected to your computer.

6 Hardware interface. Finally, Windows sends the proper commands to each piece of hardware attached to your computer. When you click the Print button in an application, that instruction is fed through the application program interface, managed by your computer's memory and microprocessor, routed through the appropriate device driver, and finally transmitted to your printer. You click the button, and a document prints; Windows does all the work in between!

How Windows Interfaces Between Your Computer Software and Hardware

1 When you're using a software program, the program doesn't interface directly with your computer hardware. Instead, Windows handles all communication from the software to the hardware—and provides all necessary resources for the program to run.

| API Graphic | API Graphic | API Graphic | API Graphic | API Graphic |

2 When a software designer creates a software program, he doesn't have to reinvent the wheel. Windows provides a library of common elements that all programs can use. For example, a programmer doesn't have to design a new menu system from scratch; he can use the common menu elements offered by Windows' application programming interfaces (APIs).

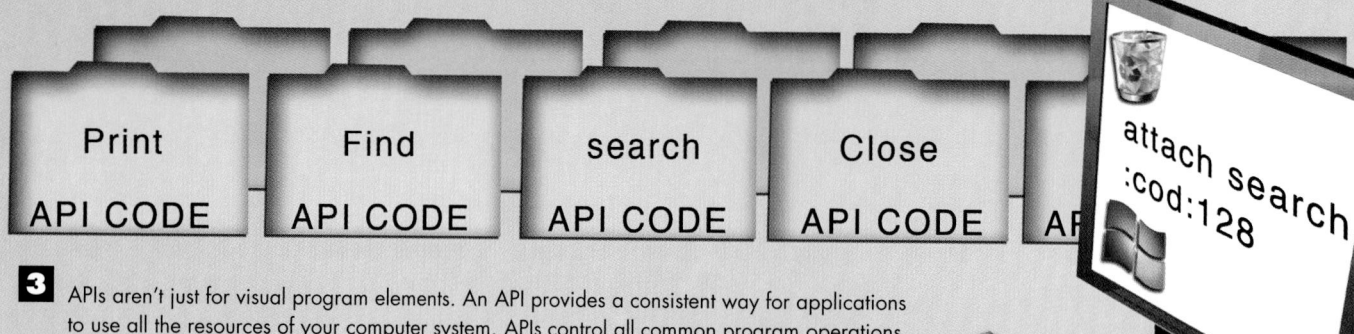

| Print | Find | search | Close | |
| API CODE | API CODE | API CODE | API CODE | |

attach search
:cod:128

3 APIs aren't just for visual program elements. An API provides a consistent way for applications to use all the resources of your computer system. APIs control all common program operations. For example, the print function in a software program uses Windows' print API, which controls all aspects of printing—and makes the print operation the same in all Windows applications. The programmer doesn't have to write a lot of complicated code to create a new print function; he writes a few lines of code to access Windows' print API and trusts Windows to do the rest.

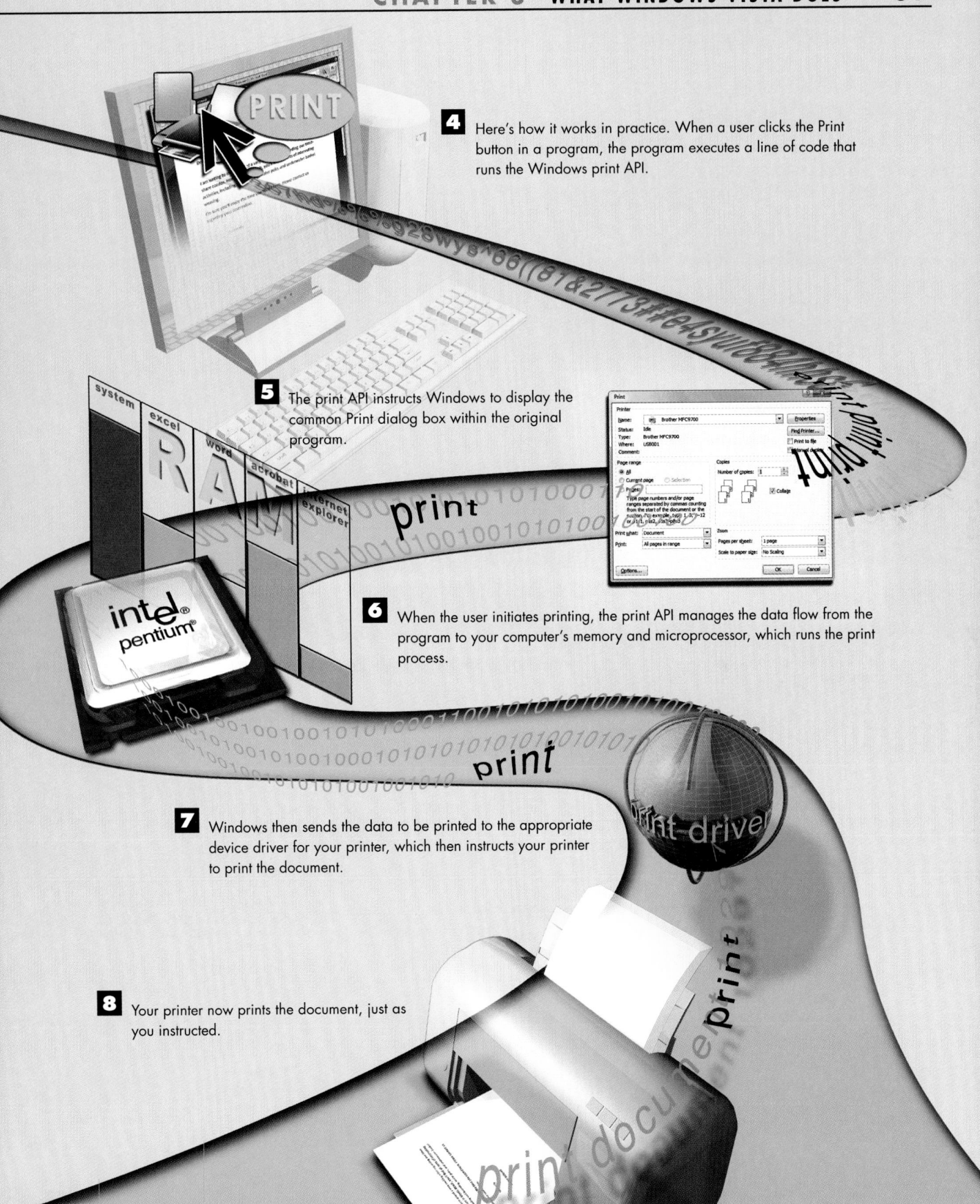

4 Here's how it works in practice. When a user clicks the Print button in a program, the program executes a line of code that runs the Windows print API.

5 The print API instructs Windows to display the common Print dialog box within the original program.

6 When the user initiates printing, the print API manages the data flow from the program to your computer's memory and microprocessor, which runs the print process.

7 Windows then sends the data to be printed to the appropriate device driver for your printer, which then instructs your printer to print the document.

8 Your printer now prints the document, just as you instructed.

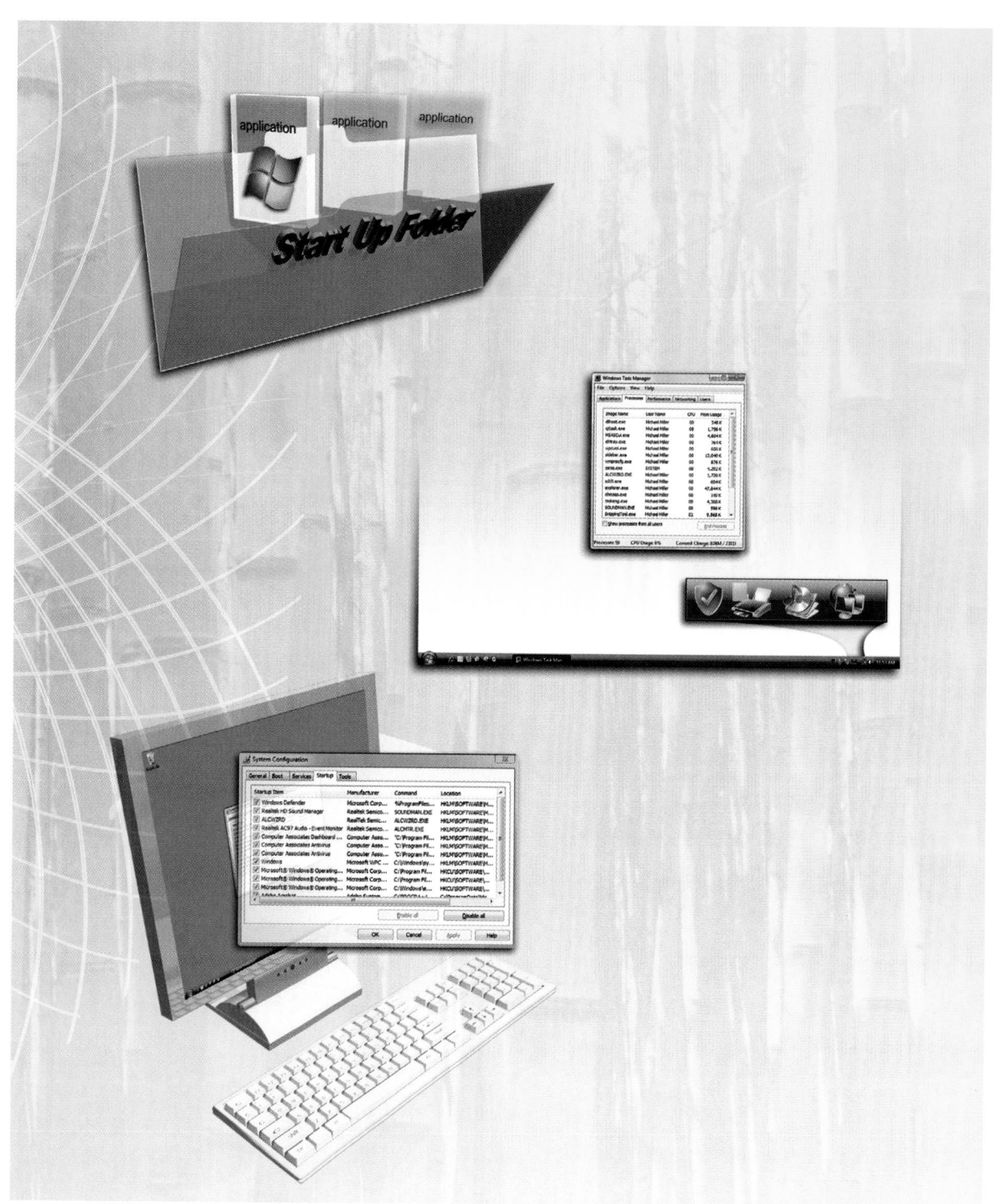

P A R T

BASIC OPERATIONS

WINDOWS Vista is an operating system. As such, it's responsible for managing all the operations on your computer system—your software, your hardware, and all the file management tasks you initiate. When you click a mouse button, Vista manages the operation. When you open a new spreadsheet, Vista manages the operation. When you surf the Web or check your email, Vista manages the operation. When you display a photo, play digital music, or just delete a file, Vista manages the operation. Whatever you do, and whatever your computer does, Vista makes it work.

In this fashion, Vista is just like any other operating system you've ever used. MS-DOS, Linux, the Mac OS—they all manage the same computer operations as Vista does. Vista might do some of these tasks a little better (or not, depending), but all operating systems must perform the same operations. That's why operating systems exist.

The first thing an operating system does is start itself. In the case of Windows Vista, the operating system launches automatically whenever you turn on your personal computer. When you press your PC's power button, the computer hardware goes through a standard power up routine, and then starts to load Vista into system memory.

For Vista to do its thing, it has to always be there. This is why key components of the operating system are designed to reside within your PC's memory; whenever something needs to be done, Vista is always in the background, waiting to manage the task.

In addition to the operating system itself, Vista also loads a variety of configuration settings and device drivers into memory. The settings are necessary to tell your computer how to look and act; the device drivers are necessary to operate the various hardware devices you have connected to your PC. Again, all these processes are just a stone's throw away in system memory, waiting in the background until they're needed.

From its location in system memory, Windows Vista is poised and ready to do whatever needs to be done. Windows manages all the system processes for your computer, from the system clock to the display adapter. It also manages the flow of information and instructions from your software programs to your hardware devices. Whenever you perform an action in a program, the program interfaces with Windows to execute the action.

The information that Windows needs to manage all these processes is stored in a huge database called the Windows Registry. The Registry stores configuration data about every program installed on your system, as well as all operating system processes and applications. So when you launch a program or open a utility, the information necessary to run that process is pulled from the Registry and put to use.

To manage all this activity, Windows must interface directly with all the devices and operations in your computer system. Vista manages your system memory, your central processing unit (CPU), your hard disk drive, your removable media drives, your display adapter, your audio system, your mouse, your keyboard, your printer—all the components that make up your computer system. Before any task is executed, Windows gets involved to direct what happens, when, and how. Nothing happens without Windows approval and instructions.

To help your programs run more efficiently, Vista includes a new memory management scheme called SuperFetch. This process automatically loads your most-used applications into memory when Windows first launches. Pre-loading these programs lets you get working quicker when you open an application.

Windows Vista also manages all the users on your computer, through the new User Account Control feature. Vista knows that only designated users can perform specific operations, and makes sure that no unauthorized use occurs. It's not just a way of creating personalized desktop experiences for each user, it's also a means of making your PC more secure.

Finally, Windows manages all the data stored on your computer—your Word documents, Excel spreadsheets, PowerPoint presentations, digital photos, digital music, digital movies, and so on. Windows manages where each file is stored, and how. It manages access to each file, and in some cases allows you to edit the file's metadata or contents. It even helps you manage your data; you use Windows Explorer to copy, move, rename, and delete all your files and folders. And this file management is made easier in Windows Vista, thanks to improved navigation pointers (in the form of a "breadcrumb" trail of folders in each window) and the ability to view "live" thumbnails of each file's contents.

All of these operations, from power on to power off and everything in-between, are managed by the Windows Vista operating system. In most case, you never even know what's going on under the surface; it's Vista's job to perform its duties without getting in the way of your day-to-day computing activities. But you'd know it if Vista wasn't around—it's what makes your computer run!

CHAPTER

4

Powering On and Powering Off

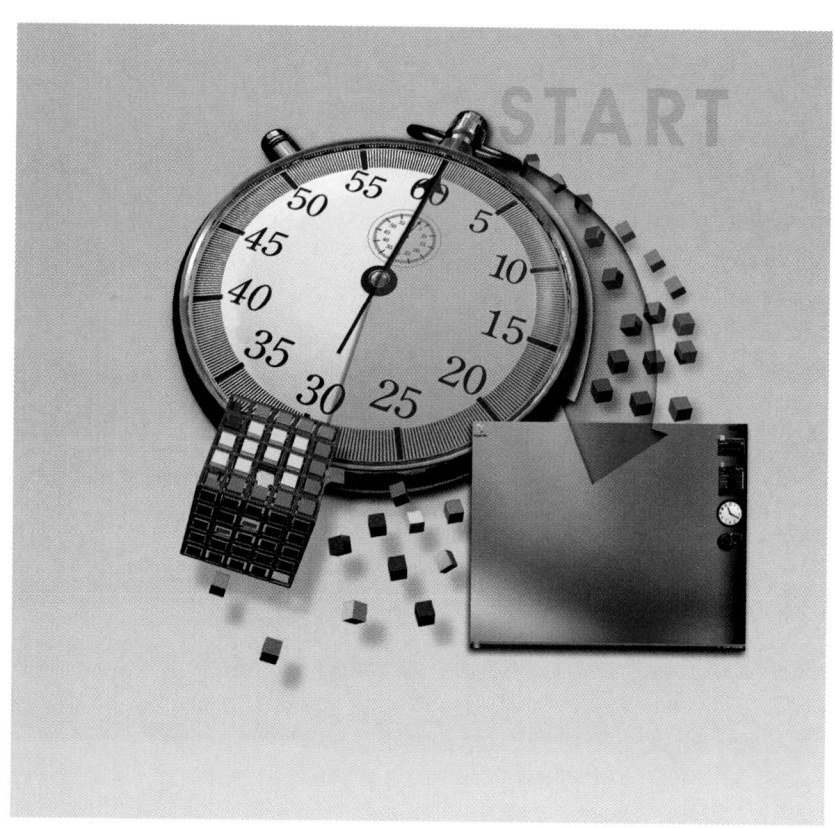

WINDOWS is there at the beginning, and it's there at the end. In computer terms, this means that Windows is involved with both the power on and power off processes. It helps manage your computer when you turn it on, and it makes sure that everything is properly closed and safely put away when you turn your computer off.

To be fair, the power on process starts before Windows loads, but loading Windows is definitely part of the process. Your computer has to boot up and perform some rudimentary tests (as directed by the BIOS on your PC's motherboard) before it accesses the hard disk, which is where the Windows program code resides. The Windows code is then read from the hard disk into your computer's memory, where it goes to work. It generally takes only a couple of seconds for the BIOS to hand over control of the system to Windows.

When Windows is loaded into system memory, it also loads all necessary configuration settings and device drivers—everything it needs to do its job. It also launches a variety of behind-the-scenes processes and (sometimes) applications—again, items that Windows needs loaded to perform essential operations. For example, Windows might load a device driver to enable your printer to print, as well as launch a process that speeds up the launching of the Adobe Reader program. These drivers, processes, and applications remain in memory, where they can quickly be called into action when needed. (Loading a process or program from hard disk takes a lot longer than it does to access that same process or program in memory.)

Windows Vista adds a few new wrinkles to the whole power on/power off process. First, Vista incorporates a new Fast Boot and Resume function that helps to speed up the whole startup process. With Fast Boot and Resume, not all processes are loaded before the Windows desktop appears; some processes are loaded in the background after the initial startup, so you can see the desktop and start working faster than you could before.

Also new in Windows Vista is the enhanced Sleep mode. With Sleep mode, you don't have to turn off your computer when you're done working for the day; when you put your computer to sleep, your hardware stays powered on (but in a low-power mode) while your open applications and documents are stored away for fast relaunching when you wake up your system. Microsoft so likes this new Sleep mode that when you click the Power button on the Start menu, you no longer turn off your PC; instead, clicking the Power button puts your computer into Sleep mode. If you're like most users, you'll find that Sleep mode is preferable to powering off your computer and then going through the whole power on process the next morning—it's a lot quicker, both on and off!

How Windows Powers On Your System

1 The first part of your computer's startup routine takes place before Windows loads. When you press your computer's "on" button, power is sent through the PC's power supply to the motherboard in the system unit, and your system reads instructions stored in your computer's *basic input/output system* (BIOS), which is stored in *read-only memory* (ROM). These instructions tell your computer to perform a *power-on self test* (POST), which checks and verifies the status of all the low-level hardware in your system—memory, controllers, and so on.

2 After the self-test, your computer looks for the first bootable drive on your PC. This is probably your hard drive C, although it could also be a diskette drive or CD/DVD drive with a bootable disc inserted. A bootable disc contains, in a sector called the Master Boot Record (MBR), those important system files necessary for your system to operate—files that are normally hidden from view, and not displayed in a normal folder listing. When your computer accesses a bootable drive (normally the C: hard drive), it reads into memory the contents of the disk's *boot sector*, which contains certain files that tell your system how to load the Windows operating system.

3 The first file found on and run from the hard disk is the Windows Boot Manager (sometimes called the *bootstrap loader*). Its purpose is simple—it tells your system to launch other Windows pre-boot applications.

4 The Boot Manager reads from hard disk a Boot Configuration Data (BCD) file. This file is essentially a "data store," in that it functions as a container for all the files and processes used in the boot sequence.

5 The Boot Manager now loads into memory the Windows kernel (the **ntoskrnl.exe** file), the hardware abstraction layer, and the contents of the Windows Registry hive.

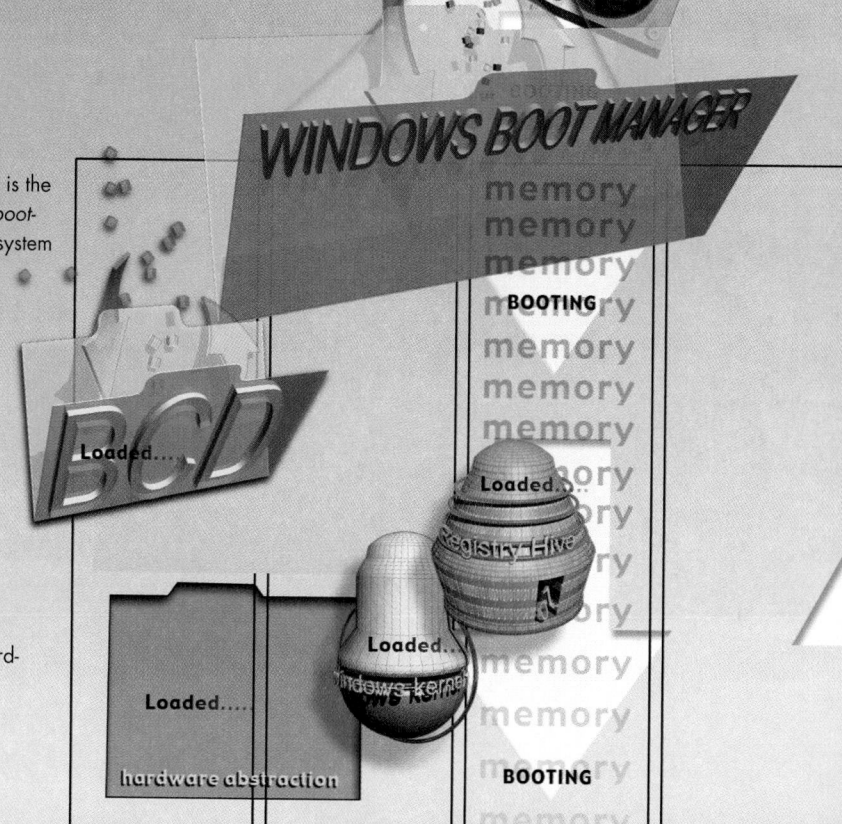

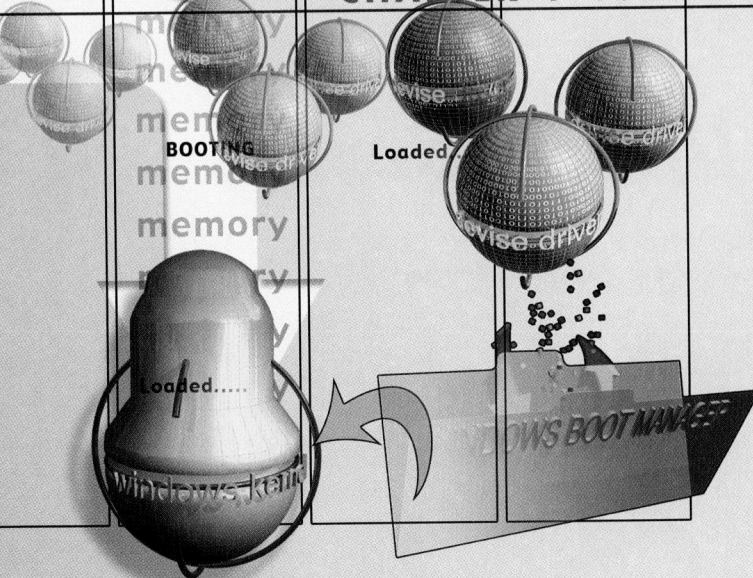

6 The Boot Loader now scans the Registry for configured device drivers and loads all boot-time device drivers into memory. These are the devices necessary to get Windows started; they're typically drivers for hard-drive controllers and file systems.

7 After the boot-time device drivers are loaded, the Boot Manager passes control to the operating system kernel.

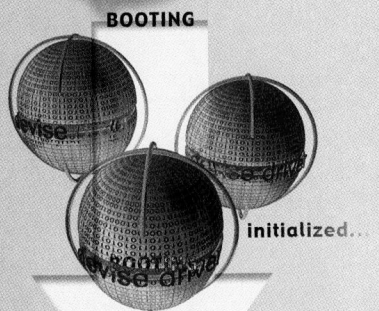

8 The kernel now takes over the boot process by initializing all relevant controllers and devices.

9 Next, the kernel scans the Registry to find and load all the other device drivers (called system drivers) into memory.

10 Windows now displays the welcome screen and prompts you to select a user account (if the PC has multiple users).

11 Once you log on as a specific user, Windows loads all the configuration and policy settings for that user from the Windows Registry.

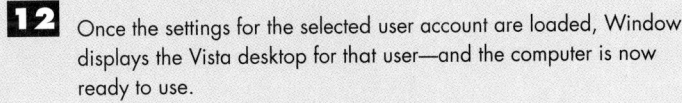

12 Once the settings for the selected user account are loaded, Windows displays the Vista desktop for that user—and the computer is now ready to use.

How Windows Loads Processes and Applications at Startup

1 When Windows first launches, it has to load all the processes necessary for the operating system to run. These include all the bits and pieces of the operating environment, as well as device drivers, background utilities, and the like. Dozens of these processes are launched on startup—without you ever knowing it.

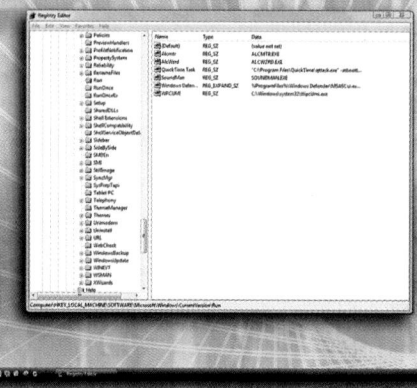

2 The processes that Windows loads on startup are specified in the Windows Registry. The Registry is a database of configuration settings for the operating system and for all Windows applications.

3 When Windows loads itself into system memory, the processes and device drivers specified in the Registry are also loaded into memory. Each process occupies a specific location in system memory so that Windows knows where to access that process when necessary.

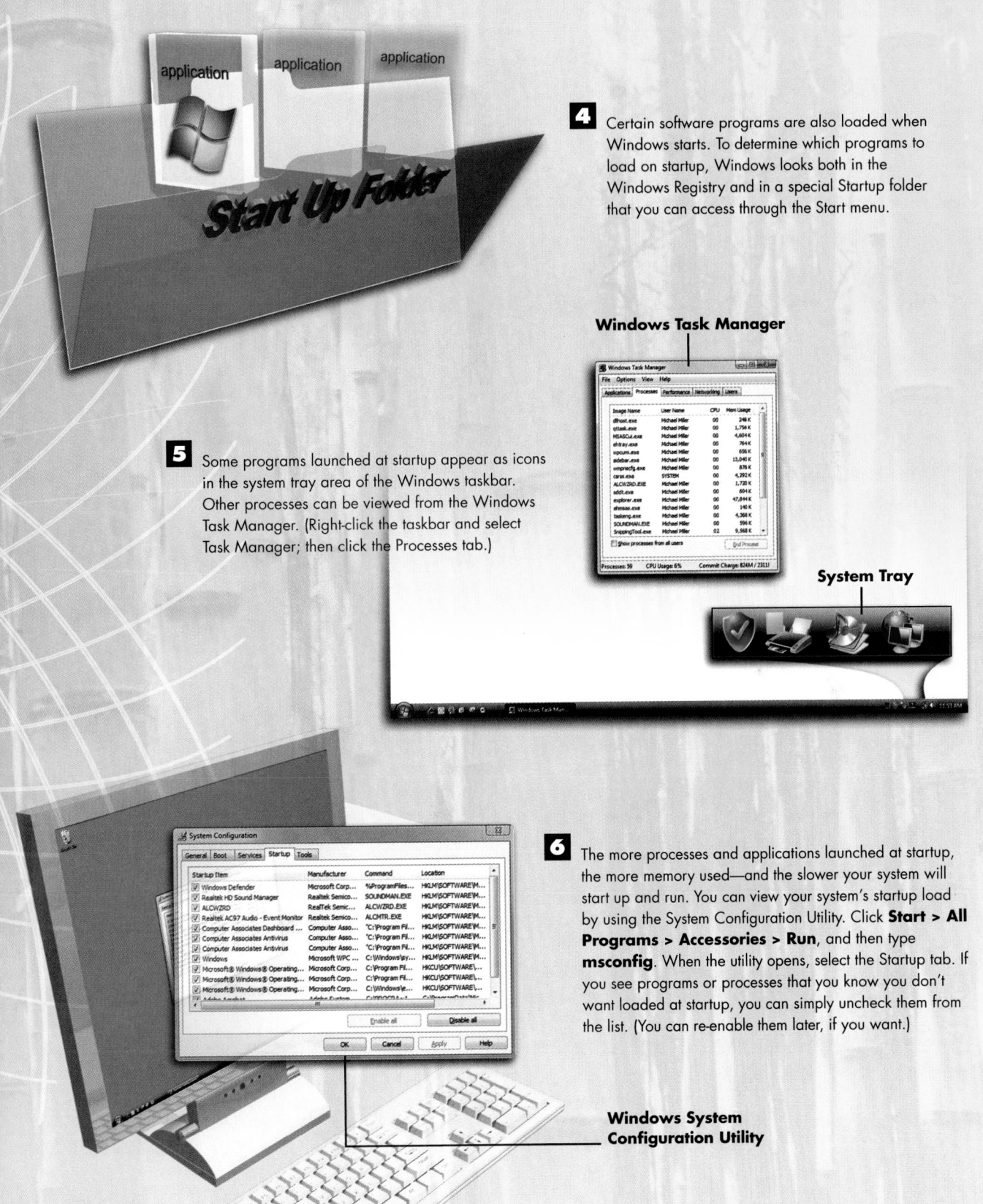

4 Certain software programs are also loaded when Windows starts. To determine which programs to load on startup, Windows looks both in the Windows Registry and in a special Startup folder that you can access through the Start menu.

Windows Task Manager

5 Some programs launched at startup appear as icons in the system tray area of the Windows taskbar. Other processes can be viewed from the Windows Task Manager. (Right-click the taskbar and select Task Manager; then click the Processes tab.)

System Tray

6 The more processes and applications launched at startup, the more memory used—and the slower your system will start up and run. You can view your system's startup load by using the System Configuration Utility. Click **Start > All Programs > Accessories > Run**, and then type **msconfig**. When the utility opens, select the Startup tab. If you see programs or processes that you know you don't want loaded at startup, you can simply uncheck them from the list. (You can re-enable them later, if you want.)

Windows System Configuration Utility

How Safe Mode Works

1 Safe mode is a special mode of operation, typically used for troubleshooting startup problems, that loads Windows in a minimal configuration. This minimal configuration runs Windows as cleanly as possible, with a low-resolution display and without any unnecessary device drivers or software. (This means that you won't be able to use a lot of your peripherals in Safe mode.)

2 You can enter Safe mode when you start or reboot your computer. When the text-based startup screen displays (just before the Windows welcome screen appears), press the F8 key on your keyboard, and then select Safe mode from the resulting startup menu.

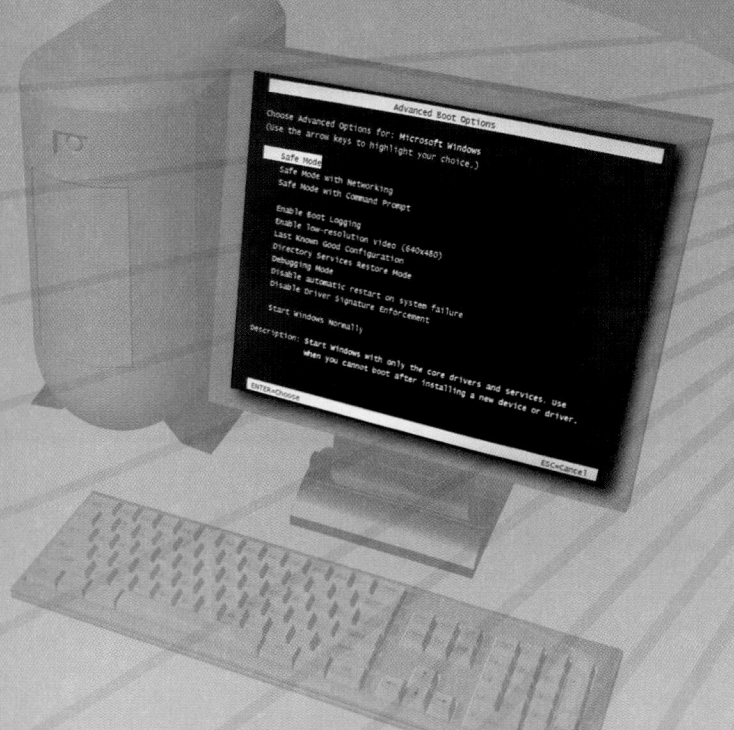

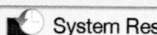

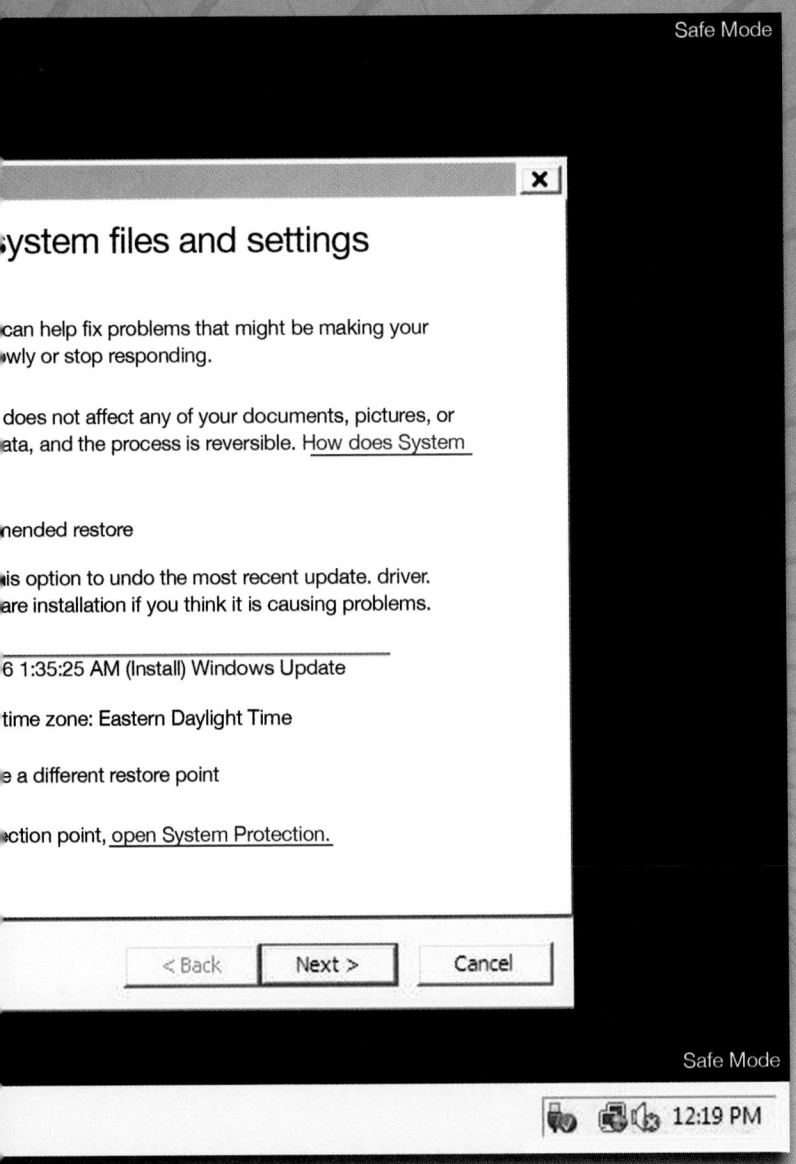

Safe Mode

ystem files and settings

can help fix problems that might be making your
wly or stop responding.

does not affect any of your documents, pictures, or
ata, and the process is reversible. How does System

nended restore

is option to undo the most recent update. driver.
are installation if you think it is causing problems.

6 1:35:25 AM (Install) Windows Update

time zone: Eastern Daylight Time

e a different restore point

ction point, open System Protection.

| < Back | Next > | Cancel |

Safe Mode

12:19 PM

3 Safe mode is used to load a basic version of
Windows when the full Windows version won't
load. The thinking is that most problems are
caused by faulty device drivers or applications or
by computer viruses, and starting Windows without these drivers (or possibly infected files) can
help you fix the problem. So if your computer
crashes or won't otherwise start, or if you can't
load Windows normally, you may be able to
access Windows by using Safe mode. (In some
instances, Windows sometimes reboots itself into
Safe mode when it encounters major problems
when loading.)

4 From within Safe mode, you can troubleshoot a
variety of problems. That's because Windows
itself still works (even if all the peripherals aren't
active), so you can make whatever changes are
necessary to get the operating system up-and-
running again in normal mode. Once in Safe
mode, you can look for device conflicts, restore
incorrect or corrupted device drivers, troubleshoot
your startup with the System Configuration Utility,
run an antivirus program, or restore your system
to a prior working configuration using the System
Restore utility.

How Fast Boot and Resume Works

1 One of the chief complaints from Windows users concerns how long it takes for Windows to start up. The long startup time is a function of how many processes and applications are automatically loaded when you turn on your computer—the more things to load, the longer it takes.

2 In previous versions of Windows, all devices and processes were loaded before the Windows interface was displayed. The Windows desktop wouldn't appear until all processes had been loaded into memory.

3 Windows Vista speeds up the startup process with the new Fast Boot and Resume feature. With Fast Boot and Resume, only essential processes are loaded at initial startup.

5 After the Windows desktop appears, lower priority processes are loaded—in the background, while the user works.

4 After the initial processes are loaded, the Windows interface is immediately displayed. This lets the user see the Windows welcome screen much sooner than was possible in previous versions of Windows.

How Windows Shuts Down Your System—or Puts It to Sleep

1 In older versions of Windows, you exited Windows and shut down your computer by clicking Start > Shut Down. In Windows Vista, to completely shut down your system, you click the Start button, and then click the right arrow (next to the Power button) and select Shut Down.

2 When you exit Windows and shut down your computer, Windows automatically closes all open applications and processes—and asks you to save all open documents. Device drivers and program files may be damaged if they're not closed in this proper fashion, which is why you never want to turn off your computer from the main power button on the system unit.

3 After closing all open processes, Windows then removes its code from system memory and sends a shut-down command to your computer. This command shuts off all power to your system hardware, including the memory and microprocessor.

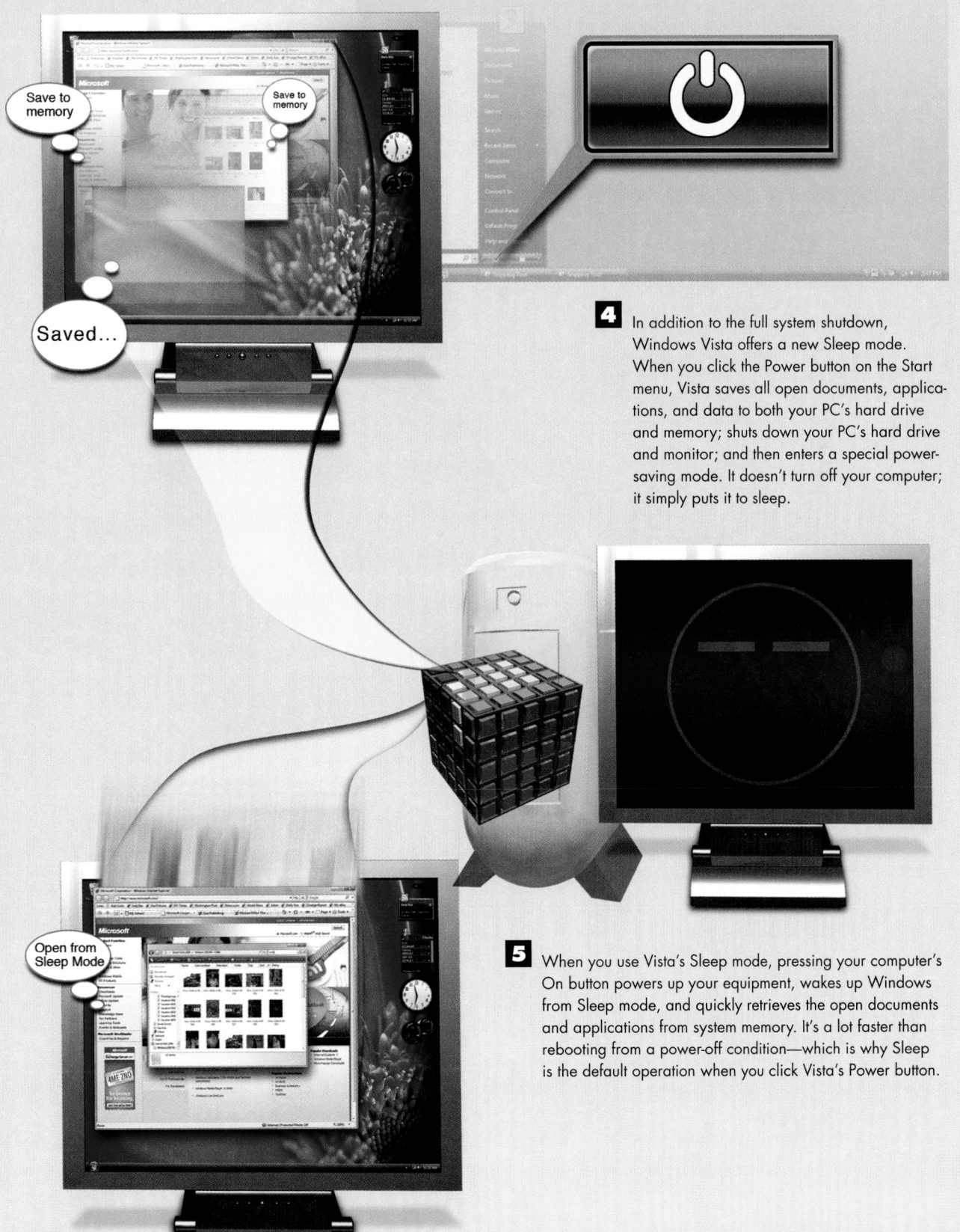

4 In addition to the full system shutdown, Windows Vista offers a new Sleep mode. When you click the Power button on the Start menu, Vista saves all open documents, applications, and data to both your PC's hard drive and memory; shuts down your PC's hard drive and monitor; and then enters a special power-saving mode. It doesn't turn off your computer; it simply puts it to sleep.

5 When you use Vista's Sleep mode, pressing your computer's On button powers up your equipment, wakes up Windows from Sleep mode, and quickly retrieves the open documents and applications from system memory. It's a lot faster than rebooting from a power-off condition—which is why Sleep is the default operation when you click Vista's Power button.

CHAPTER 5

Managing System Resources

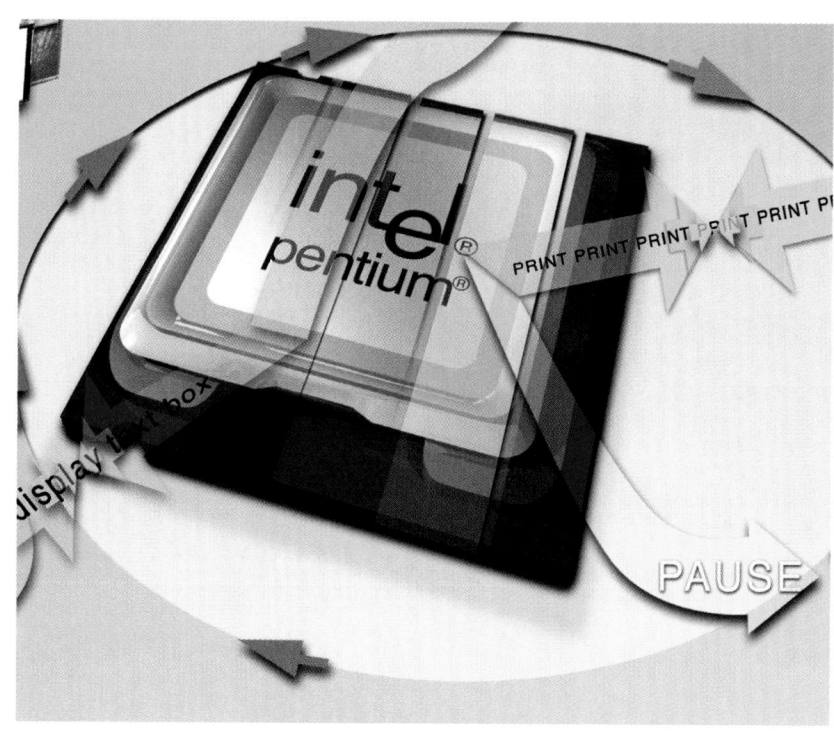

THE part of Windows Vista that you see—the Vista desktop—is just part of the operating system. Behind this interface (under the hood, if you will) is the guts of the beast. Vista is more than just a pretty interface; it's a robust engine that makes all the components of your computer system run.

The Windows Vista engine works by managing the data flow to all the different pieces of hardware (including key subsystems) of your PC. Vista manages the instructions that are fed to the central processing unit; the applications and drivers that are stored in system memory; the external and internal devices that are connected to your computer; and the disk drives that your computer uses to store your data. Think of Windows as a virtual traffic cop, managing the flow of data and instructions; it's all quite complex, yet Windows handles any given operation in the blink of an eye.

Consider, for example, the simple act of clicking your mouse to open a dialog box. When you press your finger down on that mouse button, it sends an electric signal from the mouse to your computer. That signal is translated into a specific instruction in binary code, thanks to a small software program called a device driver, which is part of the Windows operating system. Windows takes the instruction from the device driver, interprets what it means, and then forwards the instruction to your computer's CPU. The CPU processes the instruction, and then feeds the result back to Windows. Windows then accesses the currently running program, which is temporarily stored in system memory, and tells it to open the dialog box. The program does as it's told, and feeds back to Windows the necessary information about what dialog box to open, and where. Windows takes that instruction, processes it as necessary, and then feeds the graphic information about the dialog box to a different device driver—this one for your PC's video card. The video device driver translates Windows' instruction into the appropriate electronic signal, and the dialog box appears on your computer monitor screen. This whole process occurs in the blink of an eye.

Although this sounds rather complicated, it's actually an example of a very simple—and very common—operation. Windows manages dozens, if not hundreds, of these operations every hour, all in the background, all without you knowing what's going on behind the scenes. The operating system just does its thing, routing the proper instructions to the proper devices and systems, making sure that no one operation gets in the way of any other one. There's a lot of interrupting and pausing and restarting, but that's the nature of the game—and it all happens behind the scenes, without troubling you, the user.

It's all in a days work, as far as Windows Vista is concerned.

How Windows Manages the CPU

1 All operations that your computer undertakes are broken down into processes that perform some individual action. In the case of an application, such as Microsoft Word or Internet Explorer, several processes are typically involved. The application itself may contain one or more processes, but also cause several other processes to begin—typically for related tasks, such as accessing the modem, activating the printer, and so on. Your system's central processing unit (CPU) manages these processes. At any given time, Windows is running dozens of background processes to handle your system's memory management, disk management, networking, virus checking, and so on.

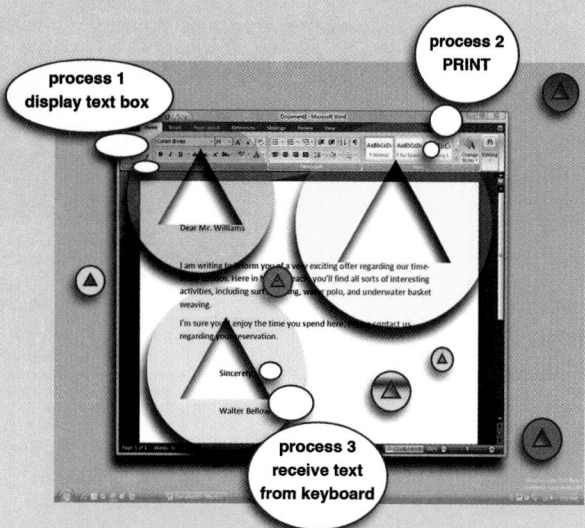

process 1
display text box

process 2
PRINT

process 3
receive text
from keyboard

display text box

2 Windows is a multitasking operating system. This means that multiple processes are run at virtually the same time; this is how you can simultaneously surf the Web, listen to digital music, and print a document. Windows' job is to arrange the execution of all these processes so that they seem to be running concurrently—when in fact, they're being processed sequentially.

3 When multiple processes are running at the same time, Windows assigns each process a slice of the CPU's time. It starts by allotting a certain number of CPU execution cycles to the first process and sends that process to the CPU.

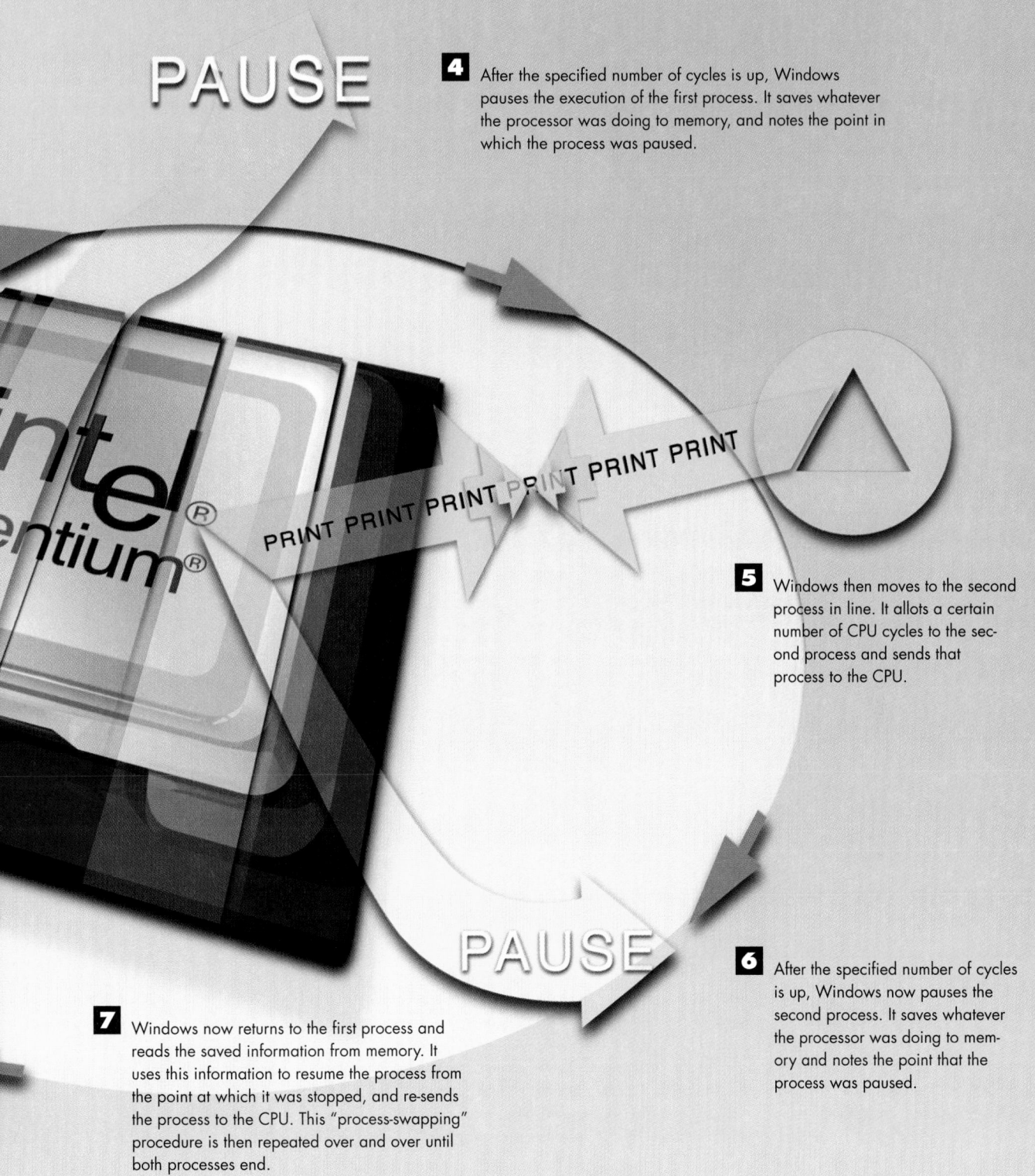

PAUSE

4 After the specified number of cycles is up, Windows pauses the execution of the first process. It saves whatever the processor was doing to memory, and notes the point in which the process was paused.

PRINT PRINT PRINT PRINT PRINT PRINT

5 Windows then moves to the second process in line. It allots a certain number of CPU cycles to the second process and sends that process to the CPU.

PAUSE

6 After the specified number of cycles is up, Windows now pauses the second process. It saves whatever the processor was doing to memory and notes the point that the process was paused.

7 Windows now returns to the first process and reads the saved information from memory. It uses this information to resume the process from the point at which it was stopped, and re-sends the process to the CPU. This "process-swapping" procedure is then repeated over and over until both processes end.

How Windows Manages Memory with SuperFetch

Kernel space

1 When Windows first starts up, the Windows kernel (that part of the operating system responsible for securely managing running programs) is the first item loaded into system memory. The kernel loads at the very top of the available system memory, "backing up" far enough to meet the needs of the operating system. This area of memory is called the *system space* or *kernel space*.

2 After loading the kernel, Windows now moves to the bottom of the pool of system memory and starts loading the various device drivers needed to control your computer's hardware subsystems.

favorite

explorer

3 The remaining memory between the device drivers and the Windows kernel is free for the loading of software applications. In Windows Vista, SuperFetch technology automatically loads your most-used applications into memory when Windows first launches—instead of waiting for you to open the program manually. By pre-loading a program into a memory, it starts up much quicker when you later open the program. SuperFetch uses an intelligent prioritization scheme to understand which programs you use most often, and it can even differentiate which programs you're likely to use at different times.

Loaded device drives

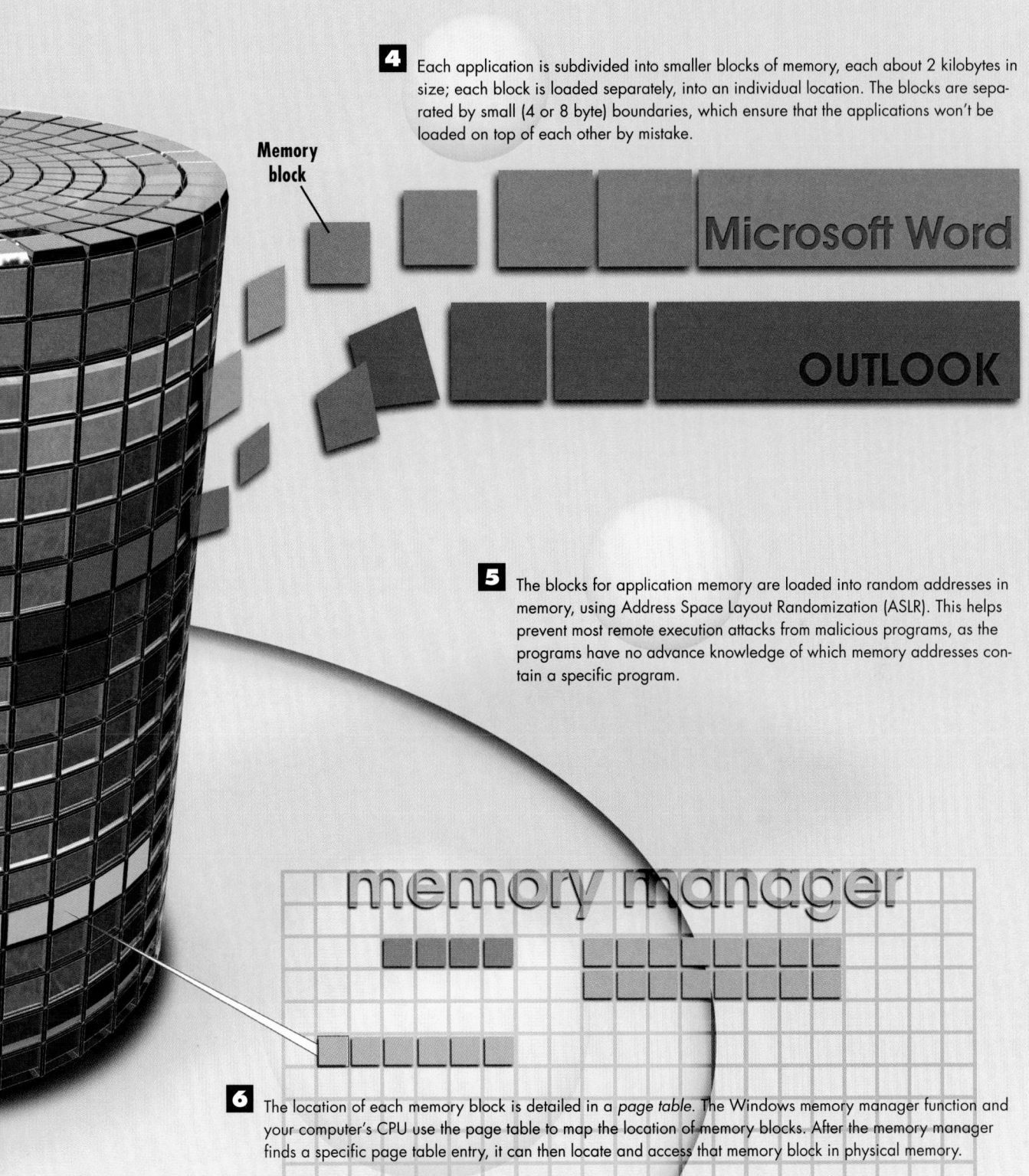

4 Each application is subdivided into smaller blocks of memory, each about 2 kilobytes in size; each block is loaded separately, into an individual location. The blocks are separated by small (4 or 8 byte) boundaries, which ensure that the applications won't be loaded on top of each other by mistake.

Memory block

Microsoft Word

OUTLOOK

5 The blocks for application memory are loaded into random addresses in memory, using Address Space Layout Randomization (ASLR). This helps prevent most remote execution attacks from malicious programs, as the programs have no advance knowledge of which memory addresses contain a specific program.

memory manager

6 The location of each memory block is detailed in a *page table*. The Windows memory manager function and your computer's CPU use the page table to map the location of memory blocks. After the memory manager finds a specific page table entry, it can then locate and access that memory block in physical memory.

How Windows Manages System Devices

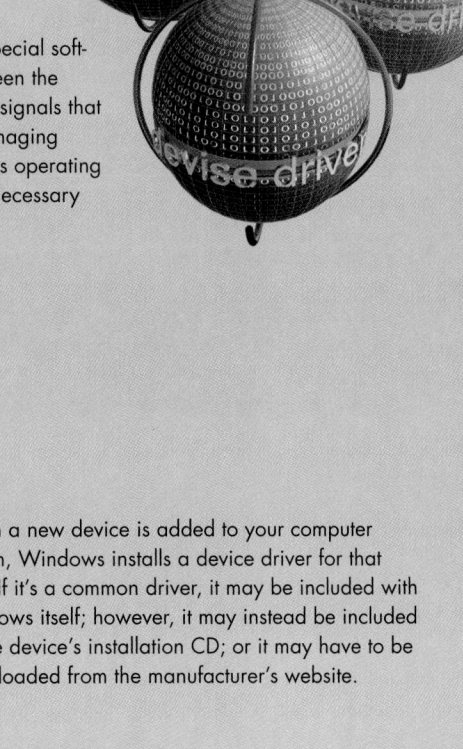

1 To manage all the hardware not on your PC's motherboard, Windows uses a special software program, called a *device driver*. The driver functions as a translator between the instructions issued by Windows (and Windows' applications) and the electrical signals that run the hardware subsystems. Without device drivers, all the instructions for managing every possible hardware device would have to be hard-coded into the Windows operating system. Because of the driver architecture, you only need to load those drivers necessary for the hardware on your specific computer system.

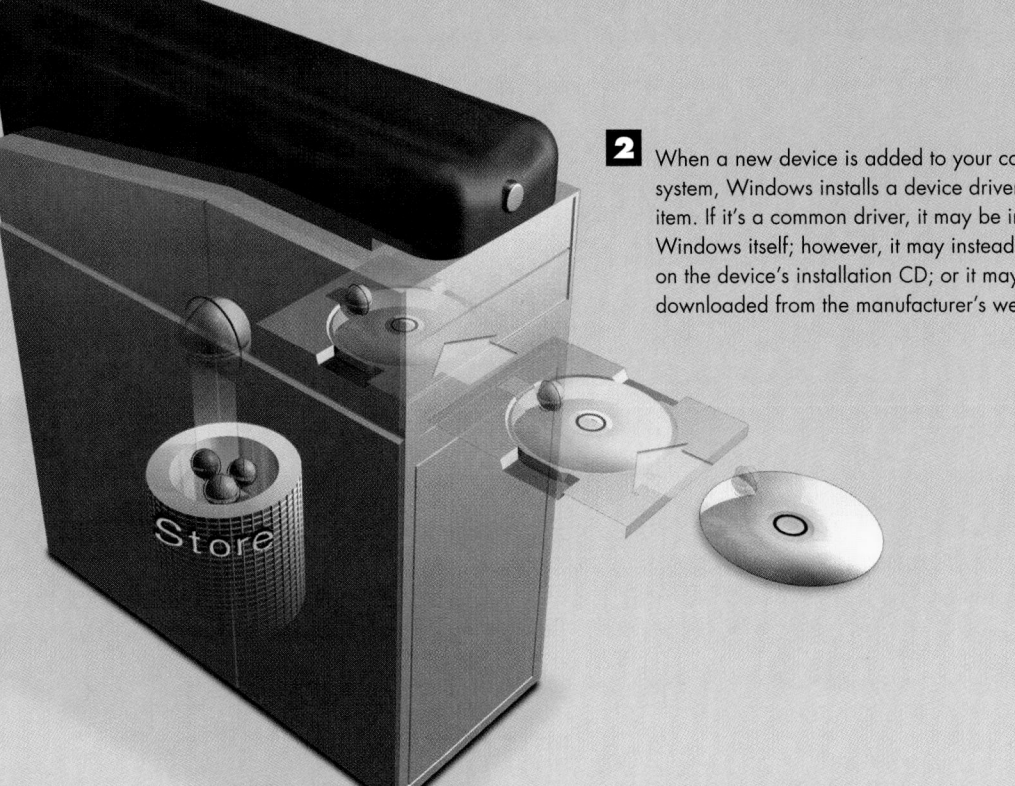

2 When a new device is added to your computer system, Windows installs a device driver for that item. If it's a common driver, it may be included with Windows itself; however, it may instead be included on the device's installation CD; or it may have to be downloaded from the manufacturer's website.

3 Once installed, each driver is added to the Windows Vista *Driver Store*. This component, new to Vista, is a repository of all installed driver packages for your particular installation of Windows. The Driver Store ensures that if you need to repair or reinstall a particular device driver, you won't need to locate and use the original installation disk; Windows will automatically access the original driver stored in the Driver Store.

4 In regular use, all installed device drivers are loaded into system memory when Windows starts up. Once loaded, the driver passes information to Windows on which device it's talking to and what that device can do. It then becomes an adjunct to the operating system, sitting dormant while it waits for a request from Windows.

Function Dispatch Table

Task Driver

Task Driver

5 Information about a particular device is stored in system memory in what is called a *driver object*. The driver object supplies data that completes the *Function Dispatch Table*, which is a database that tells Windows about each driver.

Task Driver

6 When Windows needs to perform a particular function, it first examines the Function Dispatch Table to determine which device can best do the job.

Print Driver

INPUT/OUTPUT REQUEST PACKET

7 After identifying the appropriate device, Windows sends the instruction to the device driver, in the form of an Input/Output Request Packet (IRP).

Task Driver

Task Driver

print print print print print print print

8 The device driver translates the instructions from Windows, and then commands the device to perform the appropriate function.

print

How Windows Manages Interrupts

display keystroke

INTERRUPT

1 Not all processes are sent to your computer's CPU with the same priority. Processes from some devices—such as keystrokes from your keyboard, clicks from your mouse, and the like—need an immediate response; to receive immediate attention, these device drivers generate a special type of signal called an *interrupt*.

STOP PROCESS

2 The presence of an interrupt causes Windows to temporarily halt what it is doing to divert all attention to the service that issues the interrupt signal. When Windows receives an interrupt signal, it starts by interrupting the currently running process in the CPU.

3 Information about the current process (including the address of the current operation) is placed into a special location in system memory, called a *stack*.

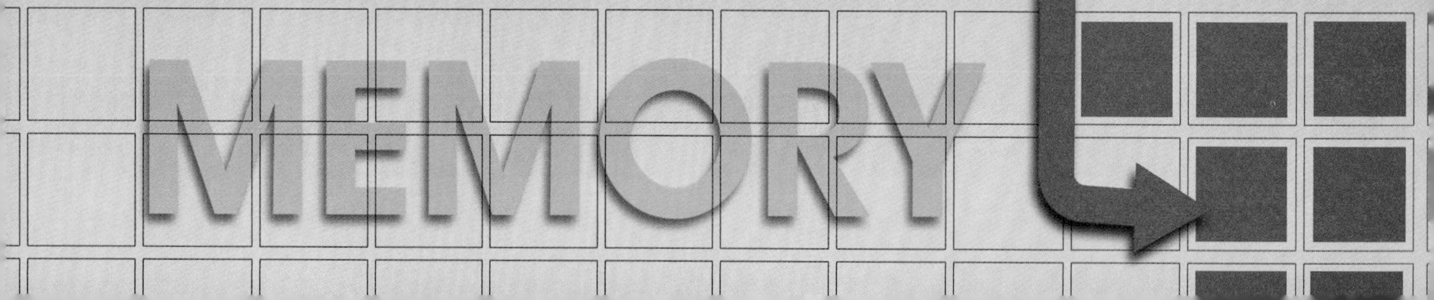

MEMORY

Non-Maskable Interrupts

Some types of interrupts are so important that they can't be ignored. These include interrupts that result from memory problems or other error conditions. These are called *non-maskable interrupts* (NMIs), and Windows deals with them immediately, regardless of what other tasks await.

4 Windows now opens a path from the device that issued the interrupt to the CPU, and then runs the necessary process.

5 When the new process is completed, Windows generates an *interrupt return* (IRET) signal.

6 The IRET instructs the CPU to retrieve the address of the previous operation from the stack and then to resume running that process from where it left off.

display keystroke

display keystroke

stop

hold

interrupt

go

intel® pentium®

processing

RESUME

7 In many instances, Windows is capable of *masking* the interrupt so as not to interfere with already running processes. When the CPU is running an important process, Windows intercepts the interrupt signal and holds it so that the current process can be finished as quickly as possible. As soon as the process is done running, Windows then puts through the interrupt request.

How Windows Manages Disk Drives and Data with NTFS

1 Windows Vista, like all operating systems, uses a file system to determine how files are named, stored, and organized on all physical disks. A file system manages files and folders, as well as the information needed to locate and access this data. The file system used in Windows Vista is called NTFS.

2 A hard drive formatted with NTFS is divided into several sectors, the first of which is the *boot sector*. The boot sector stores information about the layout of the disk and the file system structures, and also contains the boot code that launches the Windows operating system on startup.

3 Also included in each partition is the Master File Table (MFT), which is a type of database that contains all the information necessary to locate and retrieve files from the hard disk.

master file table

| cluster 0001 | cluster 0002 | cluster 0003 | cluster 0004 |
| cluster 0006 | cluster 0007 | cluster 0008 | cluster 0009 |

4 Each file is stored on your hard disk in one or more *clusters* of data. With NTFS, a cluster can range in size from 512 bytes to 64 kilobytes (KB), depending on the total size of your hard drive. For example, on a 2GB drive, the default cluster size is 2KB; on a 200GB drive, the default cluster size is 4KB. Clusters cannot be subdivided; even if the file is smaller than 4KB, it still takes up an entire cluster.

NTFS
NTFS originated with the Windows NT operating system, and stands for *NT File System*. Previous versions of Windows used either the FAT or FAT32 file systems, which utilized larger cluster sizes.

5 Large files are broken into multiple clusters. Although Windows tries to find contiguous storage space that will hold all the clusters for a file, those clusters may end up scattered in different physical locations on the hard disk.

6 When a file is stored on your hard disk, a record of that file—and the location of all its clusters—is created in the Master File Table.

7 When it needs to access a file (to open it within an application, copy it, move it, and so on), Windows accesses the MFT to locate all the clusters associated with that file.

cluster 0011	cluster 0012	cluster 0013	c
cluster 0016	cluster 0017	cluster 0018	c
cluster 0021	cluster 0022	cluster 0023	c

8 NTFS also allows for on-the-fly data compression. Because this compression is implemented within the file system, any Windows-based application can read and write compressed files just as it would noncompressed files. Compression is determined by setting a particular bit within the file header; information about the compression is stored in the data file attribute.

decompress

memory memo

memory memo

memory memo

9 When a program opens a compressed file, NTFS automatically decompresses only the portion of the file being read, and then copies that data to system memory. Because the application only accesses the data in memory, which has already been decompressed, speed of data access is just as fast as if the program were accessing a noncompressed file.

How Windows ReadyBoost Adds Instant Memory to Your PC

1 When Windows runs short on memory (also called Random Access Memory, or RAM), it uses your PC's hard disk as virtual memory, writing temporary code to the hard drive. Unfortunately, reading and writing to hard disk is much slower than reading and writing to electronic RAM, so system performance suffers.

2 Windows Vista lets you add an instant memory upgrade to your PC via ReadyBoost technology. With ReadyBoost, you can use a flash memory device to temporarily increase the amount of RAM on your personal computer. Insert one of these devices into the appropriate slot on your PC, and your system's memory is automatically increased—and your system's performance is automatically improved. Vista supports USB flash memory drives, as well as CompactFlash (CF) and Secure Digital (SD) memory cards; it can handle devices that hold between 256MB and 4GB of RAM.

3 With ReadyBoost, Windows duplicates the overflow data that is typically sent to your hard disk by also sending it to the inserted flash memory device. Windows then uses the data stored in the flash device's RAM, instead of accessing the data on the slower hard disk; a flash memory device is approximately 10 times faster than hard disk-based virtual memory. (Windows continues to write the information to the hard disk, as a backup.)

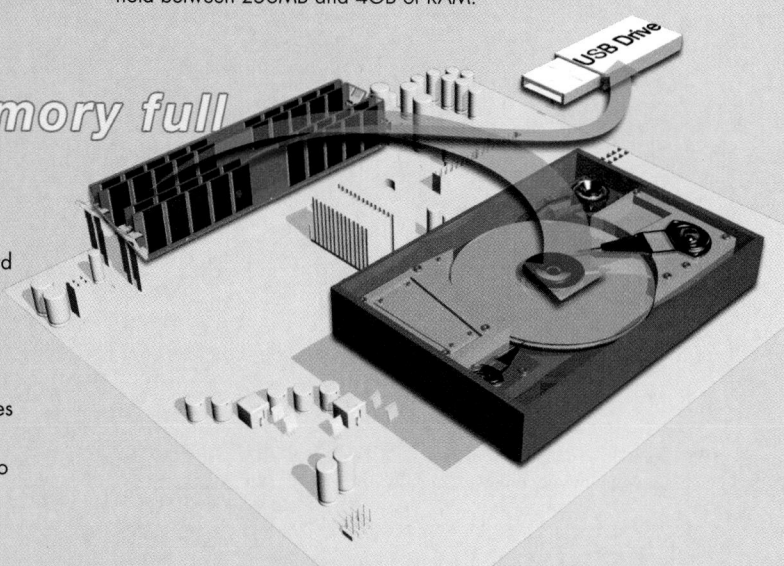

4 The RAM on the flash memory device is added to the available RAM on your computer's motherboard, thus providing more memory to run applications and open documents.

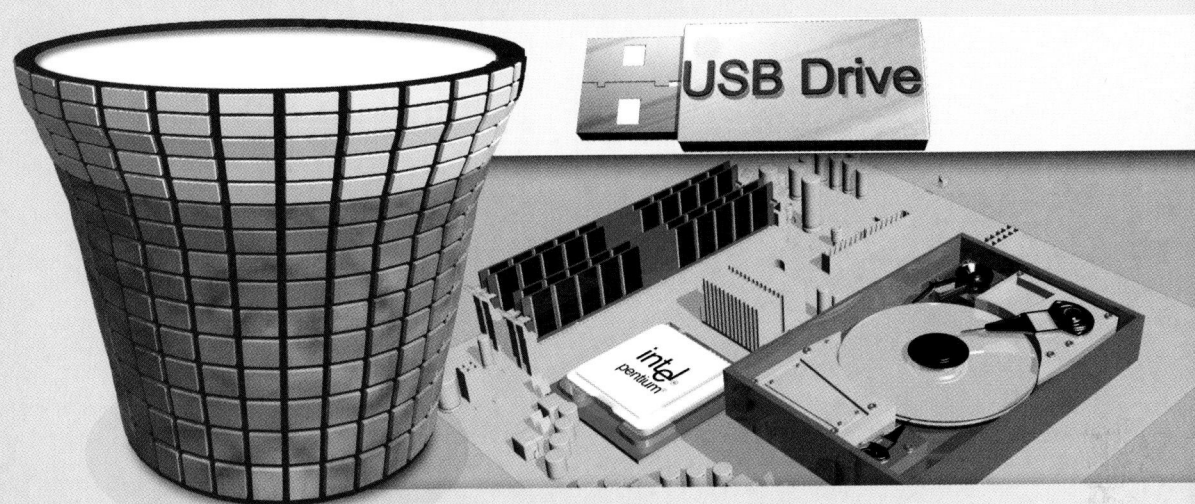

5 You can configure Vista to use all or just part of the available memory on the USB drive for your system's RAM. Just right-click on the USB drive in Windows Explorer and select Properties; from the Properties dialog box, select the ReadyBoost tab and adjust the slider to select how much space to use.

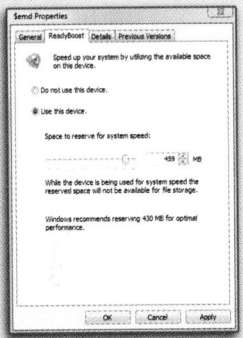

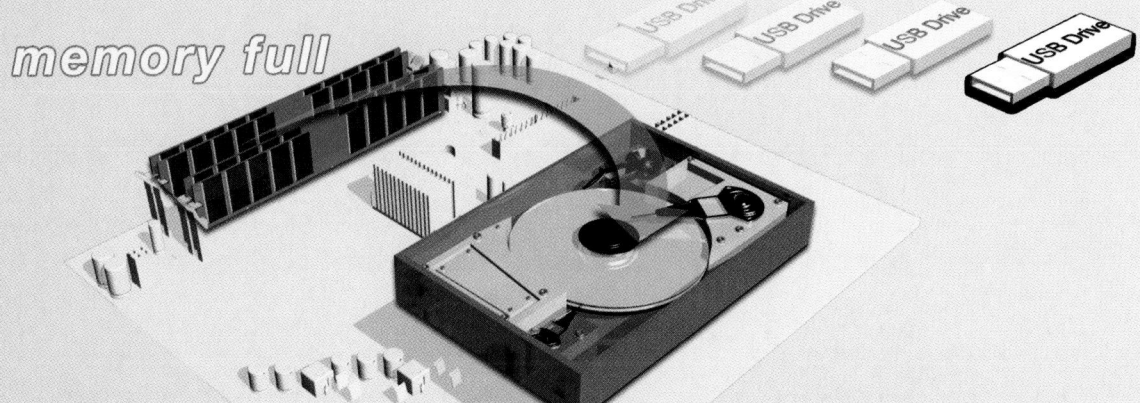

6 When you're done using the flash memory device, or if you know longer need the speed boost, simply remove the flash memory device. When the flash memory device is removed, Windows returns to using just the RAM available on the system motherboard. Any data still in use when the flash memory device was removed is now read from the hard disk, where it was duplicated during the ReadyBoost process.

CHAPTER

6

Managing System Information

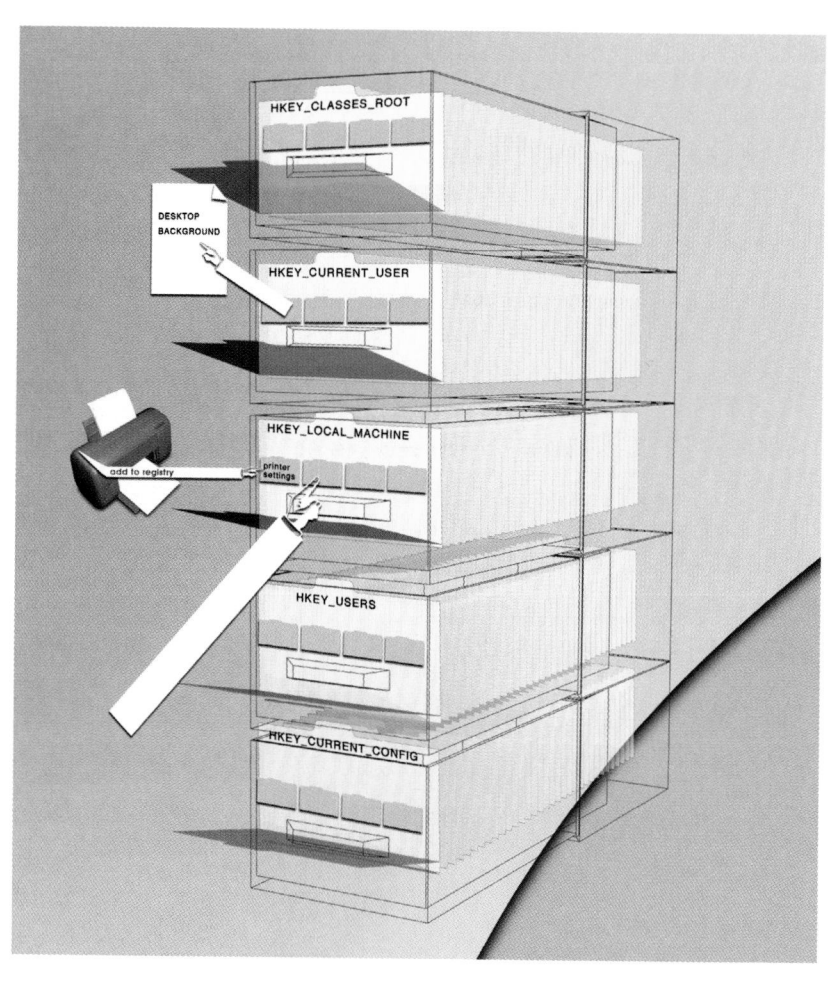

WINDOWS Vista is a complex and sophisticated piece of computer software. The operating system itself encompasses literally tens of thousands of individual system files—all of which have to be managed and monitored, as do all the devices that Vista is tasked with managing. It's a lot of information to track.

With all these files and devices to manage, it should come as no surprise that Vista is an extremely organized piece of software. To that end, thousands of individual configuration settings are stored in a single database called the Windows Registry. The Registry is where Windows turns when it needs to find out anything about any part of the system; it houses all manner of settings for everything from the window color and translucency to the brand and model number of printer you're using. This type of centralized configuration storage makes it easy for Windows to find precise settings, when necessary.

To that end, every time you make a configuration change, that information is automatically written to the Registry. Change the system time, and the Registry is updated; change your desktop wallpaper, the Registry is updated; change the home page in Internet Explorer, the Registry is updated. The Registry is also updated whenever you install a new software program or hardware device. And it all happens automatically, in the background.

You make most configuration changes from the Windows Control Panel. The Control Panel in Windows Vista is subtly different from the one in Windows XP, most noticeably in the new Control Panel Home view. Settings are grouped more logically than they were in Windows XP, and the most common tasks are accessible from the Home page, via a series of text links. Of course, if you like the old way of doing things, you can still display each of the control settings individually, by selecting the Classic view.

Windows Vista also makes a lot of other system information accessible to the average user. You're probably familiar with My Computer (called the Computer Explorer in Windows Vista), which lets you view information about your PC's hard disk and other storage devices. A lot of similar utilities in Windows Vista let you monitor or configure all sorts of system settings, from your PC's processor and memory specs to detailed information about specific device drivers. Everything you want to know about your system is available somewhere within Windows Vista—if you know where to look!

How the Windows Registry Manages Your System's Configuration

1 The Windows Registry is a database that contains configuration data about the hardware and environment of your PC and Windows Vista.

2 When Windows needs to do any-thing—open a program, display a dialog box, you name it—it accesses the Registry to obtain the proper con-figuration information. In this sense, the Registry functions like a control center for your entire computer system; it defines how every part of your system looks and works.

3 Settings are added to the Registry when-ever you install a new software program or hardware device. Existing settings are changed whenever you make a change to Control Panel settings, file associations, system policies, and the like.

4 The Registry is organized into five major sec-tions, called *hives*. Each hive is stored in its own system file on your PC's hard disk, as shown here.

5 Each hive is further organized into a variety of keys and subkeys that can be represented by a series of folders and subfolders. For example, if you want to find configuration information for which programs Windows Vista loads at launch, you would look in the following key: **HKEY_LOCAL_MACHINE\SOFTWARE\Microsoft\Windows\CurrentVersion\Run**.

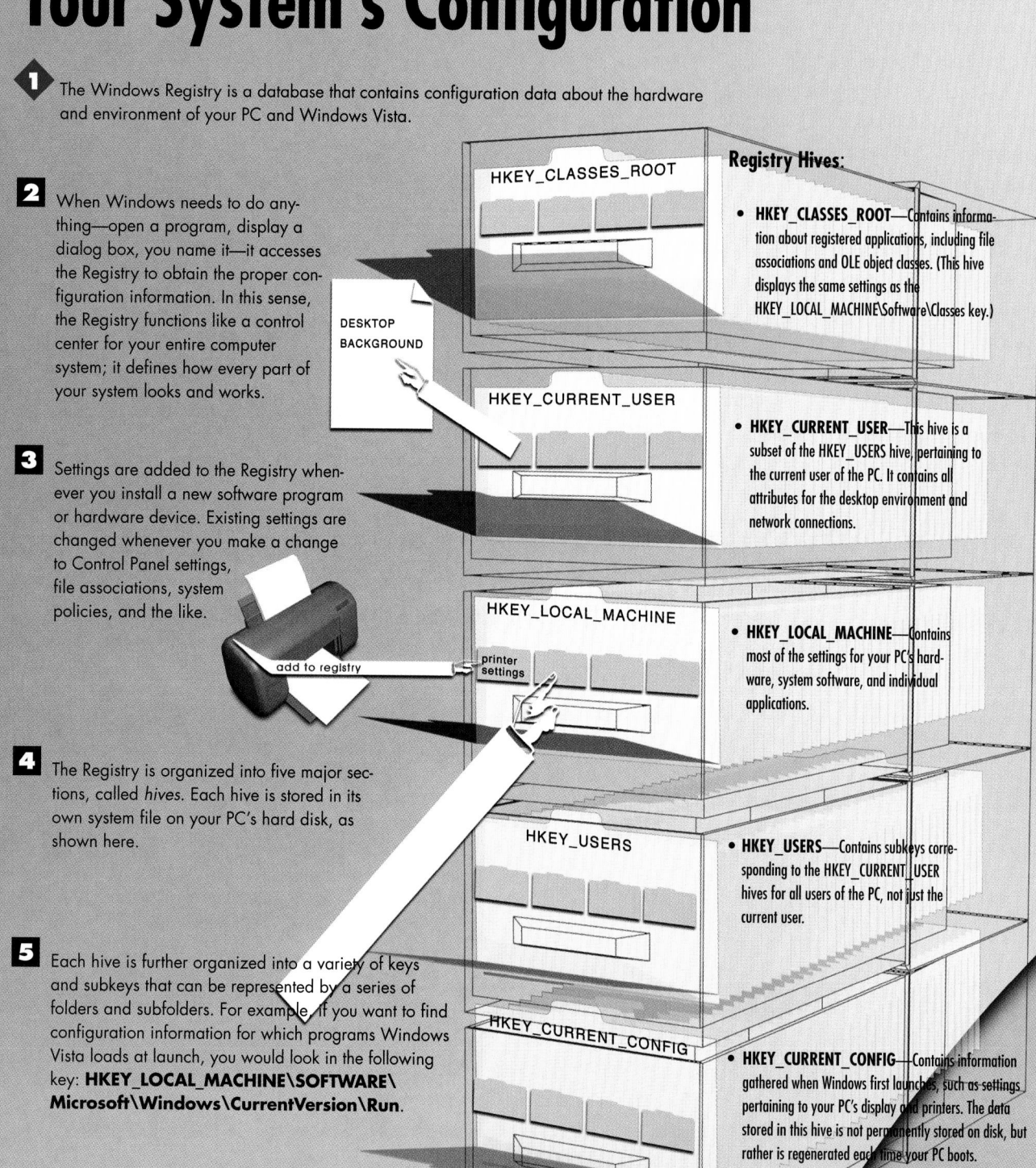

Registry Hives:

- **HKEY_CLASSES_ROOT**—Contains informa-tion about registered applications, including file associations and OLE object classes. (This hive displays the same settings as the HKEY_LOCAL_MACHINE\Software\Classes key.)

- **HKEY_CURRENT_USER**—This hive is a subset of the HKEY_USERS hive, pertaining to the current user of the PC. It contains all attributes for the desktop environment and network connections.

- **HKEY_LOCAL_MACHINE**—Contains most of the settings for your PC's hard-ware, system software, and individual applications.

- **HKEY_USERS**—Contains subkeys corre-sponding to the HKEY_CURRENT_USER hives for all users of the PC, not just the current user.

- **HKEY_CURRENT_CONFIG**—Contains information gathered when Windows first launches, such as settings pertaining to your PC's display and printers. The data stored in this hive is not permanently stored on disk, but rather is regenerated each time your PC boots.

HKEY_CLASSES_ROOT

DESKTOP BACKGROUND

HKEY_CURRENT_USER

add to registry

printer settings

HKEY_LOCAL_MACHINE

HKEY_USERS

HKEY_CURRENT_CONFIG

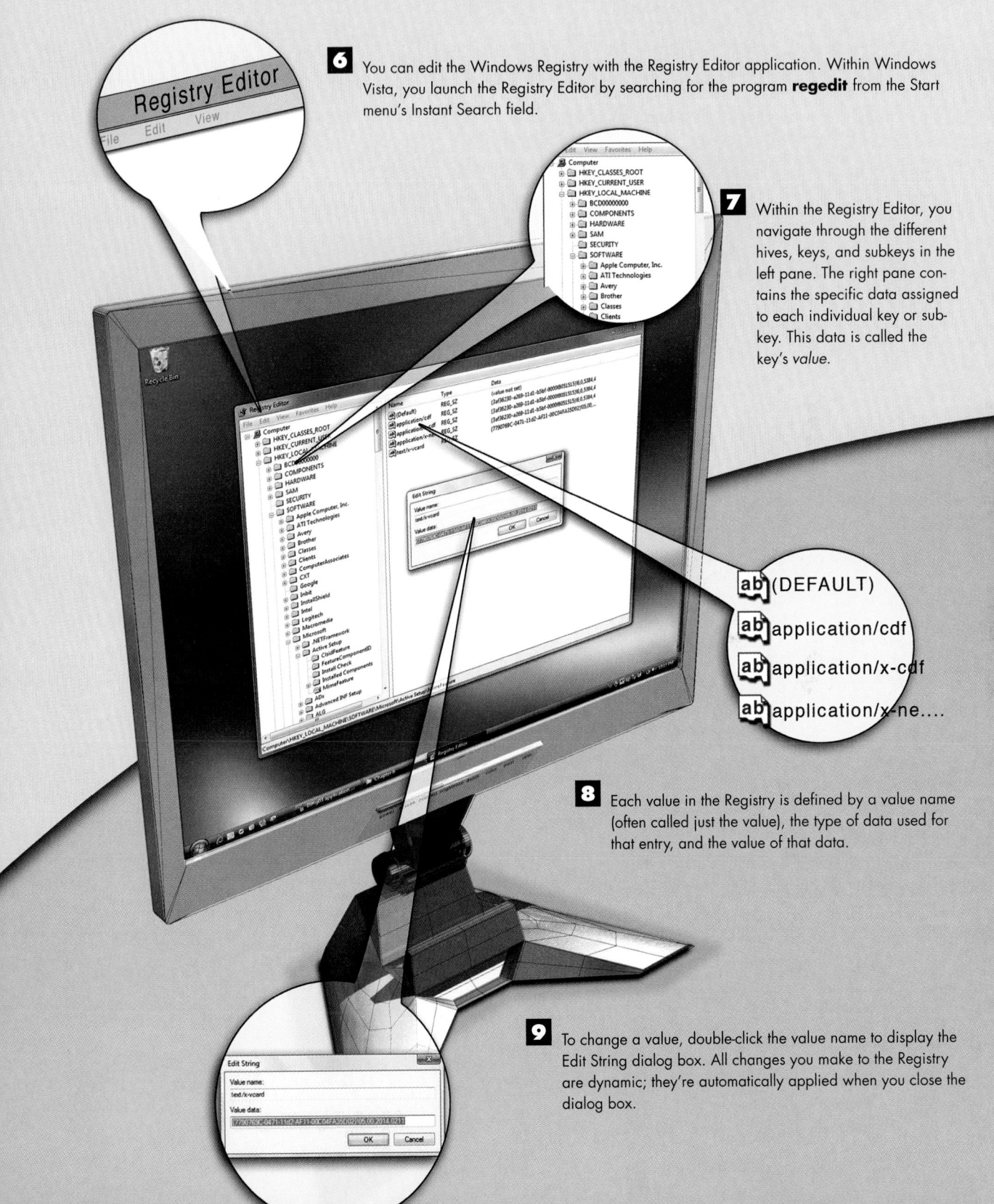

6 You can edit the Windows Registry with the Registry Editor application. Within Windows Vista, you launch the Registry Editor by searching for the program **regedit** from the Start menu's Instant Search field.

7 Within the Registry Editor, you navigate through the different hives, keys, and subkeys in the left pane. The right pane contains the specific data assigned to each individual key or subkey. This data is called the key's *value*.

8 Each value in the Registry is defined by a value name (often called just the value), the type of data used for that entry, and the value of that data.

9 To change a value, double-click the value name to display the Edit String dialog box. All changes you make to the Registry are dynamic; they're automatically applied when you close the dialog box.

How the Control Panel Changes Registry Settings

1 To change the configuration settings that are stored in the Windows Registry, you use the applets contained in the Windows Control Panel. You open the Control Panel by selecting **Start > Control Panel**.

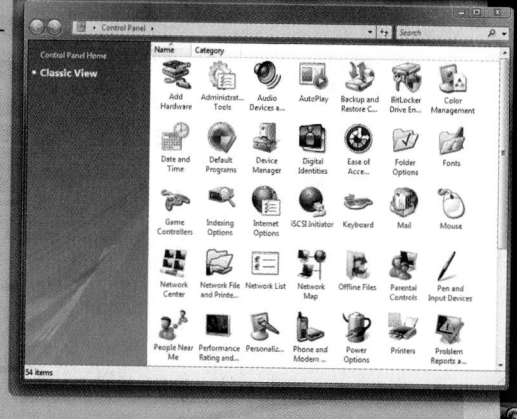

2 The Control Panel can be displayed in the new Windows Vista Home view or in the Classic view. The Classic view displays each control applet separately; the Home view groups the control applets by function.

3 The Control Panel contains individual applets for all important system settings. For example, you'll find separate applets that let you change date and time settings, display settings, folder options, Internet options, and the like. There are even control applets for adding and removing hardware and software from your PC.

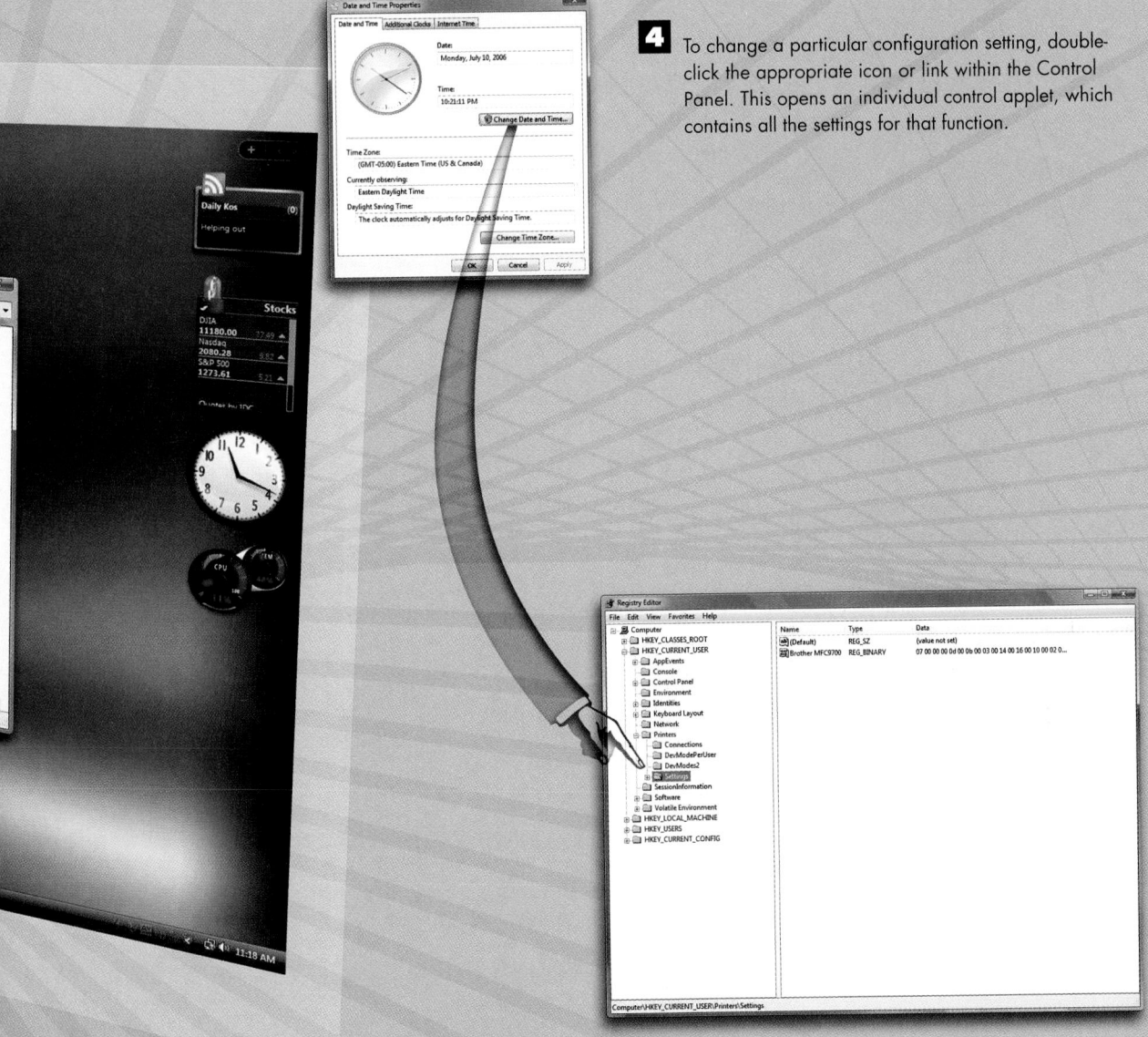

4 To change a particular configuration setting, double-click the appropriate icon or link within the Control Panel. This opens an individual control applet, which contains all the settings for that function.

5 Any setting changed within a control applet is immediately written to the corresponding key within the Windows Registry.

How to Monitor System Performance

1 Windows Vista includes numerous utilities to help you monitor and manage the performance of your computer system. Many of these utilities are centralized in the new **Welcome Center**, which displays when you first launch Windows Vista. The Welcome Center displays icons for all items that might require your attention or configuration; typical items include Set Up Devices, Add a Printer, Connect to the Internet, Add User Accounts, and so on. (Your computer manufacturer might also include offers and advertisements in this window.) Double-click an icon to open the corresponding configuration utility. (To open the Welcome Center manually, select **Start > All Programs > Accessories > Welcome Center**.)

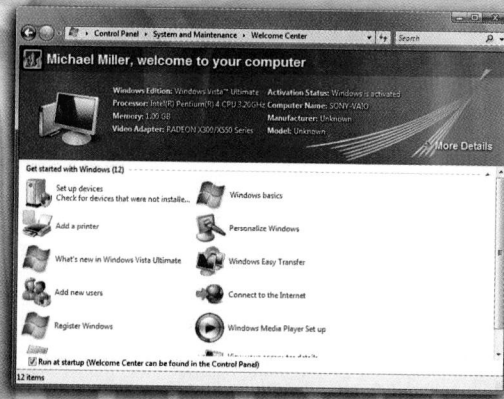

2 Perhaps the most familiar utility you can use to monitor your system is the **Computer Explorer**, previously known as My Computer. This Explorer displays information about all the storage devices attached to your system, including your main hard disk, CD/DVD drives, memory card readers, network drives, and so on. The basic window graphically displays how much storage space you have available on each drive, in the form of a bar graph. You can double-click a drive to view the drive's contents, or view detailed information about a drive by right-clicking the drive icon and selecting Properties. (To open the Computer Explorer, select **Start > Computer**.)

3 If you're not sure whether your computer has enough horsepower to run Windows Vista—or if you're experiencing performance-related problems—you should check out the new **Performance Rating and Tools** utility. This utility displays the results of the Windows System Assessment tool, which analyzes your system and displays a numeric rating of its performance potential. Ratings are on a scale of 1 to 5; the higher the rating, the more likely it is that your system can handle the demanding needs of Windows Vista. This tool also rates your system's performance in five key categories (Processor, Memory, Primary Hard Disk, Graphics, and Gaming Graphics) and alerts you if any startup programs are causing Vista to start slowly. (To open the Performance Rating and Tools utility, select **Start > Control Panel > System and Maintenance > Performance Rating and Tools**.)

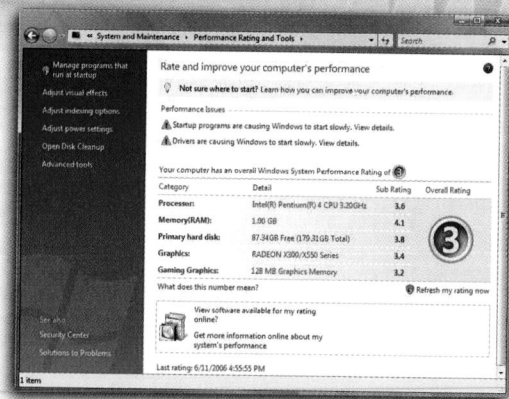

My Computer
The name change from My Computer to the Computer Explorer follows the similar naming convention changes in Windows Vista. My Documents is now the Documents Explorer, My Music is now the Music Explorer, My Pictures is now the Pictures Explorer, and so on. Each item appears on the Start menu as simply Computer, Documents, Music, and so on.

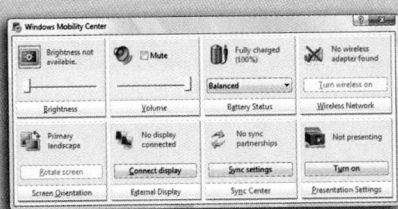

4 Users of notebook computers will appreciate Vista's new **Windows Mobility Center**. This utility centralizes all the settings relevant to mobile computing; you no longer have to open multiple utilities to make crucial configuration adjustments. Instead, you get access to a lot of useful mobility settings all in one place, including display properties, external display, sound, battery power, wireless connection, and a device synchronization manager. Click each setting to configure it separately. (To open the Windows Mobility Center on a notebook PC, select **Start > Control Panel > Mobile PC > Mobility Center**.)

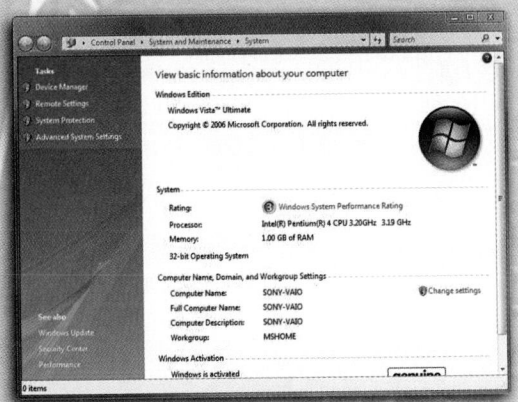

5 Experienced Windows users will recognize the **System Information** utility, which displays key information about all aspects of your computer system. Here you'll see information about your PC's processor, memory, and so forth; you can also use System Information to access other settings and utilities. (To open System Information, select **Start > Control Panel > System and Maintenance > System**.)

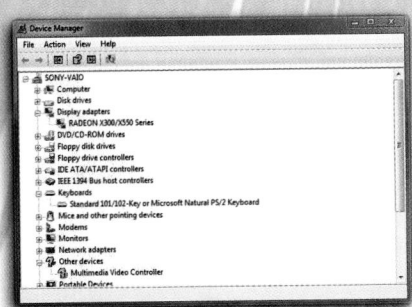

6 If you're having problems that you think are related to a particular device on your system, it's time to turn to the Windows Device Manager. The Device Manager displays key data about all the devices connected to your system—both internally and externally. Devices that have conflicts are displayed with a yellow exclamation mark through the icon; devices that aren't working have a red X through them. Double-click any device to open a Properties dialog box, which lets you update, roll back (return to an older driver version), or even delete that particular device driver. (To open the Device Manager, select **Start > Control Panel > System and Maintenance > System > Device Manager**.)

Managing Users

IF you're using your personal computer at home, chances are you're not the only person using it. When you're not pounding the keys, chances are that either your spouse or your children are perched in front of the screen. This makes your PC a multiple-user machine.

Older consumer versions of Windows (pre-XP) were not built with multiple users in mind. It was only the corporate versions of Windows (Windows NT, Windows 2000) that were built to handle multiple users on multiple computers over a corporate network; this functionality was necessary for the corporate environment.

Multiuser functionality was later incorporated into Windows XP, and is now fully integrated into Windows Vista. It's quite easy—and quite common—to configure Vista to handle multiple users of a PC and to set up the operating environment different for different users.

Why would you want to set up your computer with multiple user accounts? While you could let multiple people use your computer under a single username, the problem with this approach is that all your files would be accessible to everybody else using your PC—which probably isn't a good thing. In addition, you'd have to live with any changes to the interface made by other users, or take the trouble to reconfigure things back to the way you like them. Although communal computing is possible, it isn't ideal.

A better approach is to let the user configure Windows to his or her own personal tastes, as part of their own individual user accounts. When each user logs in, Windows displays the settings specific to that user. Plus, each user has his or her own private files, which other users can't access. This type of multiple-user setup is better for both personalization and privacy.

And, with Windows Vista's new User Account Control, each user is limited to the types of changes he or she can make to your system; it's no longer easy for users to change system settings or inadvertently install malicious software. In addition, you can use Vista's Parental Controls to manage and monitor usage of the user accounts you assign to your children. It's a great way to supervise their computer activity, without having to look over their shoulders 24/7.

How User Accounts and User Account Control Work

1 Windows Vista, like Windows XP before it, lets you create multiple user accounts—one for each person using your PC. Windows lets you easily switch from one user to another, using Fast User Switching. All the open programs and documents and settings for the first user are automatically stored when you switch to a second user; when you switch back, the first user's programs, documents, and settings reappear just as they were before the switch.

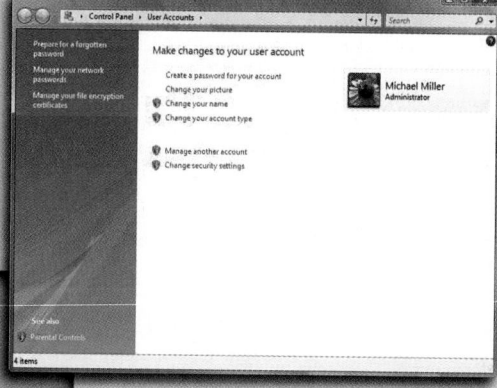

2 Each user can choose his or her own account name, picture, and password. In addition, whatever interface, desktop, and file personalization one user makes sticks with that user. Each user even gets his or her own Documents, Pictures, and Music folders, separate from other users' folders.

ADMINISTRATOR

USER

3 There are two primary levels of user accounts. An Administrator-level account has permission to perform any function, including installing programs and modifying or deleting important files. A User-level account does not have permission to install programs and delete key files; a regular user can only use the PC, not modify it.

DELETE

SOFTWARE INSTALL

ADNINISTRATOR

DELETE

SOFTWARE INSTALL

ADNINISTRATOR

ADNINISTRATOR

4 In Windows XP, all users were automatically assigned Administrator status. This resulted in rampant security problems, as users could inadvertently install malicious software and spyware on their system—and that software could then take control of the PC, using the original user's Administrator privileges.

5 To increase system security, Windows Vista utilizes User Account Control (UAC). With UAC, all users are automatically assigned User-level access, not Administrator access. This blocks the average user from executing tasks that could damage his or her system—and improves system security.

6 In Windows Vista, when a user attempts to perform an administrative-level task (such as installing a new software program, changing system settings, or deleting a system file), User Account Control presents a dialog box that asks for authorization for the task at hand. The task will not be executed until the user specifically grants permission.

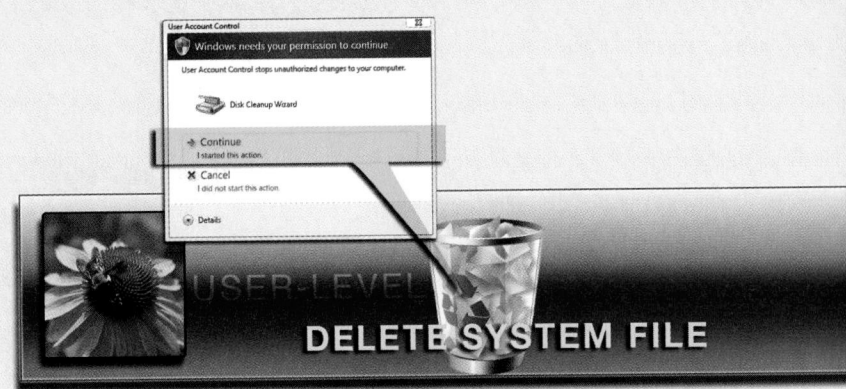

How Parental Controls Work

1 If you're a parent, you know it's not always possible to personally supervise every minute of your children's computer usage, let alone control when they can and can't access the system. That's why, when you first configure Windows Vista, it's a good idea to create separate user accounts for each of your children. This way you can use Vista's new Parental Controls feature to restrict and monitor your children's PC use—and protect them from inappropriate content.

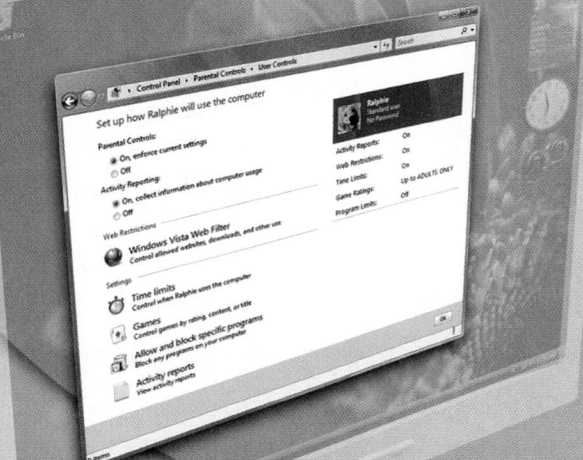

2 All of Vista's parental controls are configured and monitored from the Parental Controls Panel. From here you can, for each user, turn on general parental controls and activity reporting, as well as access activity reports, user time limits, game and application access, and a web content filter. (You access the Parental Controls Panel by selecting **Start > Control Panel > User Accounts and Family Safety > Parental Controls.**)

3 When you decide to track your children's computer usage, Windows Vista records all the activity generated by each user, including which websites they visit, who they instant message, what files they download, and which games and applications they launch—and when. This information is stored in a secure system file on your hard disk; you view this information via easy-to-read activity reports.

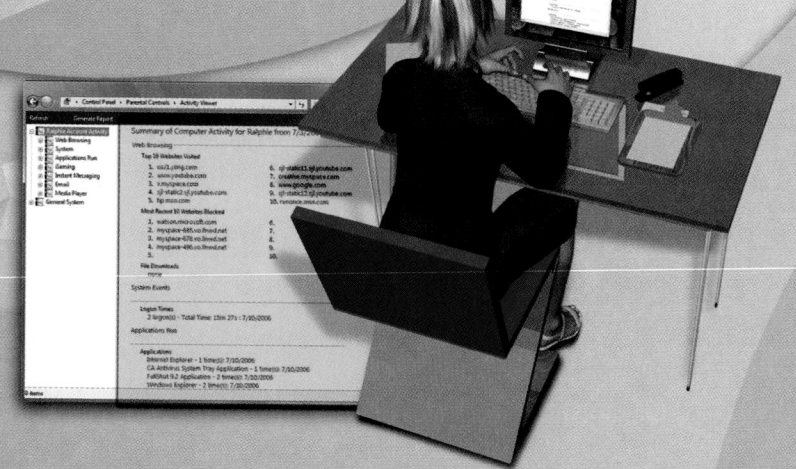

4 You don't want your children spending too much time in front of the PC. For that reason, Windows Vista offers time limits you can use to restrict computer usage. Simply determine when you want your children not to use the computer, then block out those days and times on the onscreen schedule grid. When your child is using the PC and nearing the end of an approved time period, he'll receive a 10-minute and 1-minute notification that his allowed time is just about up. If he fails to log off before his time is up, Windows will suspend his current session and display the login screen so that another user can use the computer. The next time your child logs on, his suspended session will appear onscreen, so he can pick up right where he left off.

5 As a parent, you know that some computer games are more acceptable than others. That's why the game industry rates their games for certain age levels. You can configure Windows Vista to allow or block access to games based on their age ratings; you can also allow or block access based on certain types of content, such as language or violence. Windows tracks the type of game by the content flags embedded in the game itself, and only allows that access you permit for each user.

6 Likewise, you may not want your children to have access to every application installed on your computer. For example, you may want to block access to the personal financial information stored in Quicken and Microsoft Money or to the business reports you generate with Microsoft Excel. You can use Vista's Block Specific Programs feature to display a list of all installed programs, and then choose to allow or block access to each program for this user.

7 Perhaps the scariest part of allowing your children to use a personal computer is all the inappropriate content available on the Internet. Fortunately, Windows Vista includes a built-in Web Content Filter, which can block access to specific web pages, based on each page's content. You specify what types of content you want blocked, and the Web Content Filter looks for and blocks access to pages that contain that type of content. (The filter examines the title, body text, and metadata contained in each page's underlying HTML code and compares this content with a database of unacceptable words and images.) When your child tries to access a blocked page, he or she sees a screen that explains why the site is unavailable to them.

CHAPTER

8

Managing Data

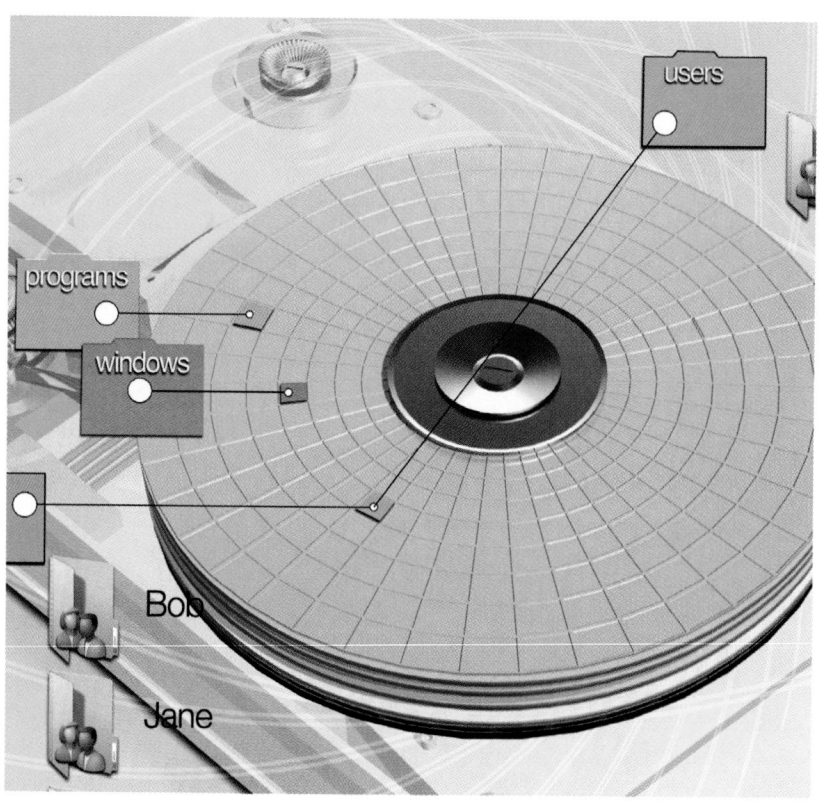

EVERY computer user has to work with files. Whether you're downloading MP3 files from the Internet or sharing Word documents with a friend or colleague, you need to know several essential file-related tasks. You have to know how to copy, delete, move, and rename files. And you have to know which file management tools to use to perform these tasks.

The way you perform these tasks has changed a little bit in Windows Vista. With Vista, the idea of separate My Documents, My Music, and My Pictures folders has morphed into a single type of folder called an Explorer, similar to the Windows Explorer found in older versions of Windows. All Explorers look and work the same, which is slightly different than how folders worked in Windows XP. For example, you won't find a Task Pane in a Windows Explorer, nor will you find a File menu. All your file operations are now accessed from a new Command Bar, and you'll probably be using the new Instant Search function to find the files and folders you want.

That Instant Search function is new to Windows Vista, and it's quite useful. Vista automatically indexes all the files on your PC, including key metadata for each file. You can then use Instant Search to quickly find specific files, based on the keywords you enter. It's a lot faster than the previous Windows search technology, and it works very well.

Windows Vista also introduces the concept of *virtual folders* to the desktop. These are folders that aren't really folders; they don't have physical contents but rather point to files stored elsewhere. You use virtual folders to group similar types of files wherever they're stored on your hard disk, without having to move them to new locations.

Microsoft intended to make even more file-related changes in Windows Vista, but they simply didn't have time to do all they wanted to do. Vista was originally slated to include a completely new file system, called WinFS (for Windows Future Storage), that would apply a relational database model to data storage for faster and more efficient searching. Unfortunately, WinFS didn't make it into Vista, which instead uses the tried-and-true NTFS file system—which means no major changes for users.

How Windows Organizes Data Files

1 Windows stores all your program and document files on your computer's hard disk, in a hierarchical series of folders and subfolders. The location of each individual file does not have to be (and seldom is) physically adjacent to other files in the same folder; the hierarchical organization of files and folders within Windows is virtual, not physical.

programs

windows

2 The main folders on a hard disk differ somewhat from system to system, but Windows Vista always includes the Programs, Users, and Windows folders. These folders are located in the root of your main hard drive (typically drive C:).

users

Bob

3 The Users folder contains all the documents and settings for each user account on your computer. (In previous versions of windows, these files were stored in the Documents and Settings folder, instead.) Each user has his or her own subfolder within the Users folder.

Jane

Miranda

4 The folder for each user contains additional subfolders for different types of files. Typical subfolders include Desktop, Documents, Downloads, Favorites, Music, Pictures, Videos, and the like—each containing files of that particular type.

 Bob

Bob's Music

 Bob's Pictures

 Bob's Contacts

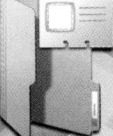 Bob's Documents

 memo1.doc

5 The files themselves are stored within a particular folder. Any folder can hold any type of file; file types can be mixed within any given folder. The ultimate location of a file is noted by the path of folders and subfolders in which it is contained. For example, the **example.doc** document contained in the Documents folder contained in the Bob folder contained in the Users folder is designated as **C:\Users\Bob\Documents\example.doc**.

 presentation.doc

presentation 06.do

How to Navigate Your Data with Windows Explorers

1 In Windows Vista, you navigate through all the folders and files on your computer with a series of Windows Explorers. These Explorers are the main tools used for finding, viewing, and managing your programs and documents. For ease-of-use, all Explorers share the same interface; common Explorers include Computer, Documents, Music, Pictures, and so forth.

2 The **Navigation Pane** on the left side of the Explorer window contains a list of common folders (labeled Favorite Links) and the folder hierarchy (called a *tree*) for the folders and files on your hard disk. Click any folder in the Navigation pane to view its contents in the main part of the Explorer window.

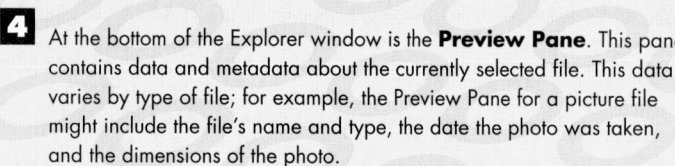

 ▶ Michael Miller ▶ Documents ▶

3 The **Address Bar** at the top of the Explorer window displays the hierarchical path you took to find the current folder. The previous folders are shown in a series of "breadcrumbs"; you can click any previous folder to open that folder, or pull down any folder to view a list of its other contents.

4 At the bottom of the Explorer window is the **Preview Pane**. This pane contains data and metadata about the currently selected file. This data varies by type of file; for example, the Preview Pane for a picture file might include the file's name and type, the date the photo was taken, and the dimensions of the photo.

Blood Sugar Monitor 2
Microsoft Office Excel 97-2003
Worksheet
Size: 543 KB   Authors: Michael Miller

File extension: Microsoft Office Excel 97-2003

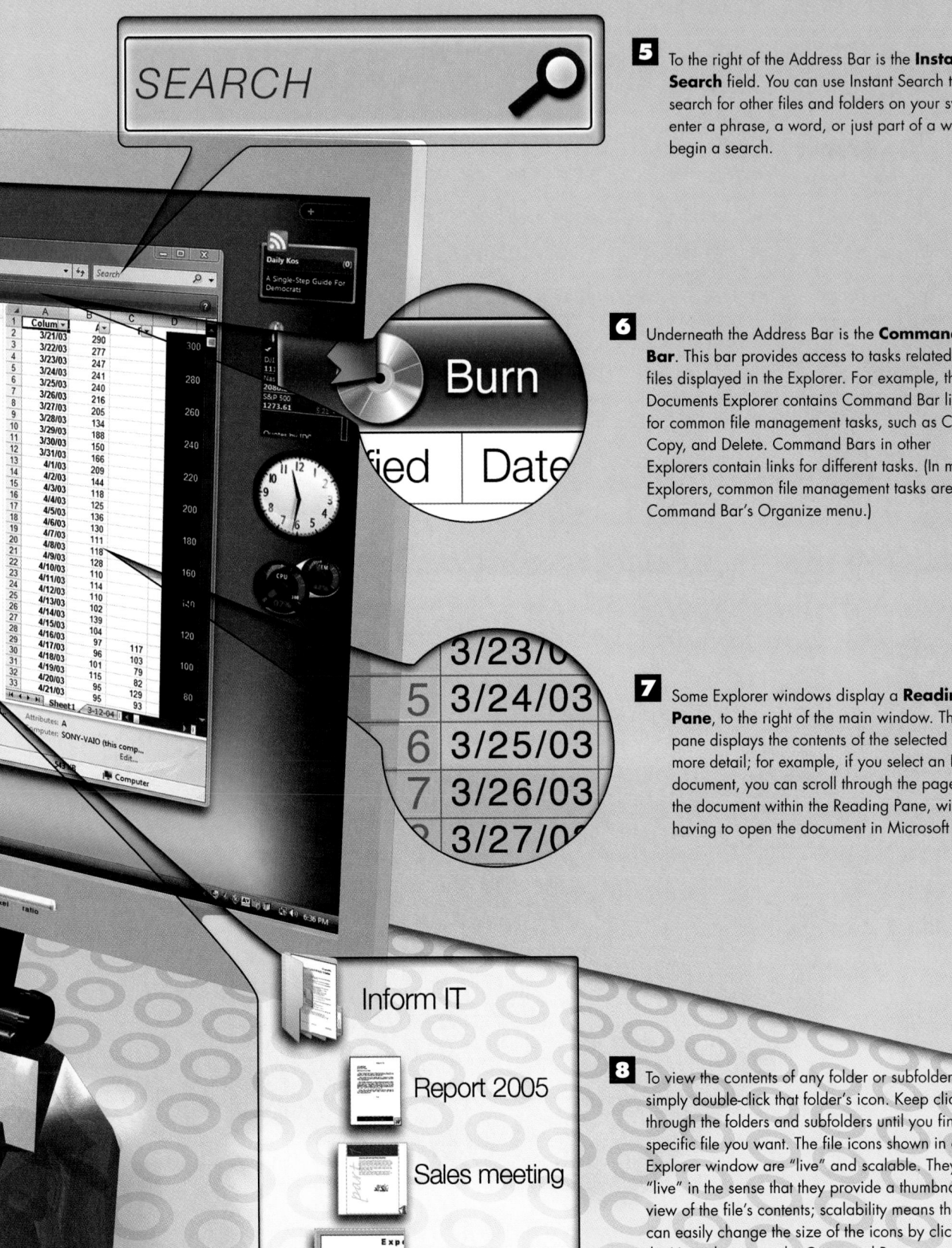

5 To the right of the Address Bar is the **Instant Search** field. You can use Instant Search to search for other files and folders on your system; enter a phrase, a word, or just part of a word to begin a search.

6 Underneath the Address Bar is the **Command Bar**. This bar provides access to tasks related to the files displayed in the Explorer. For example, the Documents Explorer contains Command Bar links for common file management tasks, such as Cut, Copy, and Delete. Command Bars in other Explorers contain links for different tasks. (In most Explorers, common file management tasks are in the Command Bar's Organize menu.)

7 Some Explorer windows display a **Reading Pane**, to the right of the main window. This pane displays the contents of the selected file in more detail; for example, if you select an Excel document, you can scroll through the pages of the document within the Reading Pane, without having to open the document in Microsoft Excel.

8 To view the contents of any folder or subfolder, simply double-click that folder's icon. Keep clicking through the folders and subfolders until you find the specific file you want. The file icons shown in any Explorer window are "live" and scalable. They're "live" in the sense that they provide a thumbnail preview of the file's contents; scalability means that you can easily change the size of the icons by clicking the Views button on the Command Bar.

How Files Are Copied, Moved, and Deleted

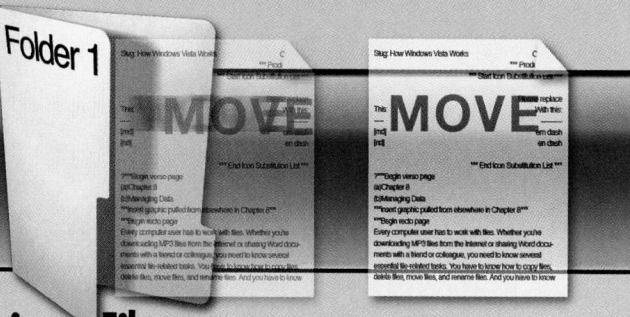

Copying a File

1 The act of copying a file makes a virtual copy of the original file and places it in another location on your system. When you copy a file, the original file remains in its original location; you end up with two separate files: the original and the copy.

2 When you select **Organize > Copy**, a copy of the original file is placed in the Windows Clipboard, which is a section of temporary system memory.

Moving a File

1 Moving a file differs from copying a file in that the original file itself is moved to a new location. After the move operation, only one file remains; the original file no longer resides in its original location.

2 When you select **Organize > Cut**, the selected file is moved out of the original folder to the Windows Clipboard in system memory.

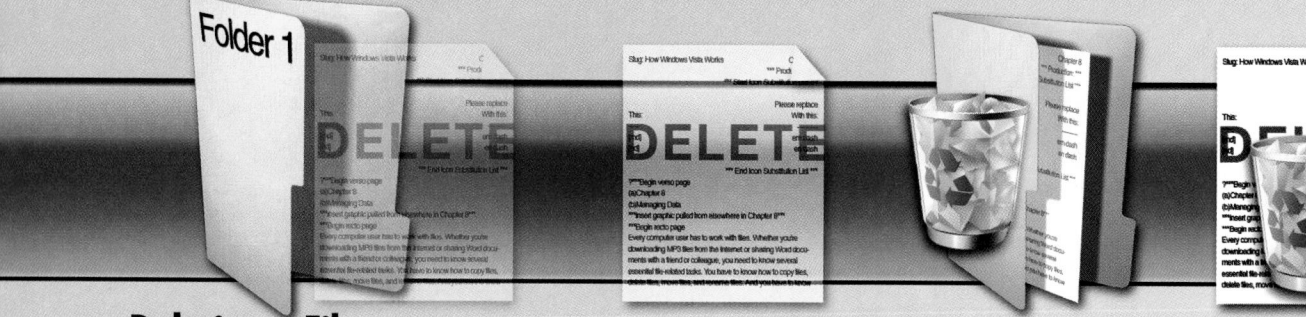

Deleting a File

1 When you delete a file from a folder, the file isn't really deleted—yet. All files you delete are temporarily stored in the Recycle Bin, which is a system file that serves as a physical cache for recently deleted files.

2 When you select **Organize > Delete**, the selected file is moved from its original folder into the Recycle Bin folder. You can undelete the file by opening the Recycle Bin, highlighting the file, and then selecting Restore This Item.

3 When you navigate to a new folder and select **Organize >
Paste**, the copy of the original file is moved from the Windows
Clipboard into the new folder.

3 When you navigate to a new folder and select
Organize > Paste, the file is moved from the
Windows Clipboard into the new folder.

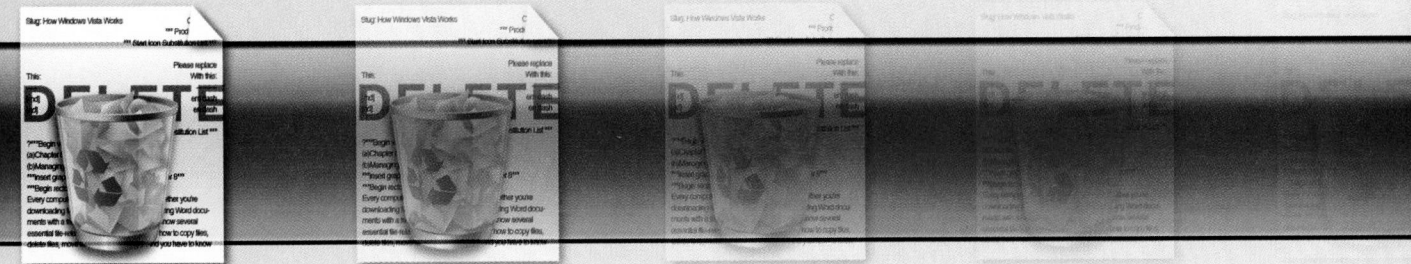

3 When the Recycle Bin fills up, files are permanently deleted on a first come, first gone basis. (You can also manually
empty files from the Recycle Bin, if you like.) When a file is emptied from the Recycle Bin, the pointer to where that file
is on the hard disk is removed, making the file invisible to Windows—and freeing up that file space for new files.

How Instant Search Works

1 Windows Vista includes a much improved (and much more visible) search tool than previous versions of Windows. The new Instant Search is useful for quickly finding any type of information on your system—files, programs, email messages, you name it.

2 The new Windows Search Engine service is running constantly, in the background, as you conduct your other computing tasks. It catalogues all the data on your hard drive, creating an index of files and metadata. It's this index that you access when you enter a query into an Instant Search box; your query is matched against entries in the index, with matching entries displayed as search results.

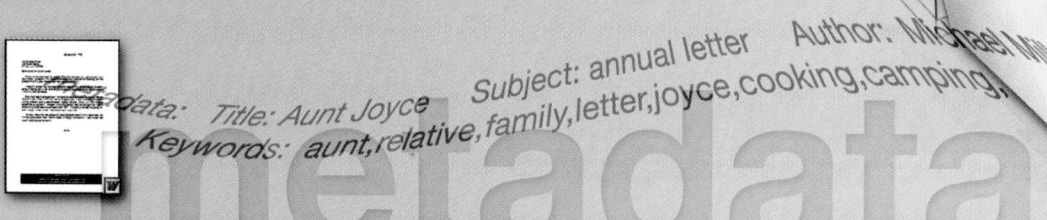

3 The Windows Search Engine not only indexes file names and message headers, it also indexes text within documents and any metadata attached to a file. Metadata are data points collected by the data files associated with a particular application. For example, Microsoft Word collects data for Title, Subject, Author, Manager, Company, and Keywords. Other programs collect similar application-related data points. The Windows Search Engine includes all these data points along with the other important information about each file in its index. You can then include metadata in your search query, to better find specific files.

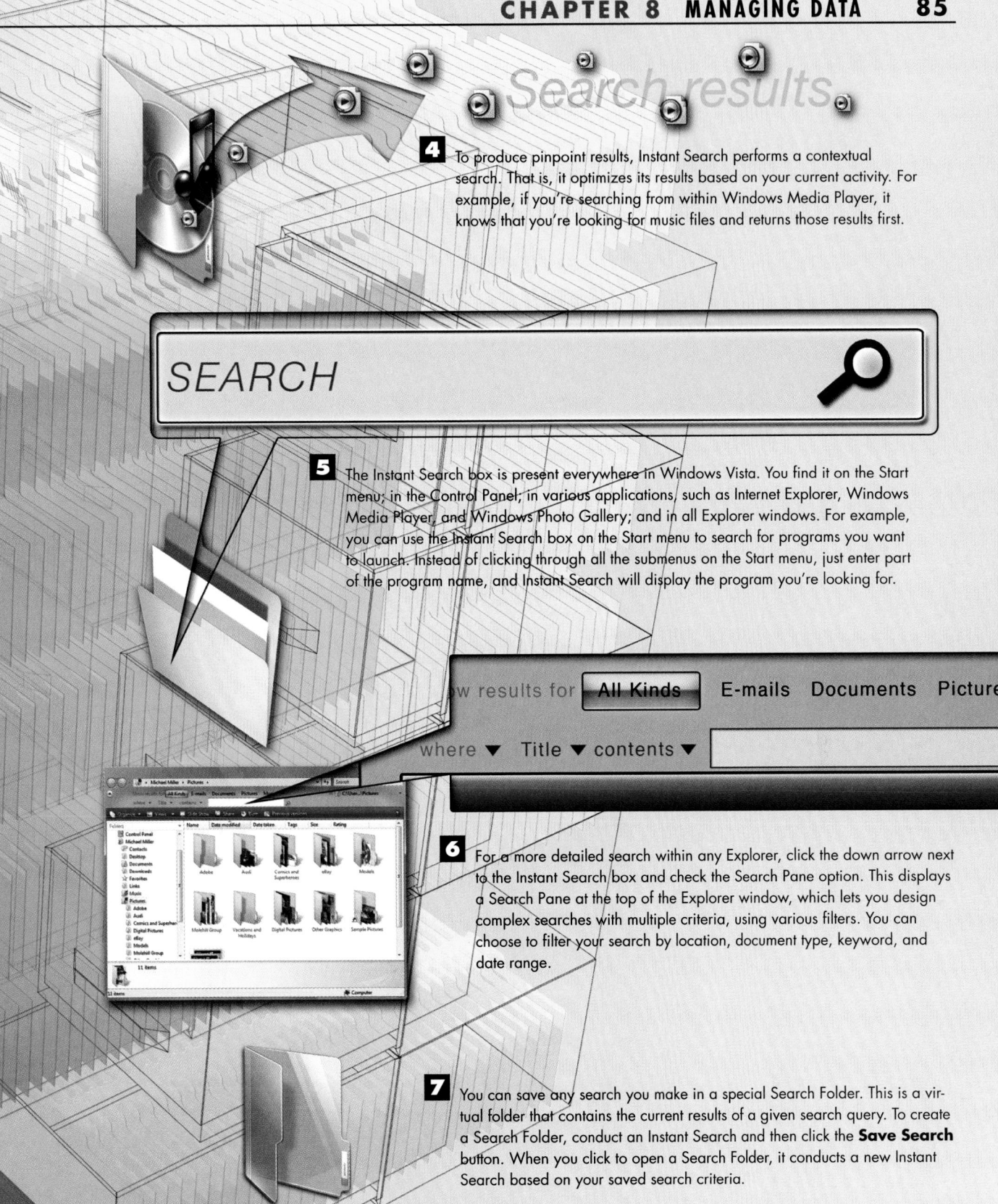

Search results

4 To produce pinpoint results, Instant Search performs a contextual search. That is, it optimizes its results based on your current activity. For example, if you're searching from within Windows Media Player, it knows that you're looking for music files and returns those results first.

SEARCH

5 The Instant Search box is present everywhere in Windows Vista. You find it on the Start menu; in the Control Panel; in various applications, such as Internet Explorer, Windows Media Player, and Windows Photo Gallery; and in all Explorer windows. For example, you can use the Instant Search box on the Start menu to search for programs you want to launch. Instead of clicking through all the submenus on the Start menu, just enter part of the program name, and Instant Search will display the program you're looking for.

ow results for   All Kinds   E-mails   Documents   Pictures

where ▼ Title ▼ contents ▼

6 For a more detailed search within any Explorer, click the down arrow next to the Instant Search box and check the Search Pane option. This displays a Search Pane at the top of the Explorer window, which lets you design complex searches with multiple criteria, using various filters. You can choose to filter your search by location, document type, keyword, and date range.

7 You can save any search you make in a special Search Folder. This is a virtual folder that contains the current results of a given search query. To create a Search Folder, conduct an Instant Search and then click the **Save Search** button. When you click to open a Search Folder, it conducts a new Instant Search based on your saved search criteria.

How Virtual Folders Work

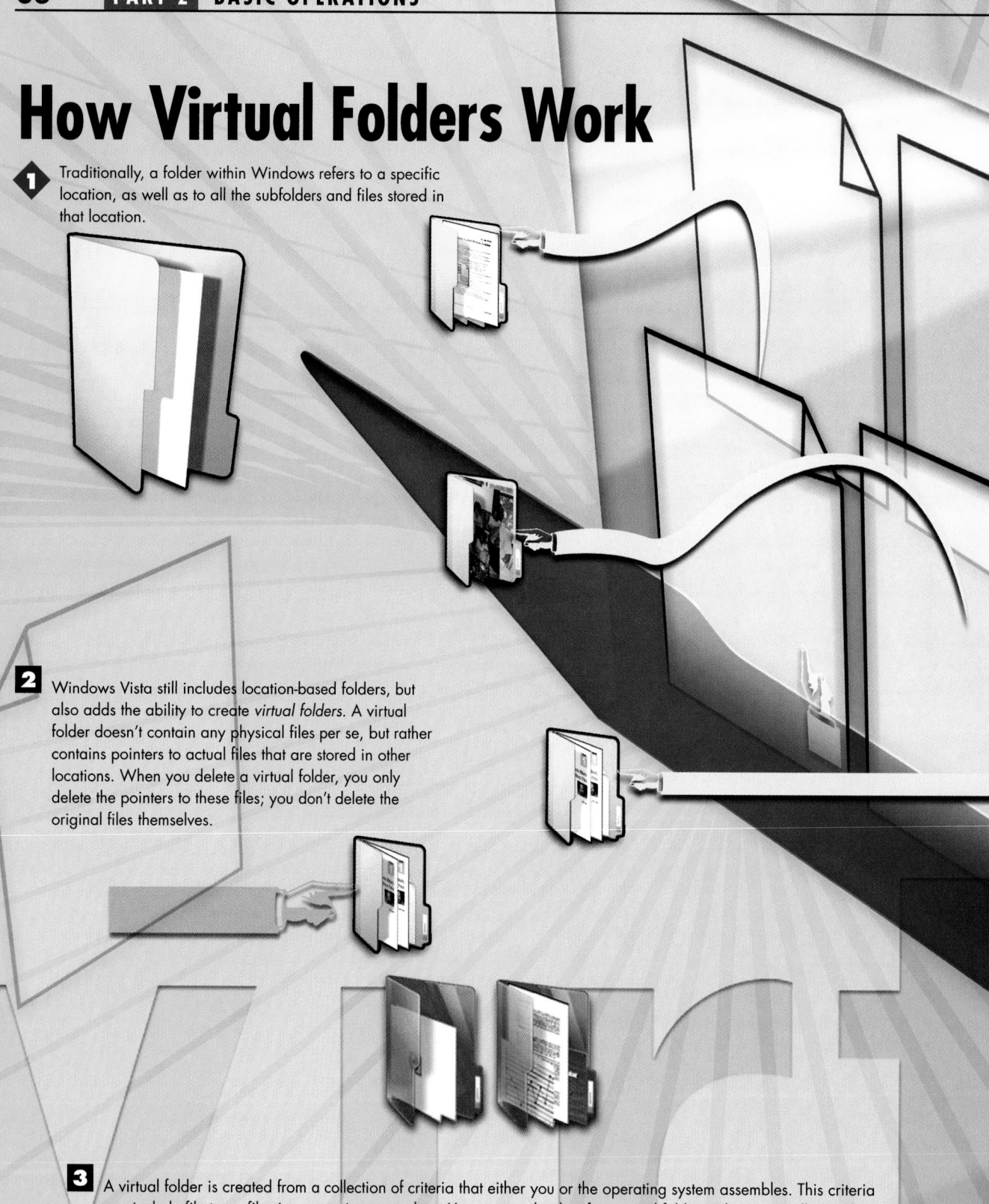

1 Traditionally, a folder within Windows refers to a specific location, as well as to all the subfolders and files stored in that location.

2 Windows Vista still includes location-based folders, but also adds the ability to create *virtual folders*. A virtual folder doesn't contain any physical files per se, but rather contains pointers to actual files that are stored in other locations. When you delete a virtual folder, you only delete the pointers to these files; you don't delete the original files themselves.

3 A virtual folder is created from a collection of criteria that either you or the operating system assembles. This criteria can include file type, file size, or various metadata. You can easily identify a virtual folder within Vista; all virtual folder icons are blue, instead of the normal yellow color.

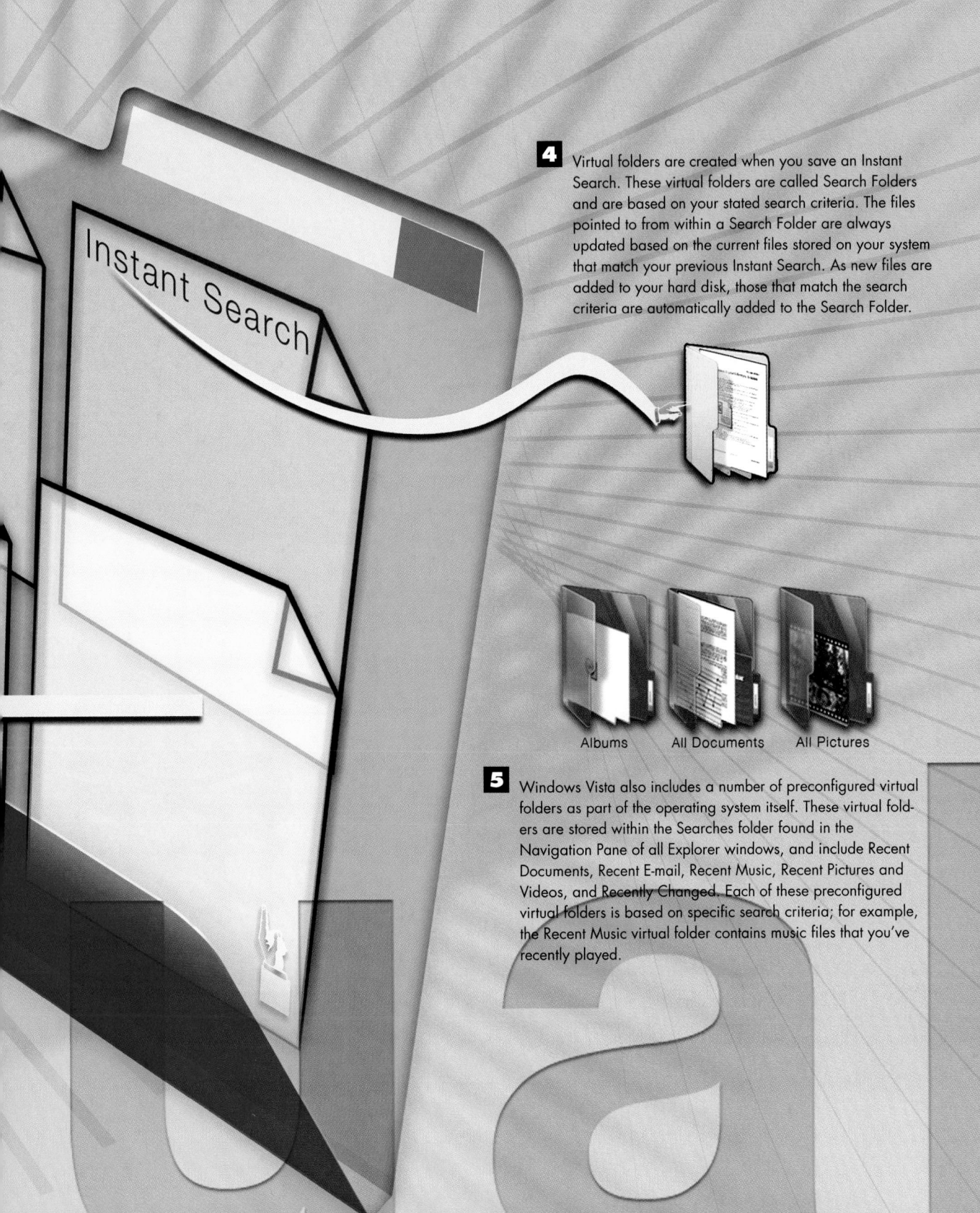

4 Virtual folders are created when you save an Instant Search. These virtual folders are called Search Folders and are based on your stated search criteria. The files pointed to from within a Search Folder are always updated based on the current files stored on your system that match your previous Instant Search. As new files are added to your hard disk, those that match the search criteria are automatically added to the Search Folder.

Albums   All Documents   All Pictures

5 Windows Vista also includes a number of preconfigured virtual folders as part of the operating system itself. These virtual folders are stored within the Searches folder found in the Navigation Pane of all Explorer windows, and include Recent Documents, Recent E-mail, Recent Music, Recent Pictures and Videos, and Recently Changed. Each of these preconfigured virtual folders is based on specific search criteria; for example, the Recent Music virtual folder contains music files that you've recently played.

How Compressed Folders Work

1   When a file is too big to transmit via email or copy to a removable disk, or it simply takes up too much hard disk space, you can use file compression to reduce its size. The concept of file compression is based on the fact that most computer files are fairly redundant—that is, they repeat a lot of the same information over and over again. By only storing the redundant information once (rather than multiple times), the compressed file is significantly reduced in size. Only the unique information remains.

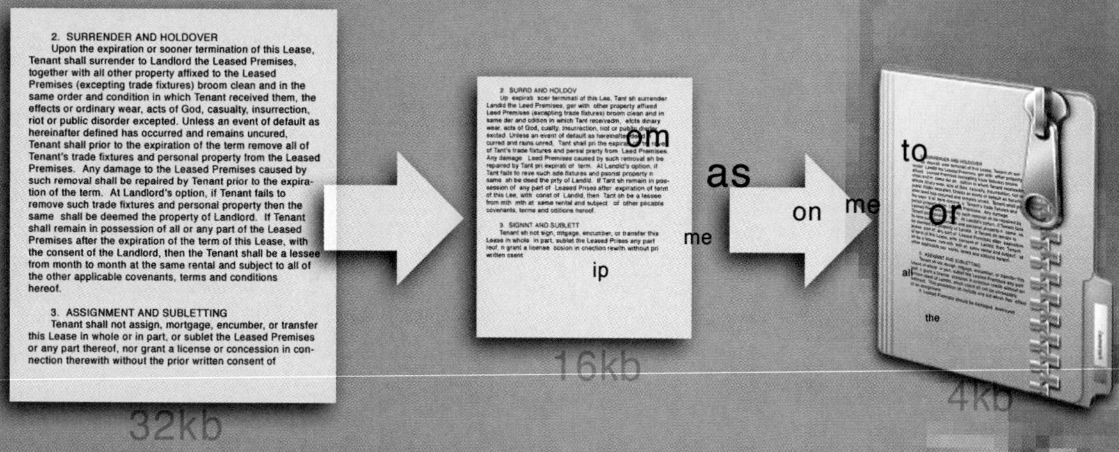

32kb

16kb

4kb

2   Windows Vista lets you reduce the size of your archived files via its *compressed folders* feature. Windows' compressed folders are actually .ZIP-format files compressed with the LZW algorithm.

LZW Compression
The LZW compression algorithm is named after Abraham Lempel, Jacob Ziv, and Terry Welch, the algorithm's creators.

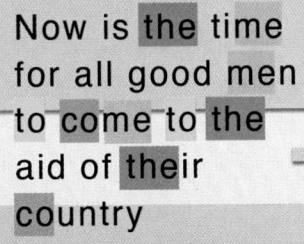

Now is the time for all good men to come to the aid of their country

3 In a text file, redundant information is identified by the LZW algorithm. LZW is an adaptive, dictionary-based algorithm. This means that redundant letter patterns are identified as the file is processed; as the process continues, it adapts to find more redundant letter patterns.

Dictionary

to   the

me   co

4 The redundant letter patterns are removed from the original text and placed in a dictionary. The compressed file now contains only nonredundant patterns, with pointers inserted where the original redundant patterns resided. Each pointer refers to a distinct letter pattern in the dictionary, which is stored as part of the compressed file.

Now is the time for all good men to come to the aid of their country

Now is ▮ ti_ for all good _n ▮ ▮ ▮ aid of _ir _untry

5 When the file is uncompressed, the pointers are replaced by the original letter patterns, as stored in the dictionary. This restores the file to its original condition, with no data loss. This type of data compression is called *lossless compression*.

6 There are similar types of data redundancies in all types of files. For example, this digital picture of a landscape contains a big blue sky—which repeats the same value of blue across a large area. You don't need to store every single blue pixel, so Windows' compression algorithm places that particular blue pixel into the dictionary, and inserts pointers where those pixels originally resided. Since the blue pixel is only stored once for the entire sky area, the file compresses into a much smaller size.

Image Compression

How the XPS File Format Works

1 When you print a normal Word or Excel document, the printed document doesn't always look identical to what's onscreen. What is printed depends on the fonts installed on the user's PC; printing the same document on different PCs can produce different results.

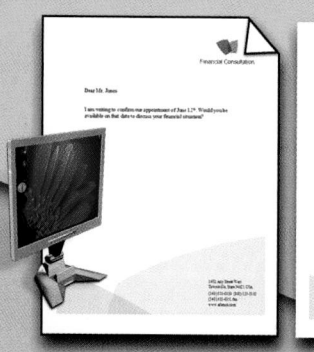

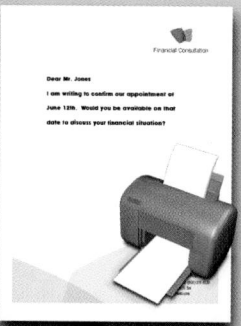

2 Microsoft's new XML Paper Specification (XPS) document format solves this problem. Like Adobe's Portable Document Format (PDF), documents created in XPS format look the same no matter what PC they're printed from. The XPS document format is an integral part of Windows Vista and of new Microsoft Office 2007 applications.

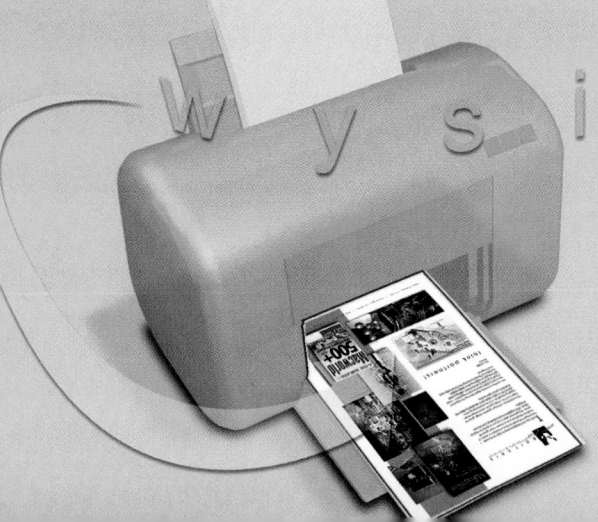

3 An XPS document is a fixed document—that is, an identical representation of what was created onscreen. An image of the entire document is rendered, and this image is viewed onscreen and sent to the printer. Because an image is created of the original document, the XPS document retains all the fonts and images of the original, as well as the exact page layout.

4 The XPS format supports high-fidelity, vector-based graphics, instead of traditional bit-mapped graphics. This enables an XPS document to be magnified many times over; the original text and graphics are simply scaled upward, with no loss in resolution.

5 Windows Vista automatically generates an XPS document anytime you print from any application. When the XPS document is sent to an XPS-capable printer, no conversion between the PC and the printer is needed. Because a single image is being printed, no individual fonts have to be loaded or accessed. This improves print fidelity while at the same time increasing print speeds.

6 XPS documents are also more secure than traditional Word or Excel files. That's because an XPS document is simply an image of a document; it doesn't contain any macros or scripts that can be run in the background. This makes an XPS document more like a sheet of electronic paper, rather than a file containing various types of data.

CHAPTER 9

Managing Applications

WHAT use is an operating system if you don't have any software to run on it?

In many ways, Windows exists as the infrastructure that enables you to run various software programs on your PC. If Windows is doing its job, you almost forget that it's there. You use the operating system to launch your programs, but after they're launched, it stays out of your way.

The way you manage programs hasn't changed dramatically in Windows Vista. All your programs are still displayed on the Start menu, they still appear in separate windows on your desktop, and you can still switch between them using the buttons that appear on the taskbar. Windows remains a true multitasking operating system so that you can run more than one application at a time. And, best of all, all Windows-compatible applications still have a similar look and feel, which makes it easy for you to learn new programs—you don't have to reinvent the wheel, as it were.

Not only do you not have to reinvent any wheels, neither do the developers of Windows-compatible applications. With Windows, Microsoft has created an architecture that supports cross-application consistency. Windows itself includes a giant toolbox of application operations and elements that are shared between all Windows applications; a program developer simply "calls" the necessary operation or element, and it automatically appears in the program—looking and acting the same as it does in all other programs. This makes for efficient application design and greater ease-of-use for you and me.

Of course, you never see all this behind-the-scenes activity. All you need to know is that you open the Start menu to launch a program and that every program you use has a similar File menu, save function, Print dialog box, and so forth. Sure, some of these elements might look a little different in Windows Vista (that's because of the new Aero interface), but everything appears where it should and does what it should. And that's what makes Windows such a user-friendly operating system.

How the Start Menu Works

1 The Start menu is where you launch all your applications and utilities. The right side of the Start menu contains links to common Windows Explorers (Documents, Pictures, Music, and so on), whereas frequently used and recently used programs are listed on the left side of the menu. The All Programs menu within the Start menu contains links to all the applications installed on your PC.

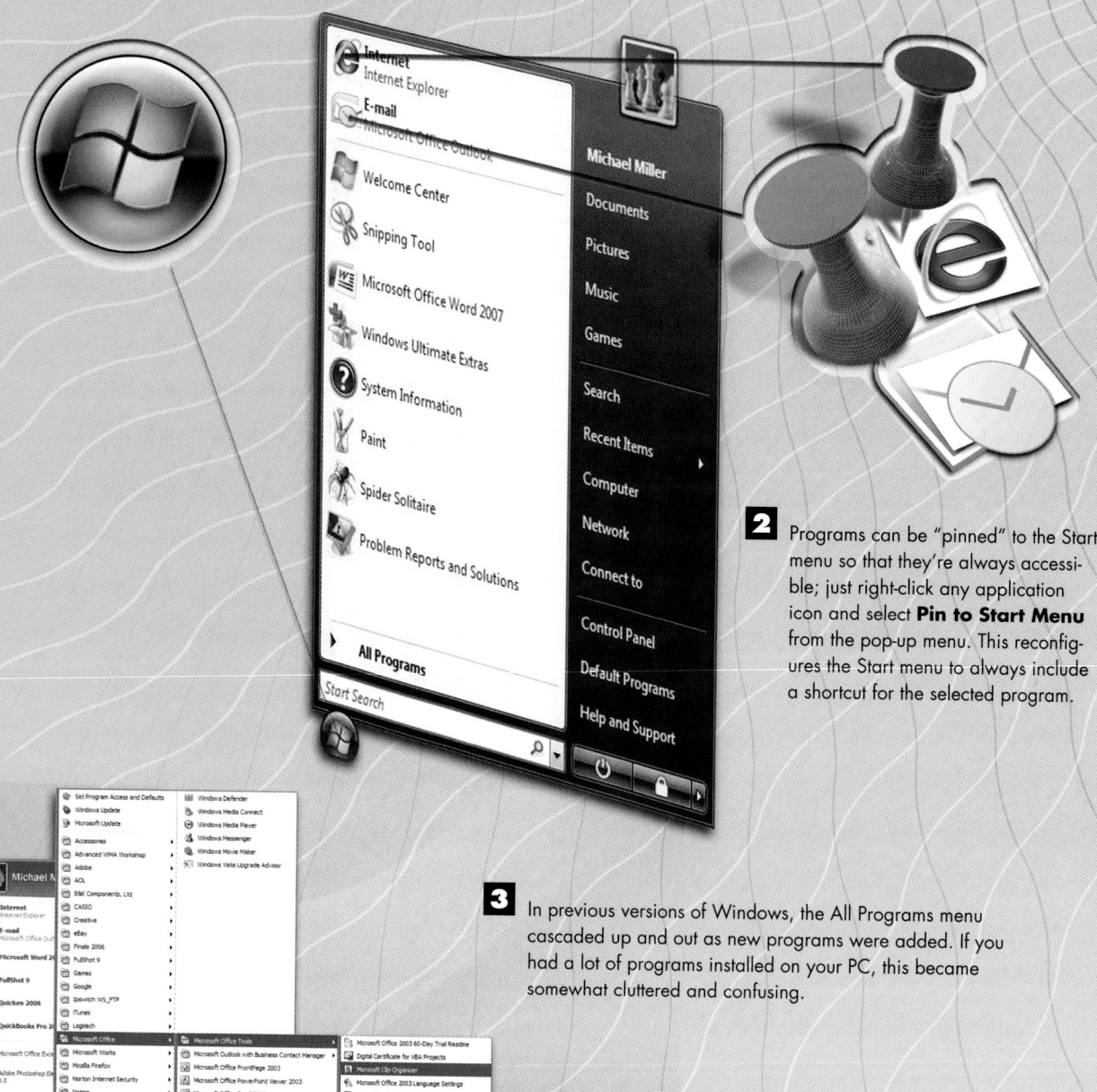

2 Programs can be "pinned" to the Start menu so that they're always accessible; just right-click any application icon and select **Pin to Start Menu** from the pop-up menu. This reconfigures the Start menu to always include a shortcut for the selected program.

3 In previous versions of Windows, the All Programs menu cascaded up and out as new programs were added. If you had a lot of programs installed on your PC, this became somewhat cluttered and confusing.

4 In Windows Vista, application clutter is contained by an All Programs menu that expands and contracts in a tree-like structure without taking up excess desktop space. Click any folder to expand it and view the applications within.

5 Windows Vista also includes an Instant Search field on the Start menu. Enter all or part of a program name into the Instant Search field, and matching applications are listed in the Programs pane of the Start menu. For example, to find the Microsoft Excel application, enter **Excel** into the Instant Search field; Vista immediately displays a shortcut to Excel, as well as other relevant links.

6 The Start menu works by displaying shortcuts that point to the actual executable files that reside on your PC's hard disk. When you click a shortcut on the Start menu, it sends an instruction to launch the program associated with the icon. The actual applications do not reside on the Start menu; when you delete a shortcut from the Start menu, it only removes the shortcut, not the actual program file.

How Windows Shares Code Between Programs

1 The Windows operating system makes it easy for developers to create efficient applications by letting each application share certain universal elements and functions. A program doesn't have to include separate code for these functions; the program code simply has to reference the universal Windows code to perform that particular function. This lets a single line of reference code replace hundreds and hundreds of lines of unique code.

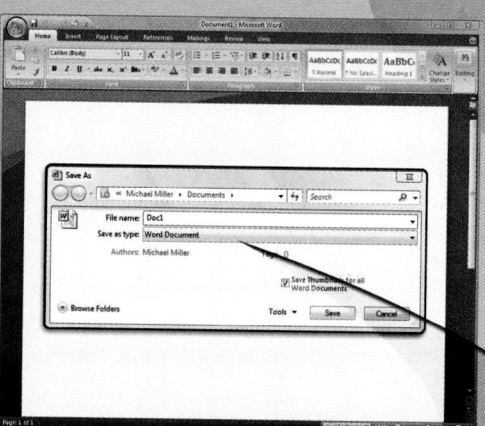

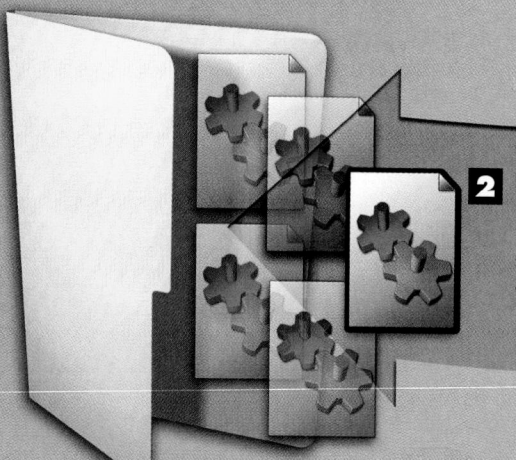

2 These packets of universal program code are stored in files called *Dynamic Link Libraries*, or DLLs. There are DLLs for all common Windows elements and functions, from displaying dialog boxes to saving open files.

3 When an application needs to access a DLL, it first refers to an *application programming interface* (API) to determine how to call that function. All DLLs have a corresponding API to enable applications to successfully call the function performed by the DLL.

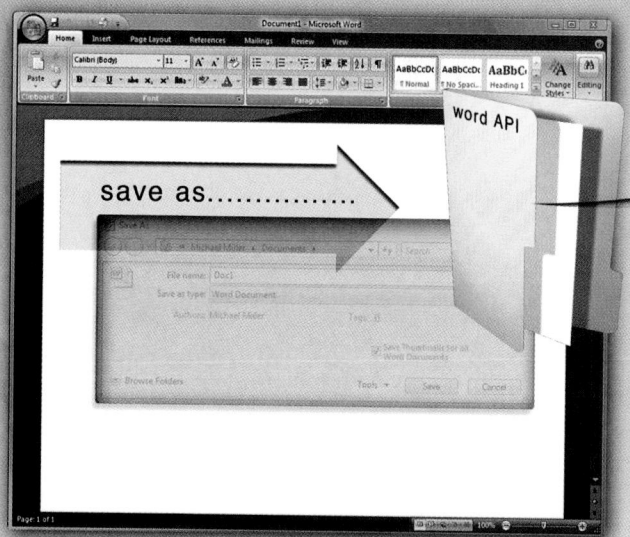

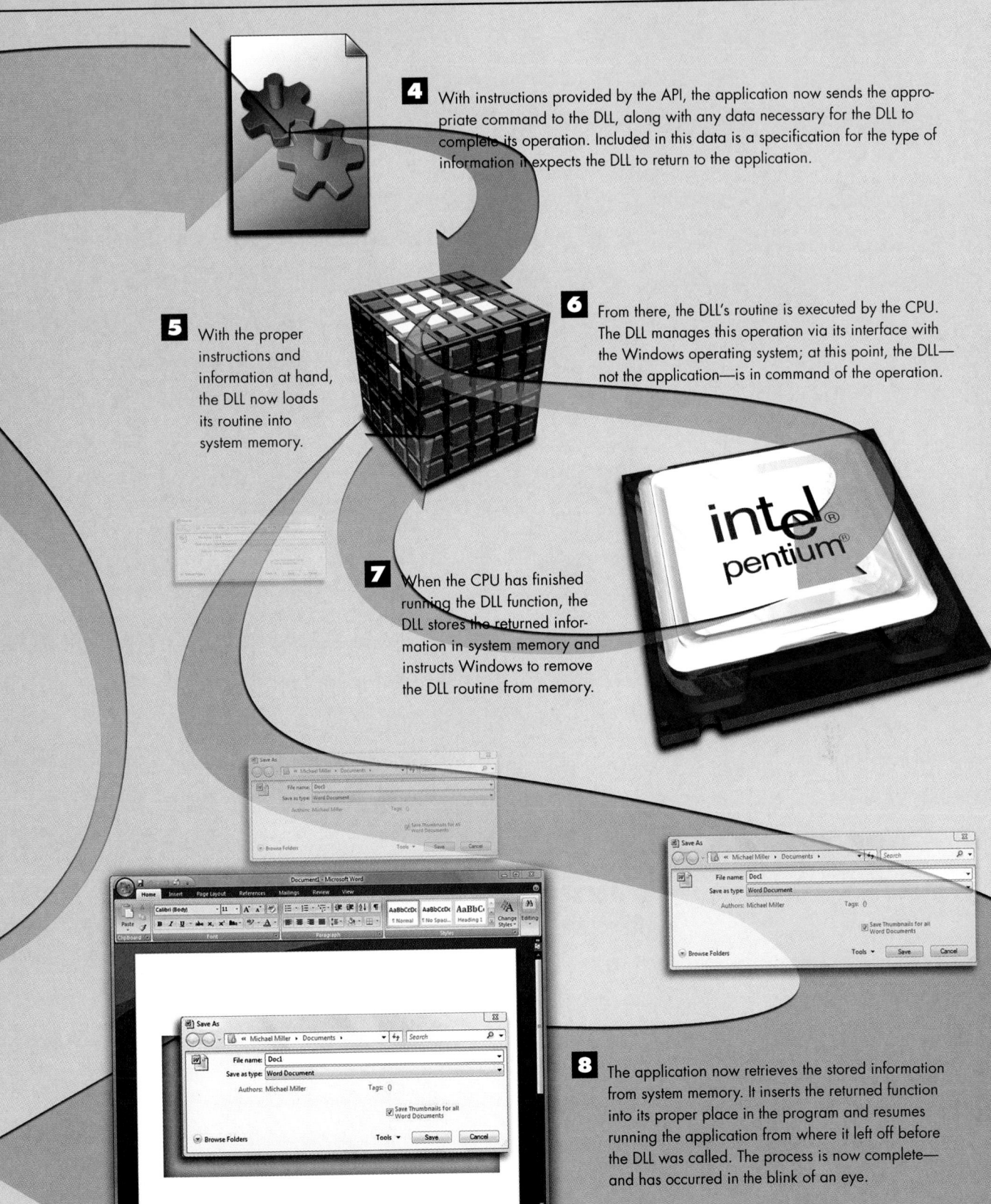

4 With instructions provided by the API, the application now sends the appropriate command to the DLL, along with any data necessary for the DLL to complete its operation. Included in this data is a specification for the type of information it expects the DLL to return to the application.

5 With the proper instructions and information at hand, the DLL now loads its routine into system memory.

6 From there, the DLL's routine is executed by the CPU. The DLL manages this operation via its interface with the Windows operating system; at this point, the DLL—not the application—is in command of the operation.

7 When the CPU has finished running the DLL function, the DLL stores the returned information in system memory and instructs Windows to remove the DLL routine from memory.

8 The application now retrieves the stored information from system memory. It inserts the returned function into its proper place in the program and resumes running the application from where it left off before the DLL was called. The process is now complete—and has occurred in the blink of an eye.

How Windows Multitasks Applications

1 Windows Vista is a multitasking operating system, which means that multiple applications and processes can be run simultaneously. It's possible to have a word processor, a spreadsheet, and a web browser all open on the Vista desktop at the same time.

1 **2** **3**

2 Each open application occupies its own space in system memory. The more memory your computer has, the more applications that can be open at the same time—without slowing down your system.

memory

3 An application's program code is stored in memory only until the PC's CPU can process that code. Unfortunately, a CPU can only process one task at a time. To process multiple applications, the processor must be fed code from each program one at a time. The appearance of multitasking is achieved by running part of one program's code, pausing that process, and then running part of a second program's code. Each application is allotted only a slice of the CPU's processing time.

4 When the CPU processes the second program, the operations from the first program are saved to a unique register within the CPU. By storing the unprocessed code in this fashion, the CPU knows exactly where the process was paused and where to resume when it's that program's turn again.

5 As shown on this simulated timeline (below), all the noncontiguous processes associated with an application are run so fast that the application appears to be running continuously—and the multiple applications appear to be running simultaneously. In reality, however, each application is starting and stopping hundreds of times a second, and Windows manages the entire operation so that none of the processes bump into one another.

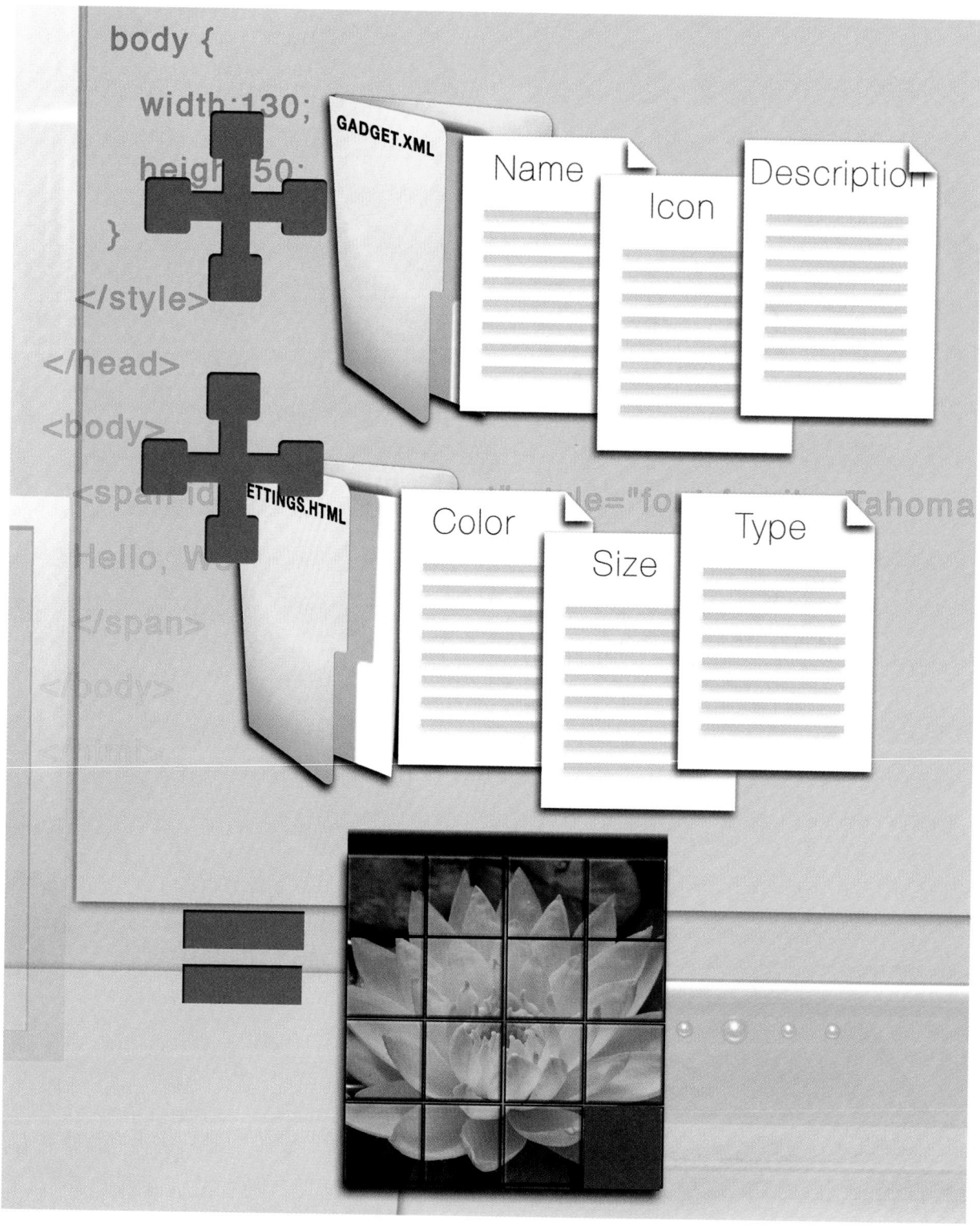

P A R T

3

WINDOWS VISTA GRAPHICS

EVEN if you don't know what's changed behind the screens, it's quickly apparent to anyone using Windows Vista that this new operating system looks different from older versions of Windows. It's not just the color scheme, or the rounded buttons, or new graphic for the Start button. Windows Vista uses a completely different graphics model, which makes for wholesale changes in the way Vista looks—and acts.

The most obvious difference between Windows Vista and Windows XP is the graphical user interface (GUI) itself. The XP interface was modern for its time (circa 2001), with gradated title bars and curved window corners, but what was once fresh now looks somewhat dated. In the intervening years, Apple has advanced the state of PC graphics, with the sleek look of its OS X Tiger. In some ways, Vista is simply catching up to the Mac in interface design; in other ways, Microsoft has done Apple one better.

The visual style of the Vista GUI is called Aero. Microsoft claims that Aero is an acronym for Authentic, Energetic, Reflective, and Open, although that's open for interpretation. The important thing about Aero is that it's a cutting edge design, complete with sleek lines, sophisticated animations, and transparent visual effects. It's a clean, appealing interface that makes previous versions of Windows look positively clunky.

To create these three-dimensional, translucent graphics and fancy window animations, Microsoft has had to up the ante in terms of graphics hardware requirements. If you have an older or lower-end PC, chances are it won't be able to display some of these sophisticated new graphics. In fact, you'll need a fairly powerful graphics card to display all the Aero effects. Microsoft recommends that you have a graphics card that meets the following requirements:

- 128MB of dedicated graphics memory (for a 1600 x 1200 pixel display)
- 3D hardware acceleration
- DirectX 9.0 capable
- Pixel Shader 2.0 capable

Most newer high-end desktop PCs that have a separate video card (as opposed to motherboard-based graphics) meet these requirements. Unfortunately, most notebook PCs *don't*—and you can't change video cards on most portable PCs. For this reason, you probably won't be able to run Vista's Aero mode on your notebook PC; instead, you'll probably be running the Vista Basic user interface, which offers a similar look and feel but without the transparencies, window animations, and other advanced visual effects. (And here's another reason not to use the Aero mode on your portable PC—it uses a lot of power, which quickly drains your notebook's batteries.)

Aside from looks, the basic functionality of the user interface has also changed somewhat in Windows Vista. The Start menu itself is organized a bit differently, with the All Programs menu now arranged in a hierarchical folder tree, rather than the cascading series of submenus used in Windows XP. With Windows Aero, the "live" contents of open applications are displayed as thumbnails above their taskbar buttons, and switching between programs is now similar to flipping through a stack of cards, thanks to the new Flip3D feature. And, everywhere you look, square corners have been replaced by rounded corners, rectangular buttons are now rounded, and a variety of control buttons (such as the old Start button) are now completely circular. It's a series of subtle changes that add up for big effect.

Also new is the ability to display a variety of small applications, called *gadgets*, directly on the Windows desktop. These gadgets are part of the new Windows Sidebar, which is a panel on the right side of the screen, similar to the Dashboard in Apple's Mac OS. At first glance, these gadgets might appear to clutter an otherwise-clean desktop; in reality, they let you view important information without opening a lot of separate application windows. It's a step forward in ease-of-use, if used judiciously.

Not all these graphical elements are available in all versions of Windows Vista, however. In particular, Windows Vista Home Basic does not include the Aero mode; with this version of Vista, you're limited to the Basic user interface, without all the translucent and 3D effects. If you want to display everything that Vista has to offer, you'll need to upgrade to at least the Home Premium Edition—and make sure that your computer has the necessary graphics horsepower.

CHAPTER

10

Understanding Vista Graphics

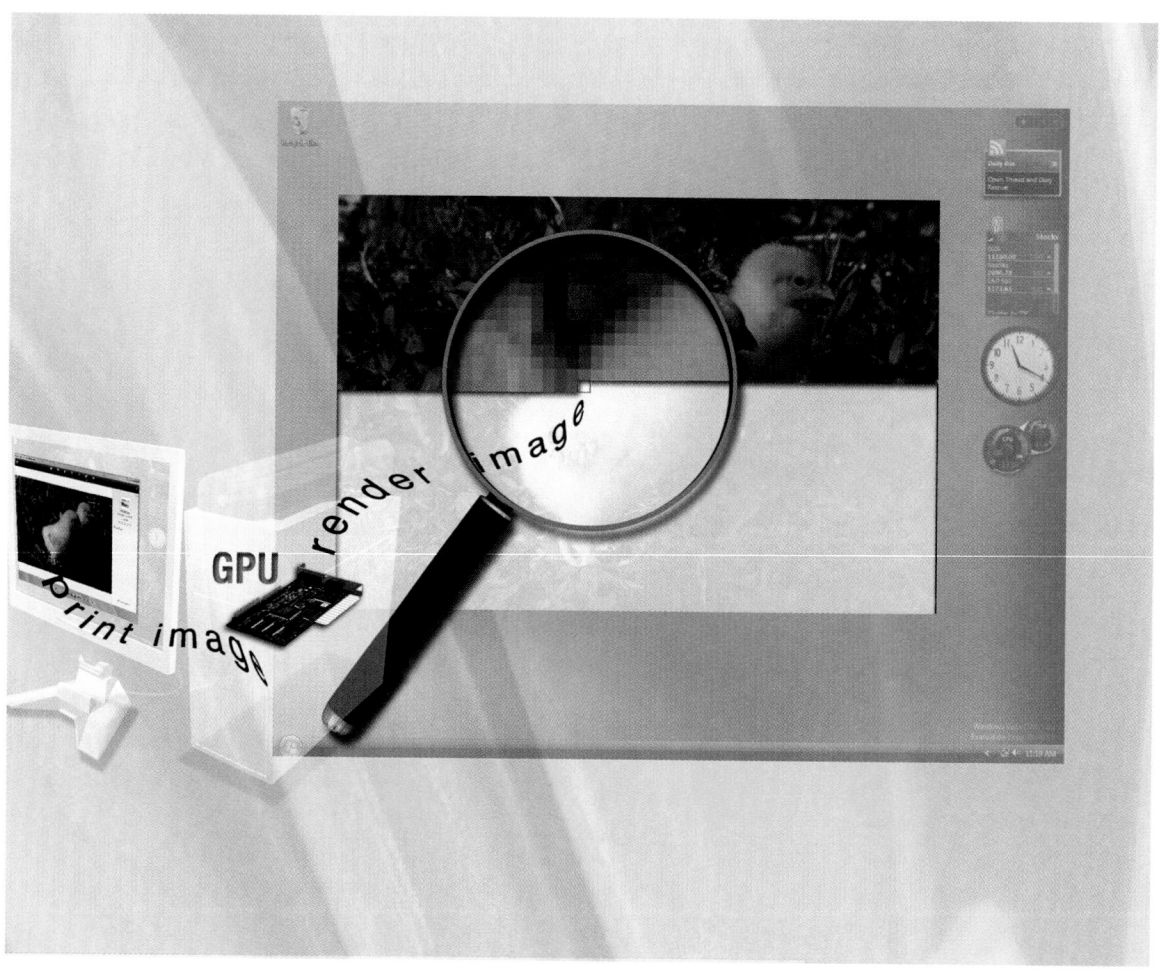

WINDOWS Vista uses a completely new graphics model to display its Aero user interface. This graphics model is called the *Windows Presentation Foundation* (WPF), and it changes the way that Windows handles graphics.

WPF is a graphical subsystem that utilizes the latest DirectX technology, called Direct3D. This subsystem takes full advantage of the independent processing power of modern graphics hardware to create rich, visually stunning graphics for the Vista desktop and all compatible applications. WPF also takes full advantage of advances in ClearType technology to render smoother and more accurate type onscreen.

What WPF does is route all graphics processing to the GPU (Graphics Processing Unit) found on your PC's video card. Prior to WPF, the PC's main CPU handled all graphics processing; by offloading graphics processing to the GPU, instead, the CPU is freed up to perform more essential computing tasks. In addition, the video card's GPU provides the additional graphics processing power necessary to create Aero's three-dimensional, translucent effects.

Another important aspect of WPF is the ability to render the Vista desktop as a series of vector graphics. Unlike traditional bitmapped (raster) graphics, which are composed of a fixed number of pixels, vector graphics are composed of a series of mathematically generated lines that can easily be scaled larger while maintaining a high resolution. In short, vector graphics let you resize practically any visual element in Vista on-the-fly, without having the graphics break up and become jagged.

Application developers who want to take advantage of Vista's Aero interface can utilize the new XAML (Extensible Application Markup Language), which is also a part of the Windows Presentation Foundation. In XAML, every visual element maps onto a class in the underlying API (Application Programming Interface), which makes it easy to design and apply all manner of three-dimensional elements.

How Windows Vista Renders Graphics

1 Previous versions of Windows rendered desktop elements as a series of bitmapped, or raster, graphics. A bitmap is a digital representation of an image, using a series of hundreds and thousands of colored dots, called pixels. The problem with bitmapped graphics is that they can't easily be resized. With a fixed number of pixels for each bitmapped element, enlarging the element displays these same pixels at a larger size, which looks jagged and low-res.

2 In contrast, Windows Vista displays all desktop elements as vector graphics. Vectors don't use individual dots to define an image. Instead, vector graphics use mathematical expressions to define the lines and curves of an image. For example, to draw a circle using vector graphics, Vista generates a formula that uses the following pieces of information: the circle's radius, the location of the center point of the circle, the line style and color for the edge of the circle, and the fill style and color for the inside of the circle. This technology renders smooth lines at any resolution; resizing an image is simply a matter of changing the appropriate data in the original equation.

3 In previous versions of Windows, all graphics were rendered by the PC's main CPU; demanding graphics can eat up processing time and slow down the operation of your entire system. With the new Windows Presentation Foundation graphics model, graphics rendering is performed by a separate Graphics Processing Unit (GPU) contained on your PC's video card. The dedicated GPU renders graphics faster than a shared CPU and frees up the CPU to run applications and other system processes.

4 The texture and shading of the Vista Aero interface is created by pixel shading technology. A pixel shader is a graphics function that calculates visual effects on a per-pixel basis. Per-pixel shading can create an extraordinary amount of surface detail, and enables the subtle glass effect of the Vista Aero interface.

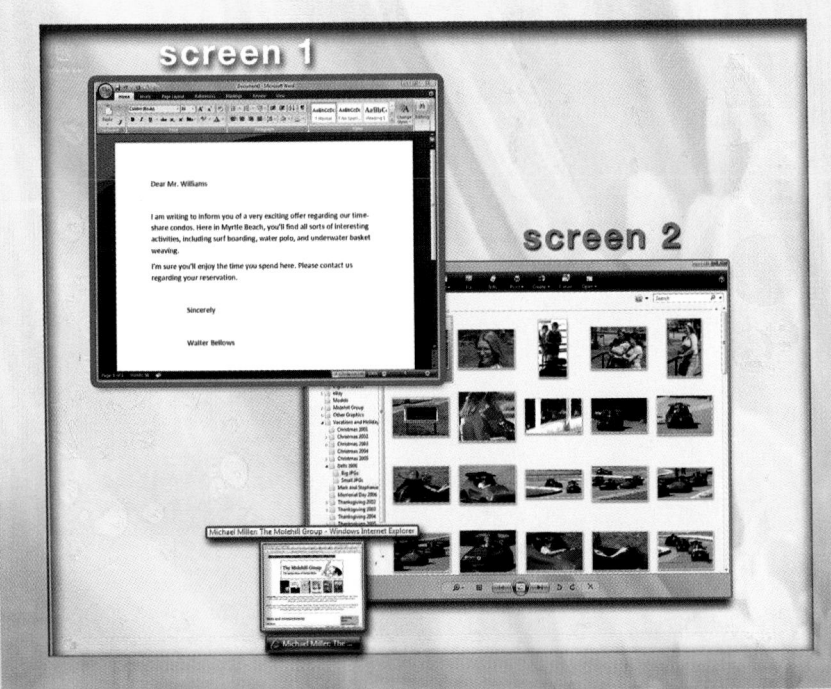

5 Each screen element is calculated separately by the graphics engine, and treated as a separate object. Individual objects can then be layered on top of each other and moved around the desktop independently without the tearing and blending common with bitmapped images. The object is moved as a whole—not as a collection of pixels.

How DirectX and Direct3D Work

1 Vista's Windows Presentation Foundation graphics subsystem is built on Microsoft's **DirectX** API. DirectX was originally used to develop computer games for the Windows environment, but has since been extended to both general and high-level graphics functionality. DirectX is actually a collection of APIs—each designed to handle a distinct function.

2 Within DirectX, two-dimensional graphics are rendered via the **DirectDraw** API. DirectDraw creates bitmapped, or raster, graphics, as used in pre-Vista versions of Windows.

3 Three-dimensional graphics are rendered via DirectX's **Direct3D** API. Direct3D incorporates several powerful 3D graphics features, including pixel shading, vertex shading, geometry shading, fog, bump mapping, and texture mapping. The Windows Vista graphics subsystem relies heavily on the Direct3D API to render the three-dimensional vector graphics of the Vista desktop.

Install DVD

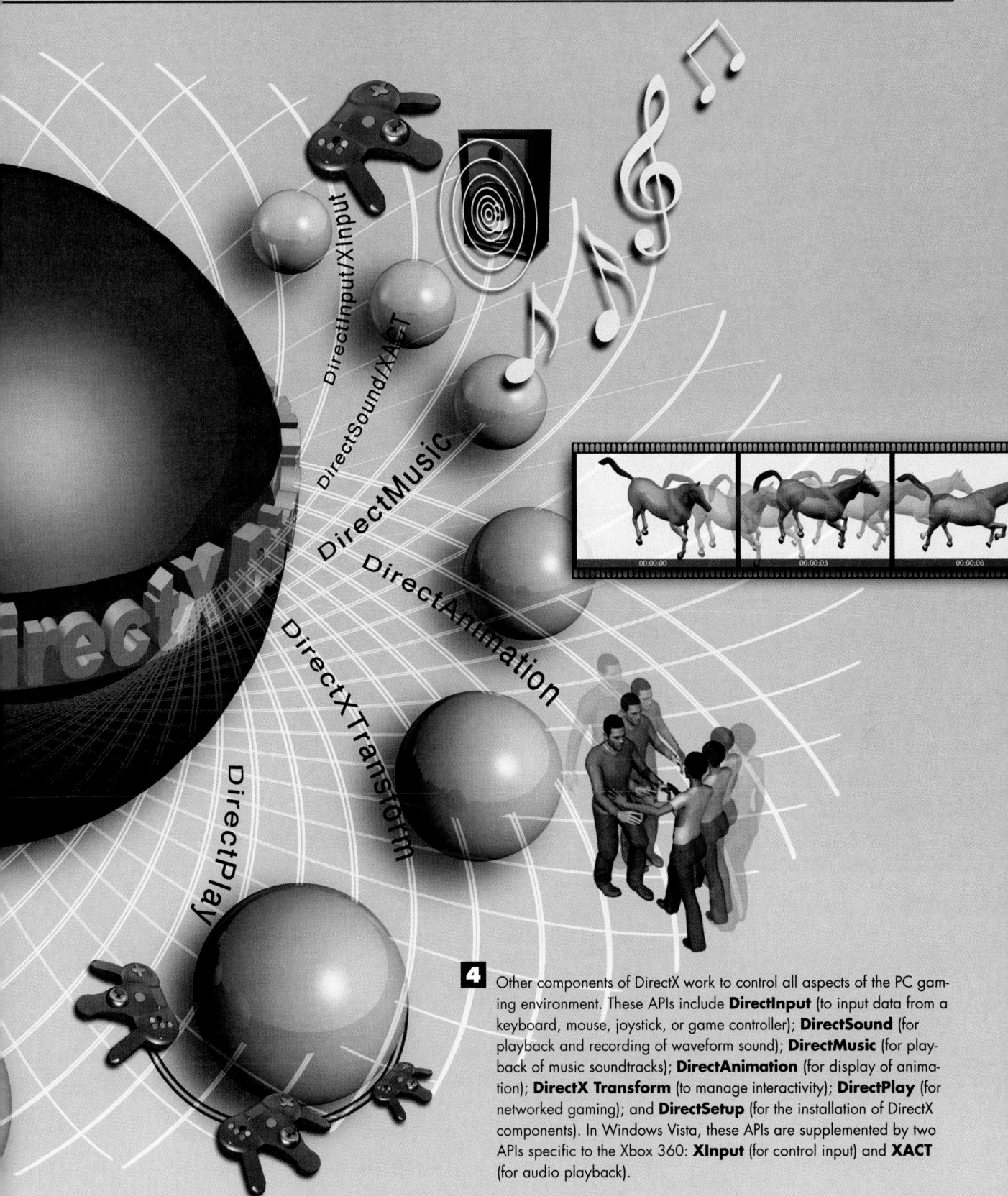

DirectInput/XInput

DirectSound/XACT

DirectMusic

DirectAnimation

DirectXTransform

DirectPlay

4 Other components of DirectX work to control all aspects of the PC gaming environment. These APIs include **DirectInput** (to input data from a keyboard, mouse, joystick, or game controller); **DirectSound** (for playback and recording of waveform sound); **DirectMusic** (for playback of music soundtracks); **DirectAnimation** (for display of animation); **DirectX Transform** (to manage interactivity); **DirectPlay** (for networked gaming); and **DirectSetup** (for the installation of DirectX components). In Windows Vista, these APIs are supplemented by two APIs specific to the Xbox 360: **XInput** (for control input) and **XACT** (for audio playback).

How ClearType Works

1 Direct3D utilizes Microsoft's **ClearType** technology to improve the appearance of onscreen text. ClearType is based on the fact that each pixel on a computer monitor is composed of three separate subpixels, one for each color—red, blue, and green. The lighting of all three subpixels creates black or (at the appropriate mix) colored type.

2 Without ClearType, text is displayed by lighting up entire pixels. As such, round edges on individual characters are comprised of a series of rectangular blocks. At large type sizes, text created from these fixed pixels can appear jagged and hard to read.

3 ClearType smoothes the rough edges of onscreen type by using antialiasing technology at the subpixel level. Instead of lighting all three subpixels (red, green, and blue), ClearType lights only those subpixels through which the curve or line of a character passes.

4 By fine-tuning character reproduction to the subpixel level, ClearType effectively triples the sharpness of the image, making the edges of text look smoother than before. This technology works because human vision is more sensitive to variations in light intensity than it is to variations in color. By sacrificing a small degree of color accuracy around the edges of a piece of type, ClearType improves the contrast between light and dark. The overall effect, as seen by the human eye, is an increase in sharpness.

ClearType Limitations
ClearType is only used for the display of text onscreen; it is not used for text printed on paper. In addition, ClearType's antialiasing technology works best on LCD screens, due to the rectangular pixel grid used on these displays. The effect is minimal (and often off-putting) on traditional CRT-type monitors, which align their round pixels in a triangular shape.

5 The only drawback to ClearType comes from the sacrifice of color fidelity for sharpness. On close examination, text reproduced with ClearType will show color fringing around the edges, due to the nonlighting of some colored subpixels. This effect is typically not noticeable at normal viewing distances, however.

C H A P T E R

11

The Vista Interface

buffer 1
buffer 2
buffer 3
buffer 4

IN Windows Vista, the Windows interface gets a complete overhaul. Every element of the screen has changed, from the design of dialog boxes to the color (and transparency) of window titles and borders. Microsoft calls this new interface Aero, and it's a more graphics-intensive, higher-resolution interface than anything previously seen in Windows.

Aero is more than just a facelift for the Windows GUI, however. Aero subtly transforms the entire user experience, visibly presenting the former two-dimensional desktop as a collection of three-dimensional elements. The Windows desktop is finally represented like a real desktop, with one object stacked on top of another, and with each object easily and independently moved through the stack and around the desktop.

The three-dimensional nature of Aero is expressed via a series of translucent windows. The title bar and border of each window looks like a pane of translucent glass so that you can see what's directly beneath that window. As you move the window around the desktop, what you see through the translucent border changes to reflect the window's changing position. It's as if each window is a physical object that you're moving around with your mouse.

The Aero interface takes advantage of Vista's new Windows Presentation Foundation (WPF) graphics engine and Windows Driver Model (WDDM) video drivers. WPF and WDDM work together to utilize the increased graphics horsepower of modern video cards to represent each window on your desktop as a separate graphics element, in its own individual layer. The desktop itself is dynamically recomposed many times a second by Vista's Desktop Windows Manager (DWM), providing the illusion of smooth movement whenever a window is moved or resized.

The result is a desktop environment that makes it easier to discern individual windows and elements. No longer do subsidiary elements get lost behind larger windows; you can see through each window to discover other open windows beneath. This improved functionality means that Aero is more than just a pretty face for the Vista operating system—Aero is a whole new way of approaching the Windows desktop.

How Vista's Different Interfaces Work

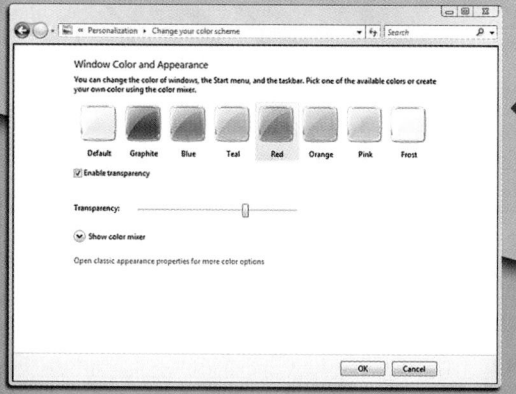

1 Windows Vista comes with several different interfaces, designed for PCs with different levels of graphics processing power. These interfaces (called "color schemes") are selected from the Appearance Settings dialog box, which is accessible from the Vista Control Panel.

2 The main interface, Windows Vista Aero, features translucent windows that let you see through the window frame to other windows or the desktop below. The Aero interface also features three-dimensional windows and sophisticated animation effects. To display the Aero interface, your PC's video card must support video drivers based on Microsoft's new Windows Display Driver Model (WDDM).

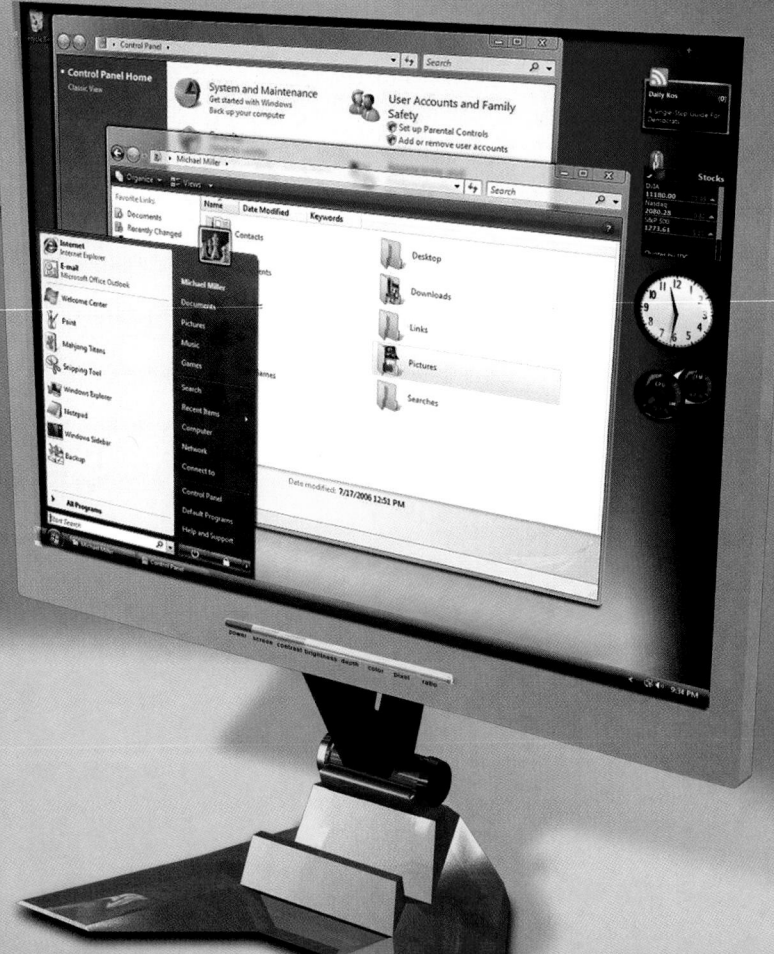

3 For users with older or less-powerful video cards incapable of running WDDM video drivers, Microsoft offers the Windows Vista Basic interface. This interface features nontranslucent windows that retain the basic Aero look and feel, but without the 3D effect. Vista Basic also lacks fancy window animations and features a slightly different Start menu. As most notebook computers lack adequate video processing, this is the interface that most portable PC users will see.

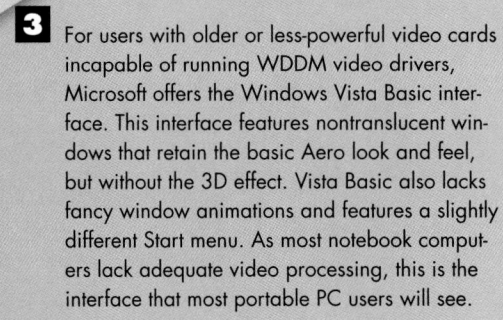

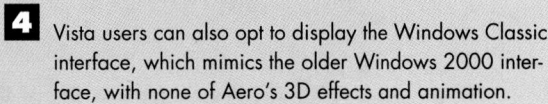

4 Vista users can also opt to display the Windows Classic interface, which mimics the older Windows 2000 interface, with none of Aero's 3D effects and animation.

How the Aero Interface Works

1 In the Aero interface, windows and other screen elements are translucent. Any element—including other windows and the desktop itself—can be seen through the glass-like windows. In Vista, even the Windows taskbar and Start menu are translucent.

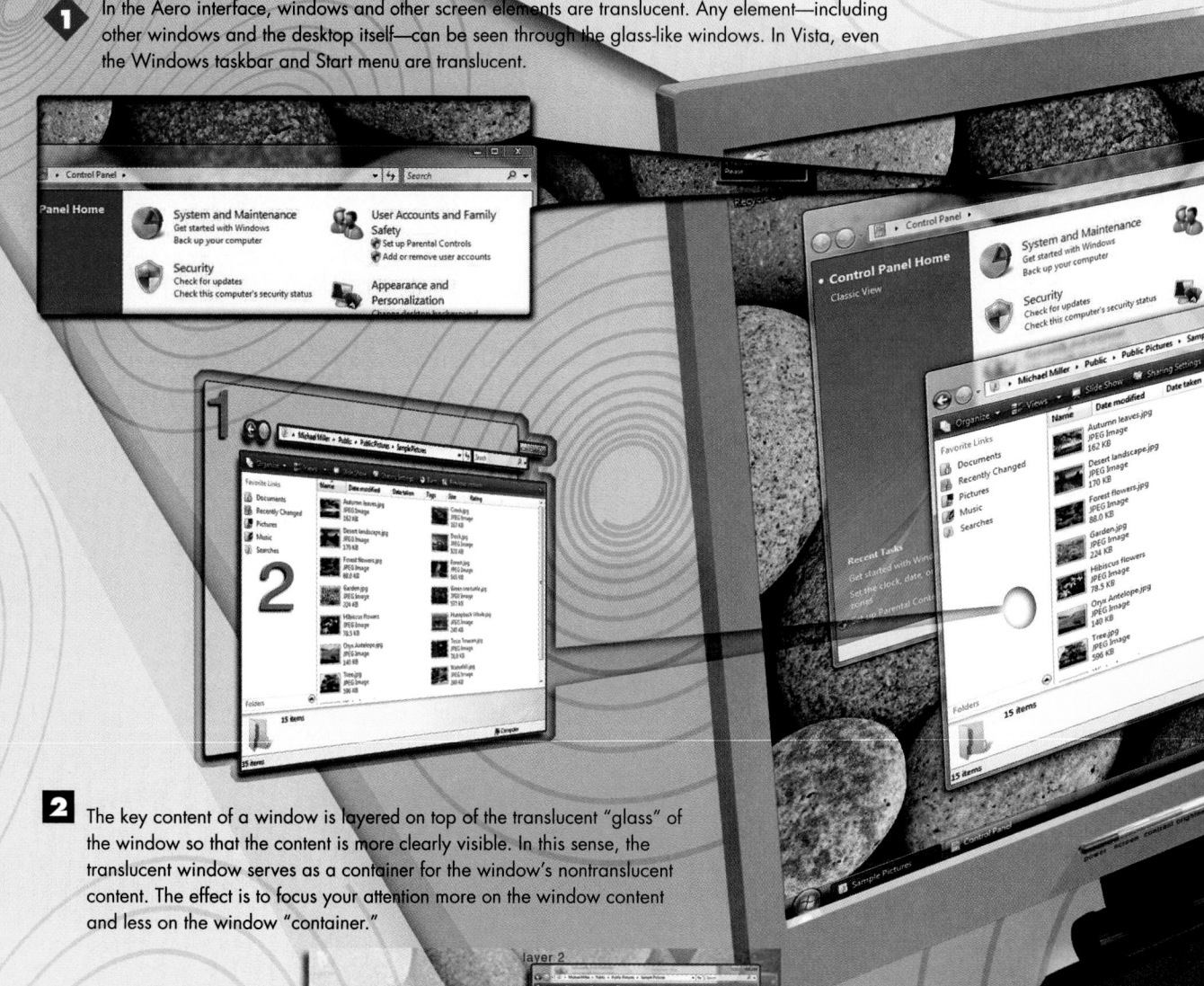

2 The key content of a window is layered on top of the translucent "glass" of the window so that the content is more clearly visible. In this sense, the translucent window serves as a container for the window's nontranslucent content. The effect is to focus your attention more on the window content and less on the window "container."

3 Each window on the screen exists on its own separate graphics layer. As such, windows can be stacked on top of each other in a three-dimensional fashion. Windows behind other windows are partially obscured; windows on top of other windows display a drop shadow on the lower elements.

4 The Maximize, Minimize, and Close buttons in Windows Vista have gone through subtle redesigns. The buttons now "light up" when hovered over or selected; the Maximize and Minimize buttons glow blue, whereas the Close button glows red.

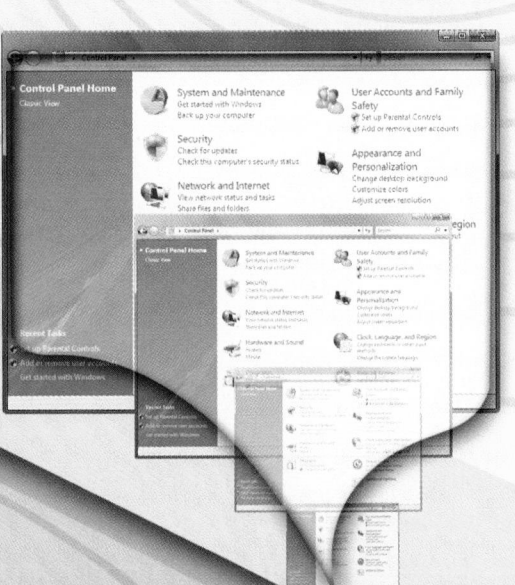

5 All Windows in the Aero interface are dynamic. When you minimize or maximize a window, it animates to or from a specific location on the taskbar. And all window movement is much smoother in Vista than it was in Windows XP; windows easily glide across the screen without any redraw or "tearing" effects.

Waterfall.jpg

6 Microsoft has also switched to a new system font in Windows Vista. While previous versions of Windows (starting with Windows 98) used the Tahoma font, the Vista Aero interface uses the Segoe UI font. Segoe UI has slightly rounder letters than Tahoma, and is optimized for use with ClearType technology and today's larger LCD computer displays. The default font size has also been increased from 8 to 9 points, to improve readability.

How the Desktop Windows Manager Works

1 In previous versions of Windows, applications were rendered directly to the PC's video card. And only that part of an application that was to be visible on the screen was painted to the PC's video card; a background window only got painted when the foreground window moved. This often resulted in uneven movement and window "tearing."

2 With the Aero interface, the way that elements are drawn on the screen is fundamentally different. In Aero, desktop composition is handled by Vista's new Desktop Windows Manager (DWM). DWM requires an application to paint its entire surface to a separate offscreen buffer—*not* to the video card itself.

3 Once all the windows are stored in their own offscreen buffers, DWM then "composes" all the surfaces and renders a complete screen image. This complete image is then sent to the video card.

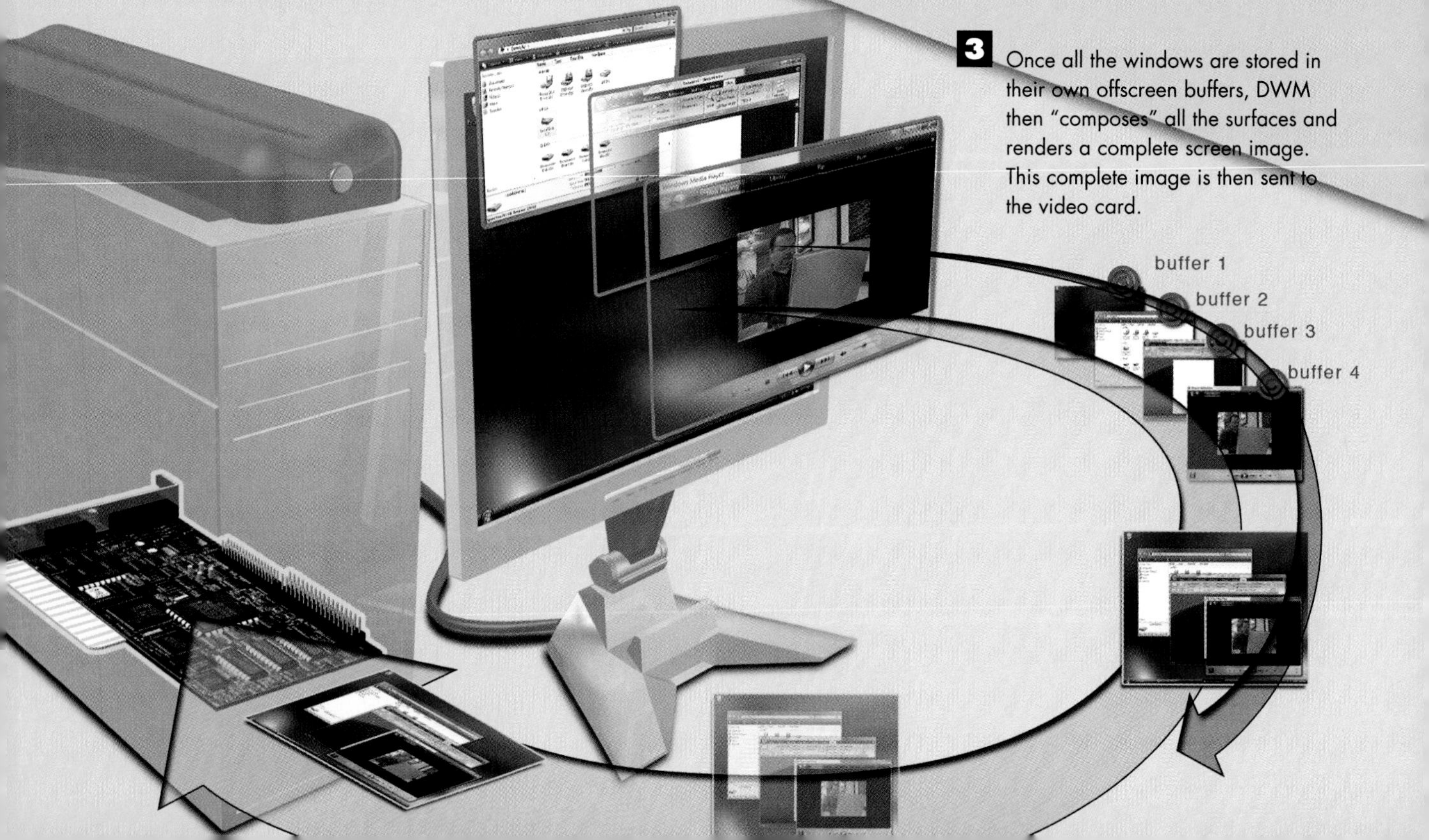

buffer 1
buffer 2
buffer 3
buffer 4

4 With the DWM, an underlying window is not forced to repaint when a foreground window moves since the complete background window has already been rendered for the offscreen buffer. The result is much smoother onscreen movement, with no tearing or streaking, and the ability to stack fully rendered windows on top of each other on the desktop.

5 Because all applications are completely rendered and stored offscreen, these offscreen representations can be used in places other than the desktop proper—such as the taskbar thumbnails and Flip 3D window stack.

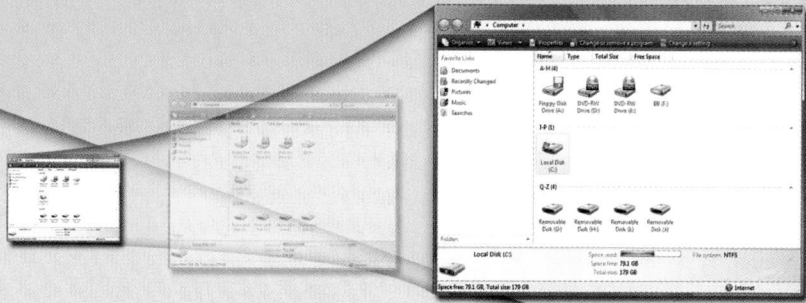

6 Because all screen elements in Vista are rendered as vector graphics, all applications are agnostic of the size of the current window or the monitor resolution they're running at. The offscreen representation of an application window is automatically scaled by the Desktop Windows Manager to fit the appropriate onscreen space, with no loss of resolution, no matter the screen size.

How Windows Flip 3D Works

1 In previous versions of Windows, pressing the Alt+Tab keys cycled between all open programs. Icons for the programs were shown in a small pane on the desktop. In Windows Vista, pressing Alt+Tab lets you cycle through all open programs via the new Windows Flip pane. Windows Flip displays live thumbnails of all open programs, along with the name of the current document or application. This makes it easier to identify a specific program or document.

2 The Aero interface also includes a new and improved method for changing programs, called Flip 3D. When you press the Windows+Tab keys, all open windows (including the desktop itself) are dynamically displayed in a three-dimensional stack.

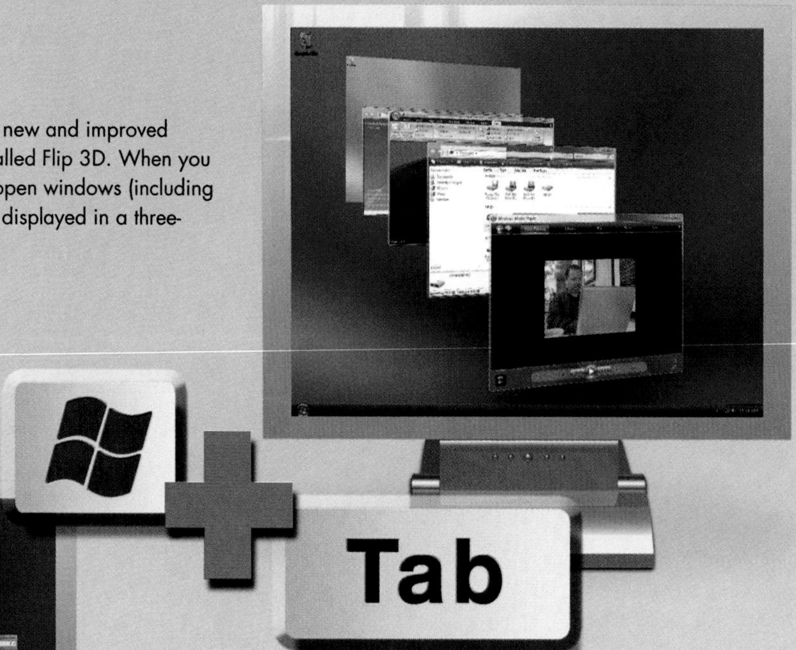

3 Pressing Windows+Tab repeatedly rotates through all the open windows, until you find the one you want. You can also rotate through the windows by using your keyboard's arrow keys or the scroll wheel on your mouse.

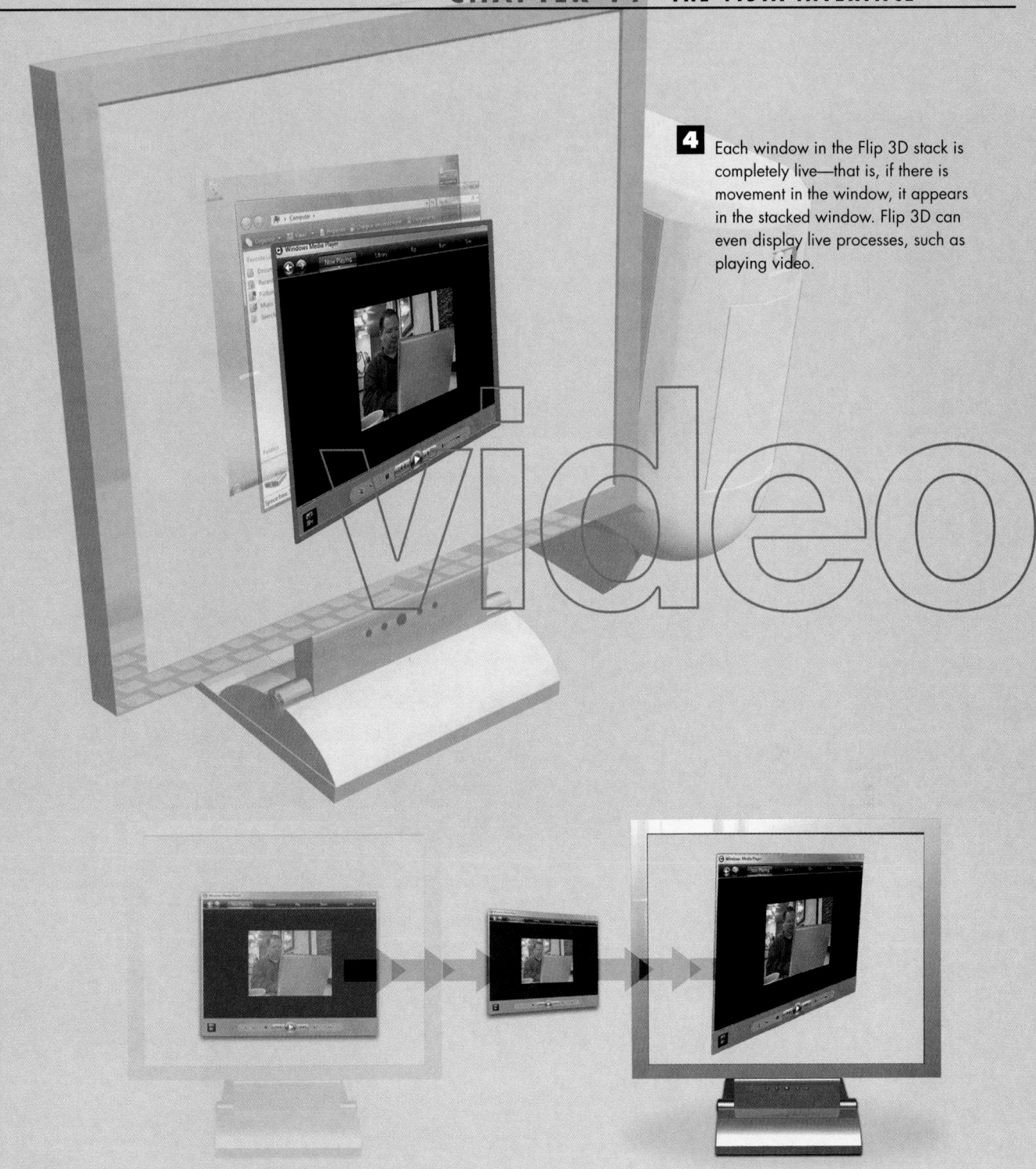

4 Each window in the Flip 3D stack is completely live—that is, if there is movement in the window, it appears in the stacked window. Flip 3D can even display live processes, such as playing video.

5 Flip 3D is possible because of Vista's new Windows Presentation Foundation (WPF) graphics engine, which utilizes the horsepower of the separate Graphics Processing Unit (GPU) found in most high-end video cards. All open applications are run as if they were in the prominent window, but the windows themselves are displayed via vector graphics. The vector graphics enable WPF to easily resize and rotate each window in real time to become a single element in the Flip 3D window stack.

CHAPTER

12

The Vista Desktop

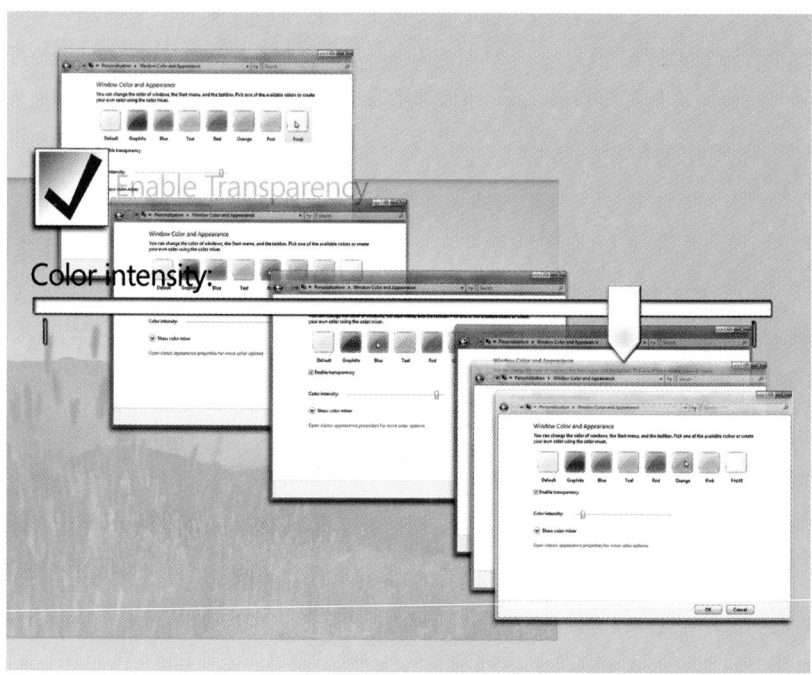

THE Windows desktop is the home base for all Windows users. Everything you need is there, from the Start menu to the taskbar to any icons you place on the desktop itself. (And that's not even mentioning the pretty pictures most people use for their desktop backgrounds.)

With Windows Vista, the desktop is different, in some subtle and not-so-subtle ways. For example, the look and feel of the Start menu and the taskbar have changed to reflect the Vista Aero interface; they're both just a little bit translucent.

A more major change comes in the form of the Windows Sidebar. This is an area of the desktop (typically docked on the right side of the screen) that is used to hold a variety of "gadgets." These gadgets are actually small utility applications that perform a single simple function. For example, the Weather gadget reports the current weather conditions and forecast for your area.

These gadgets can stay docked to the Sidebar, or they can be dragged off to sit on the desktop itself. In either position, you can configure their opacity—each gadget can have a solid background, or it can be see-through, to match the Vista interface.

If you have a new notebook PC, the Windows desktop might extend beyond your screen to a small display on the outside of the notebook's case. This display, called the Windows SideShow, lets you perform selected operations without the need to open or start up your PC. Just use the gadgets built into the SideShow display to check your email, confirm appointments, or listen to digital music.

Of course, the Vista desktop is just as customizable as the Windows XP desktop was. You can change desktop wallpaper, opt for a solid-color background, or even change the color and translucency of Vista itself. So there's no reason to stick with the default look of Windows Vista; you can personalize all the various elements to suite your own tastes and moods!

How to Personalize the Vista Desktop

1 If you don't like the Windows Vista interface as it appears by default, you can change just about all the elements you see onscreen. All the configuration settings you need are located in the Personalize Appearance and Sound Effects window, which you can display by right-clicking anywhere on the desktop and selecting Personalize. (You can also open this window by selecting **Appearance and Personalization** from the Vista Control Panel.)

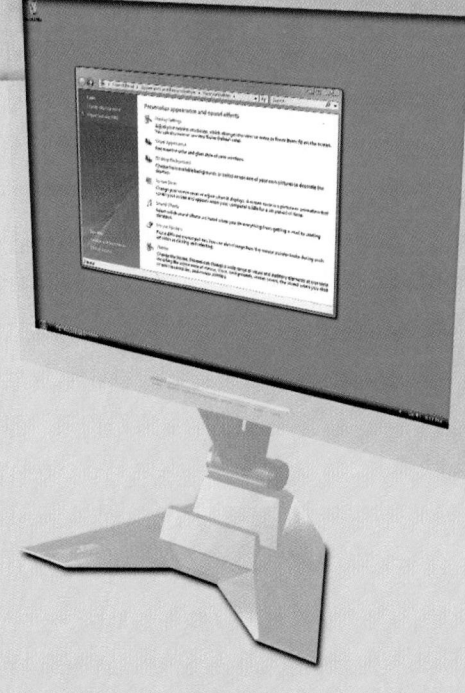

2 The easiest way to change the Vista desktop is to select a new *theme*. A theme is a combination of desktop wallpaper, window colors, screensaver, and the like. To change themes, open the Personalize Appearance and Sound Effects window and select **Theme**.

3 You can also change individual elements of the desktop. The most obvious form of personalization is the desktop background itself. Vista lets you choose from a variety of solid colors, light auras, vistas, textures, paintings, and black and white images. To select a new background, open the Personalize Appearance and Sound Effects window and select **Desktop Background**.

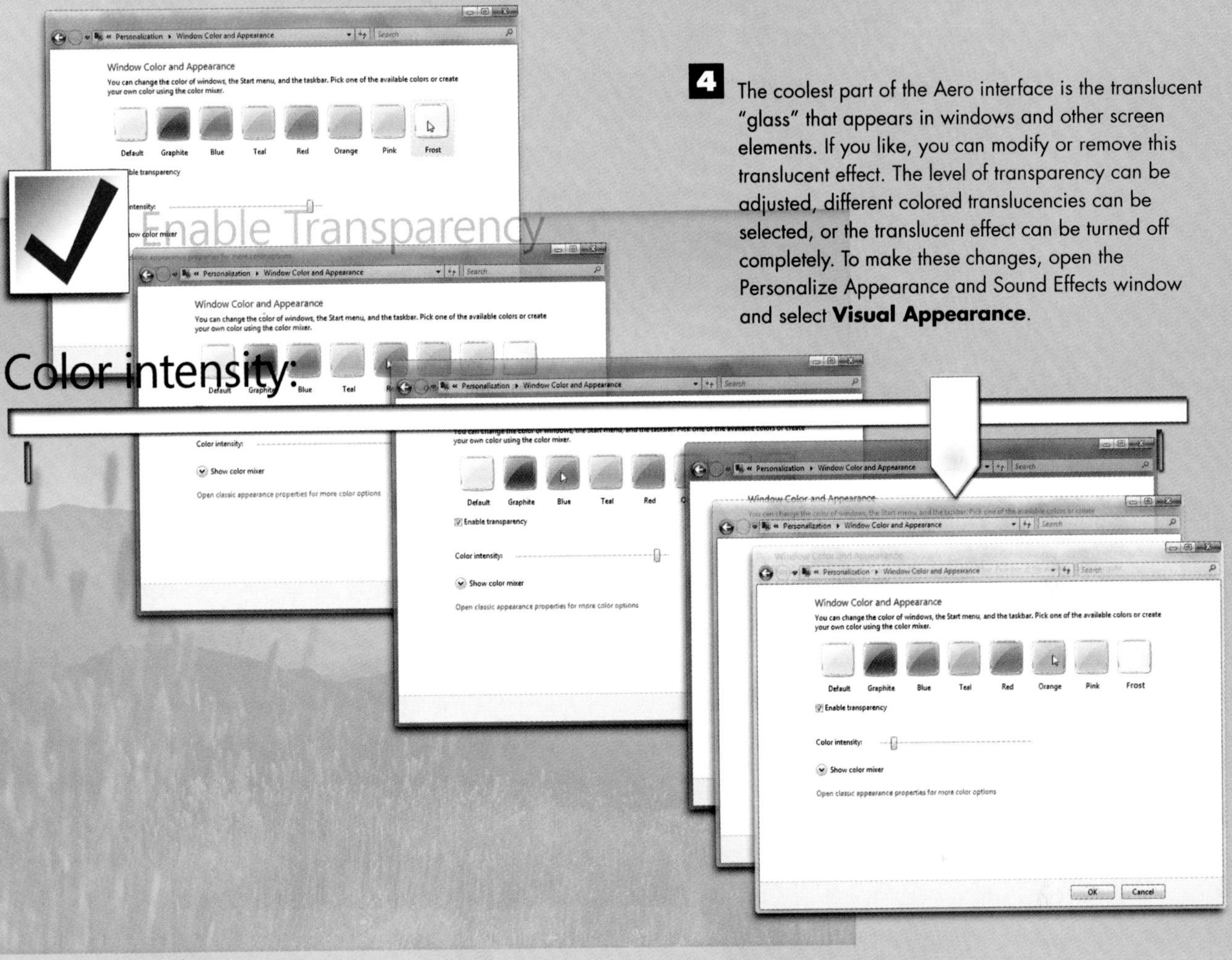

4 The coolest part of the Aero interface is the translucent "glass" that appears in windows and other screen elements. If you like, you can modify or remove this translucent effect. The level of transparency can be adjusted, different colored translucencies can be selected, or the translucent effect can be turned off completely. To make these changes, open the Personalize Appearance and Sound Effects window and select **Visual Appearance**.

5 Just as you can change the size of file and folder icons in any Explorer window, you can also change the size of icons on the Vista desktop. Just right-click the desktop, select **View** from the pop-up menu, and then chose an icon size: small, medium, large, or extra-large.

How the Windows Sidebar Works

1 Another way to personalize your Vista desktop is to display the new Windows Sidebar, along with a variety of Sidebar gadgets. The Sidebar is a special pane that appears on the far right side of the Vista desktop, taking advantage of the added screen real estate of today's widescreen monitors.

2 The Sidebar functions as a repository for small single-purpose utility programs called *gadgets*. Gadgets can be freestanding utilities, or they can connect to the Internet to offer real-time information and services. By displaying gadgets in the Sidebar, you don't have to clutter your desktop with several open applications that perform the same functions.

3 Gadgets can be displayed in the Sidebar or detached to float anywhere on the desktop. Individual gadgets and the Sidebar can be configured to rest behind all open windows or to remain on top of all other desktop elements.

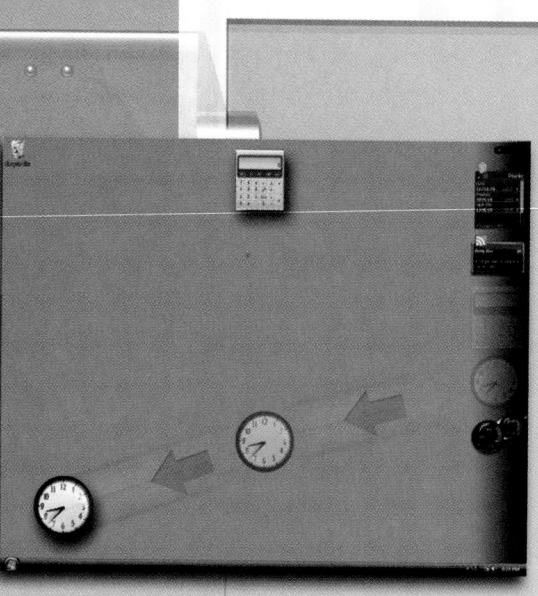

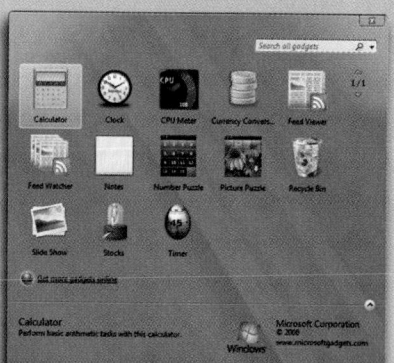

4 Windows Vista comes with Calculator, Clock, Currency Conversion, Feed Viewer, Weather, and similar gadgets included—all accessible from the Gadget Gallery. Additional gadgets are available online.

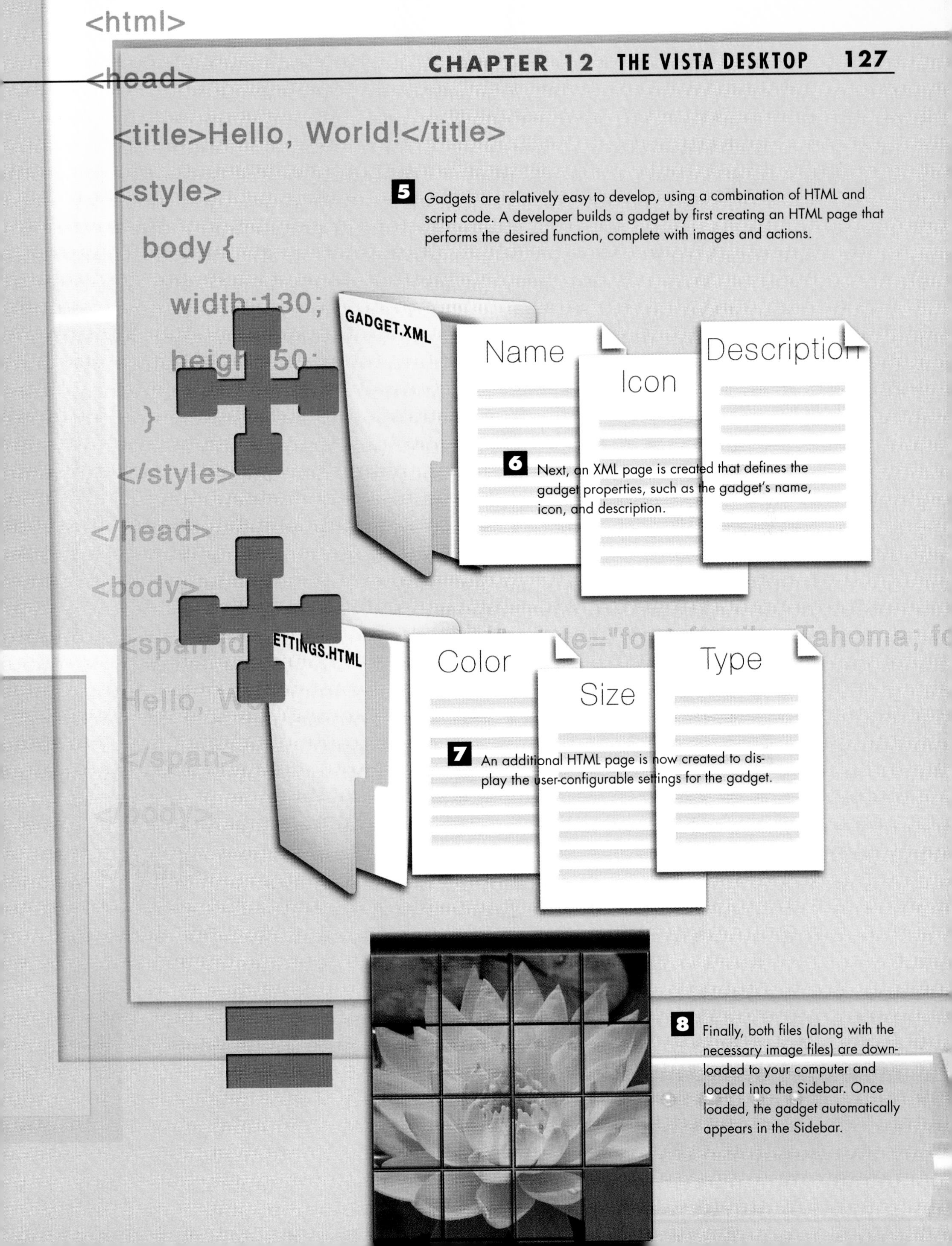

```
<html>

<head>

<title>Hello, World!</title>

<style>

  body {

    width:130;

    height:50;

  }

</style>

</head>

<body>

<span id  ETTINGS.HTML                        de="font f           Tahoma; fo

Hello, W

</span>

</body>
```

5 Gadgets are relatively easy to develop, using a combination of HTML and script code. A developer builds a gadget by first creating an HTML page that performs the desired function, complete with images and actions.

GADGET.XML

Name

Icon

Description

6 Next, an XML page is created that defines the gadget properties, such as the gadget's name, icon, and description.

Color

Size

Type

7 An additional HTML page is now created to display the user-configurable settings for the gadget.

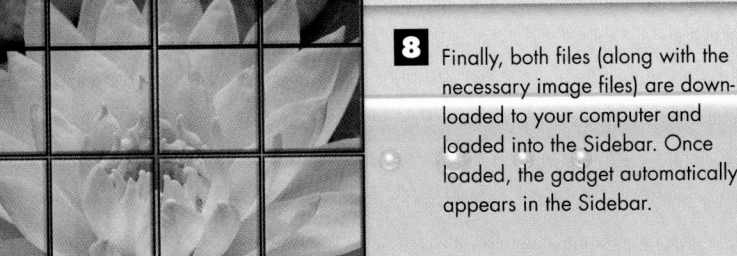

8 Finally, both files (along with the necessary image files) are downloaded to your computer and loaded into the Sidebar. Once loaded, the gadget automatically appears in the Sidebar.

How Windows SideShow Works on a Notebook PC

1 The Windows Sidebar isn't the only place you'll find gadgets in Vista. New notebook PCs are being developed that include a small exterior display called Windows SideShow. The SideShow display lets you run freestanding gadget applications from outside the notebook PC case.

2 Windows SideShow runs independently of Windows Vista. You can run SideShow gadgets without opening or powering on the notebook PC. This lets you perform specific functions even if the PC is closed or turned off—reading email messages, looking up an address or phone number, listening to digital music, and so forth. Using Windows SideShow is designed to save time (no need to wait for Windows to start up) and power (the main PC doesn't have to power on).

Microsoft Windows Email
Unread messages:4

Last updated: 8:30 AM, 9/20/2006

Thur 9/21 9:04 AM

3 SideShow runs the same type of gadget mini-applications as found in the Windows Sidebar. Windows Vista includes SideShow gadgets for Windows Mail and Windows Media Player, as well as a gadget that displays battery level, wireless signal strength, and the current time.

4 The SideShow display can also function as an auxiliary display in conjunction with your PC's main display. For example, the SideShow might display instant messages that you can read while running a full-screen application on your main display.

memory cache

5 For SideShow to run when your PC is turned off, it must access cached data previously saved from your PC. For example, Windows SideShow might save all your emails in a memory cache while your computer is running. Then, when you access SideShow when your computer is turned off, it simply accesses the messages stored in the cache. Or, if you want to listen to digital music, SideShow access all WMA and MP3 files stored in the SideShow cache. (SideShow can be configured to periodically wake your PC to update the data used by the SideShow gadgets.)

text message:
AFK...ATM..LTNS
LYLAS

You have 4
email messages

Music
TV
live tv
04:45
Odd...tree
Aux Plugins
Settings
guide

6 SideShow technology can also have other uses, outside the PC arena. For example, a SideShow-enabled computer keyboard might display a list of unanswered emails, or a SideShow-enabled remote control unit might display song or television channel information for the currently playing program on a Media Center PC.

P A R T

DIGITAL MEDIA

A PERSONAL computer today is used for more than just personal computing. Today's PCs function as digital photo and movie editors, digital music jukeboxes, and even digital video recorders for television programming. It's all about digital media—which makes your PC the ultimate digital entertainment machine.

Digital media is different from older analog media. It's the difference between a compact disc and a vinyl record. With analog media, you're limited in terms of resolution and fidelity; copies don't sound as good as the original, and they degrade over time. In the digital realm, all content is encoded digitally, using a series of 1s and 0s that represent the original recording. Digital copies are virtually identical to the original, and they retain their quality no matter how many times they're played.

Digital media is also easily edited. In the old analog days, if you wanted to edit a photograph, you had to perform arcane darkroom magic; if you wanted to edit an audio recording, you had to attack the original audiotape with a razor blade and Scotch tape. Not so in the digital world, where editing is a simple matter of moving those bits and bytes around. Photo editing can be done with the click of a mouse from an easy-to-use digital photo editing program; digital audio editing software lets you manipulate the very waveform of a recording.

These new digital media are everywhere—digital compact discs, digital music downloaded from the Internet and played on digital music players, digital movies on DVDs, digital home movies recorded on digital camcorders, digital photos taken with digital cameras—it's all digital, all the digital time.

Digital media is so important that Microsoft has been, for some time, building into its Windows operating system the means to play and edit various types of digital files. The management of digital media reaches a zenith in Windows Vista, with new or improved utilities for digital music, digital videos, and digital photos, all built into the operating system.

Let's start with digital music. To play and manage digital music on your computer, you need a digital music player program. In Windows Vista, that program is Windows Media Player 11, a significant upgrade to the program that's been around for over a decade. WMP is capable of managing entire digital music collections, playing back downloaded or ripped digital music and CDs, and creating and playing music playlists. The Windows Vista version of WMP features a much-improved interface and enhanced ease-of-use, making it perhaps the most advanced media player program on the market today.

Windows Media Player is also a video player; it can play DVDs and videos downloaded from the Internet. Windows Vista also includes Windows Movie Maker, a program you can use to edit your digital movies, and Windows DVD maker, which you can use to burn your digital movies to DVD.

For the management and editing of digital photos, Windows Vista includes a new utility called Windows Photo Gallery. Photo Gallery not only serves as a digital photo viewer, it also lets you edit your photos; you can brighten or darken a picture, crop to new dimensions, adjust color and tint levels, and even remove red eye. In fact, Photo Gallery has much of the functionality of freestanding (and expensive) photo editing programs, such as Adobe Photoshop Elements. And, like the rest of Vista's digital media tools, it's part of Windows itself—you get to use it, free of charge.

If you're really into digital media, however, you're incorporating digital entertainment into your living room home theater system. Wouldn't it be great to be able to play back all your downloaded digital music on your home audio system or view a slideshow of your digital photos on your big-screen TV? You can do all these things—and a lot more—when you connect a PC to your home theater system and that PC is running Windows Media Center. Media Center (included as part of Vista's Home Premium and Ultimate editions) puts a 10-foot interface on top of Windows' existing digital media features so that you can sit on your couch and select your playback options via remote control.

Windows Media Center includes functions for the playback of CDs and digital music libraries; the viewing of digital photos, complete with background music; the viewing of home movies you've created or videos you've downloaded from the Internet; and commercial movies on DVD. And, if your PC has a built-in television tuner, Windows Media Center can be used to view live and recorded television programs—and to pause and rewind "live" programming while you're watching it. Even better, all this is accomplished from an easy-to-use Electronic Program Guide, displayed onscreen and updated daily over the Internet.

Put it all together, and you see that Windows Vista can turn your personal computer into the ultimate digital entertainment machine. All you have to do is choose the appropriate built-in application, and then sit back and enjoy!

CHAPTER

13

Windows Media Center

WHEN you want to use your personal computer for home entertainment purposes, especially in a living room environment, you need Windows Media Center. Media Center is an interface that runs on top of the core Windows Vista operating system; it's designed as a 10-foot interface for use in the living room environment.

Windows Media Center lets you perform most common home entertainment operations with the click of a button on the Media Center remote control unit. It's really not designed for desktop applications (although it can be used on a desktop PC); there's no built-in web browser, word processor, or email client. But if you want to listen to music, watch DVDs, or record television programs, Media Center is the perfect interface. It's simple; it's intuitive; it's easy to read from across the room: It's a computer interface that doesn't look like a computer interface. And you don't need to take a training course to learn how to use it. It's easy enough to use that your parents (or grandparents!) can probably figure it out.

The ideal use for a PC running Windows Media Center is to feed all manner of digital media to your home theater system. Media Center's 10-foot interface is designed for use on widescreen and high-definition TVs, and a Media Center PC can feed high-quality music to any home audio system. In fact, a Media Center PC can replace several of the audio/video components you're currently using—you can listen to music CDs, view movie DVDs, watch and record television programming, listen to digital music files, view all your digital photographs, and much, much more. And it's all accomplished via Windows Media Center, from the comfort of your living room couch.

Of course, not everyone wants to put a personal computer in their living room. To that end, you may want to consider a Media Center Extender, instead. An Extender connects to your home network to access all the digital media files stored on your desktop PC, and then feeds all that media to your living room TV—using the Media Center onscreen interface. In fact, you may already have an Extender in your home; Microsoft's Xbox 360 does double-duty as both a videogame console and a Media Center Extender.

In previous versions of Windows, you had to buy a dedicated Media Center PC to get the Windows Media Center interface. With Windows Vista, however, Media Center is built into the Home Premium and Ultimate editions of the operating system. You can launch Media Center from the Windows Start menu—or configure Windows to launch Media Center automatically whenever you power up your computer.

How Windows Media Center Works

1 Windows Media Center is an interface that sits on top of Windows Vista and manages all of the user's digital entertainment functions—listening to music, recording and viewing television programming, viewing DVDs, viewing digital photos, and the like. Media Center is included with both the Home Premium and Ultimate editions of Windows Vista.

2 Although Media Center includes some unique operating features, most of its operations are conducted by passing instructions through to the underlying Windows Vista operating system. For example, when you play music in Media Center, Windows Media Player is actually doing the playing; Media Center simply provides the interface for that operation.

3 Media Center was designed specifically for use in living room home theater systems and optimized for widescreen and high-definition television displays. It includes a "10-foot interface" with larger and simpler screen elements than are found in the typical desktop computer "10-inch interface."

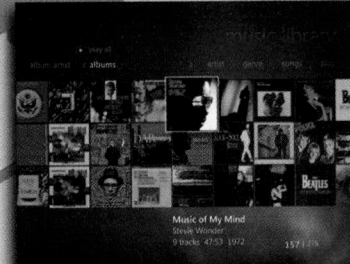

4 For convenience in the living room environment, the Media Center interface is navigated with a handheld remote control unit. For most day-to-day operations, there is no need for typical computer mouse or keyboard input; instead, all you have to do is click the appropriate buttons on the remote control.

5 Media Center's **Music** menu lets you play back digital music stored on your PC's hard disk, play music CDs, rip CDs to your hard drive, burn your own custom music CDs, and listen to Internet radio stations.

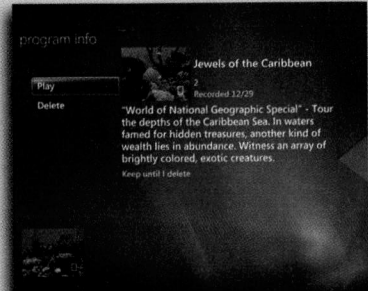

6 You use Media Center's **TV** menu to watch live TV, as well as schedule the recording of any television program and watch recorded programming.

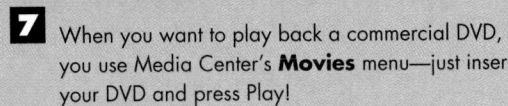

7 When you want to play back a commercial DVD, you use Media Center's **Movies** menu—just insert your DVD and press Play!

8 The **Photos + Video** menu lets you view digital photographs and videos stored on your PC's hard drive; photos can be viewed one at a time or in an onscreen slideshow.

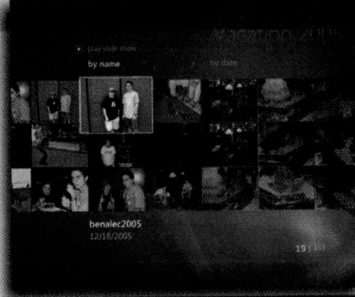

9 Even more applications are available on Media Center's **Spotlight** menu, which offers on-demand programming from AOL, CinemaNow, Comedy Central, Fox Sports, MTV, NPR, and other media partners.

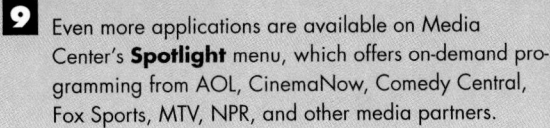

How Media Center Manages Digital Music

 In Media Center, all music-related functions are found on the Music menu.

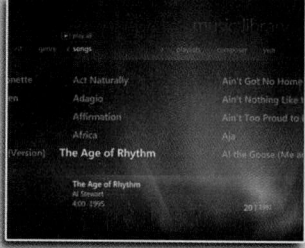  

2 The Music menu displays a collection of album cover thumbnails, representing the digital music that is stored on your PC's hard disk. You can choose to access your music by album, song, artist, genre, year, or playlist.

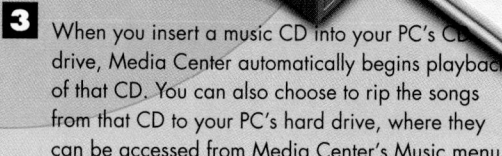

3 When you insert a music CD into your PC's CD drive, Media Center automatically begins playback of that CD. You can also choose to rip the songs from that CD to your PC's hard drive, where they can be accessed from Media Center's Music menu.

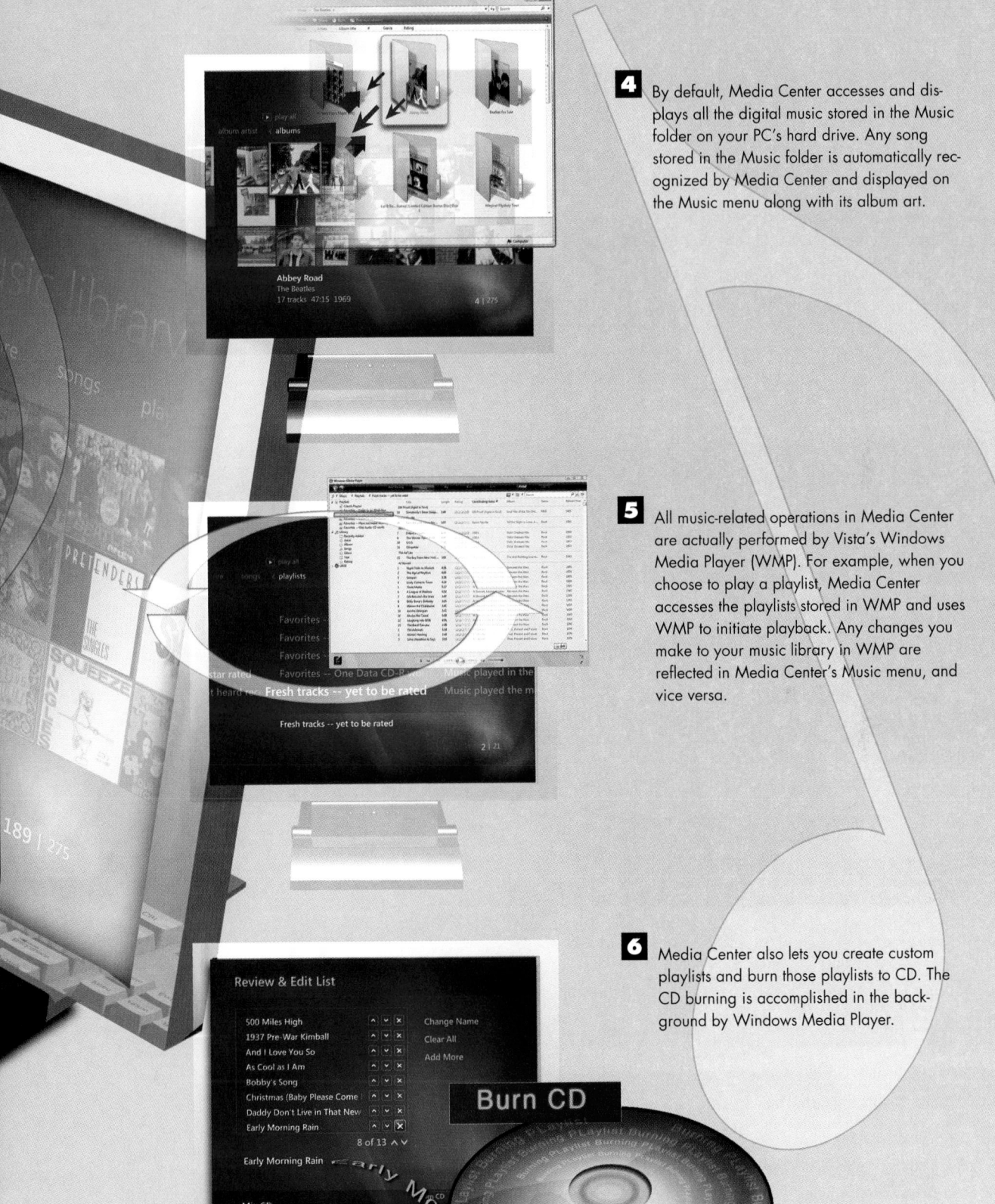

4 By default, Media Center accesses and displays all the digital music stored in the Music folder on your PC's hard drive. Any song stored in the Music folder is automatically recognized by Media Center and displayed on the Music menu along with its album art.

5 All music-related operations in Media Center are actually performed by Vista's Windows Media Player (WMP). For example, when you choose to play a playlist, Media Center accesses the playlists stored in WMP and uses WMP to initiate playback. Any changes you make to your music library in WMP are reflected in Media Center's Music menu, and vice versa.

6 Media Center also lets you create custom playlists and burn those playlists to CD. The CD burning is accomplished in the background by Windows Media Player.

How Media Center Manages Television Programming

1 If your PC has a built-in TV tuner, you can use Media Center to watch live television and record television programming. All this functionality is accessed from Media Center's TV menu.

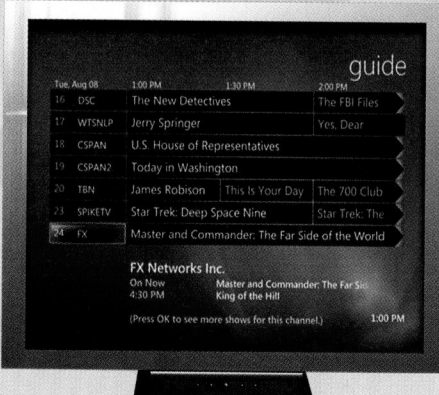

2 All television programming is accessed via Media Center's Electronic Program Guide (EPG). The EPG displays a schedule of local, cable, or satellite programs up to two weeks in advance; the guide is automatically updated via the Internet on a daily basis. Navigate to and select a program to watch it live or schedule it for later recording.

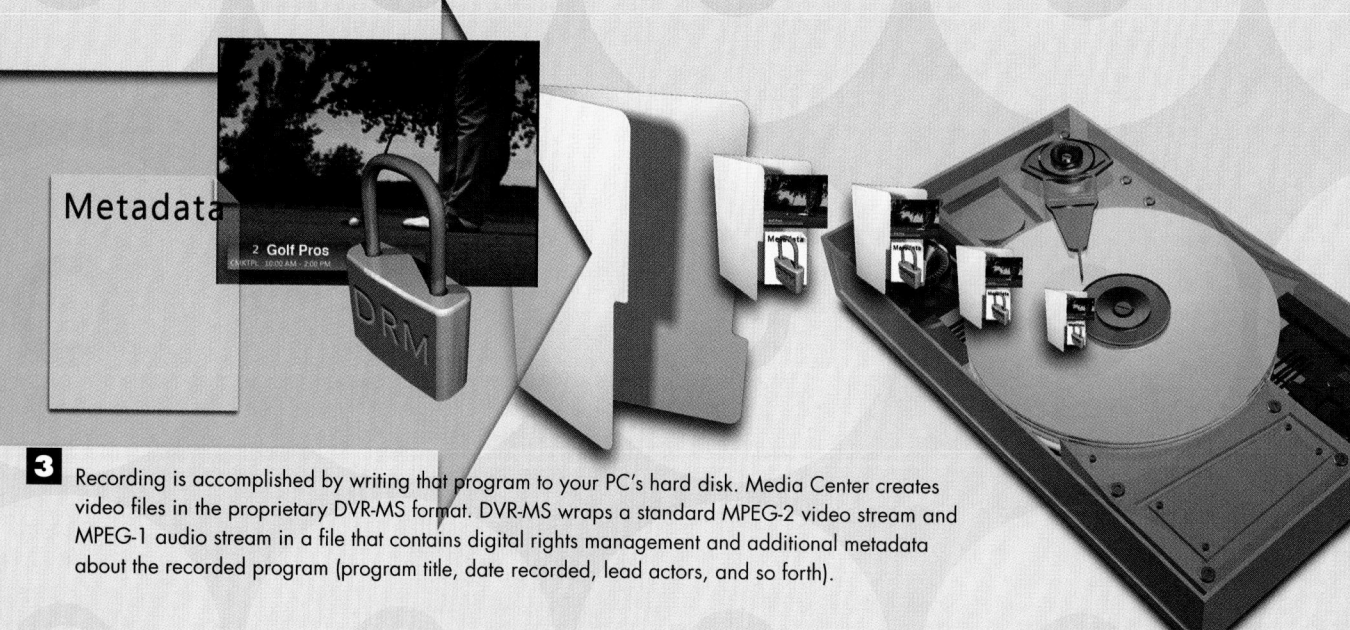

3 Recording is accomplished by writing that program to your PC's hard disk. Media Center creates video files in the proprietary DVR-MS format. DVR-MS wraps a standard MPEG-2 video stream and MPEG-1 audio stream in a file that contains digital rights management and additional metadata about the recorded program (program title, date recorded, lead actors, and so forth).

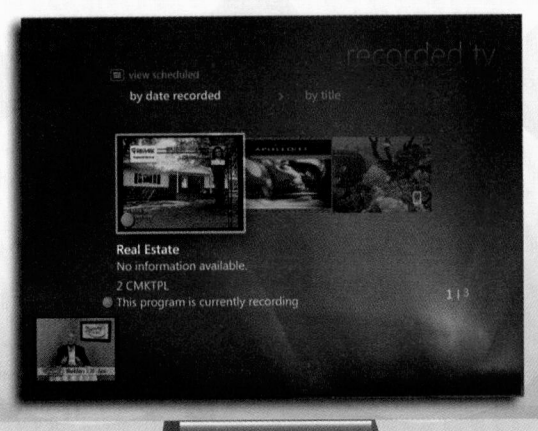

4 Media Center displays convenient thumbnails of all programs recorded to your PC's hard disk. To begin playback, simply navigate to and select a program thumbnail.

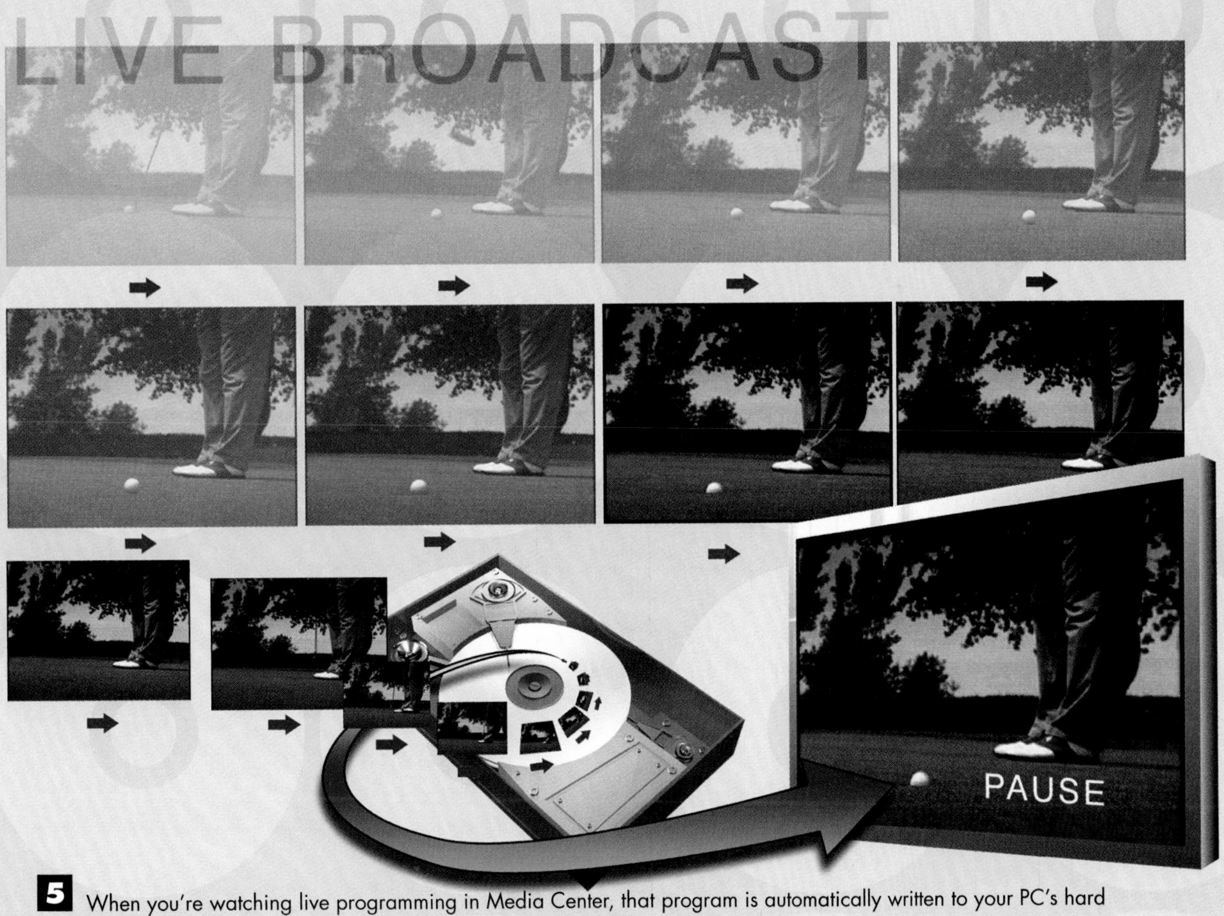

LIVE BROADCAST

PAUSE

5 When you're watching live programming in Media Center, that program is automatically written to your PC's hard disk in the background. You actually watch the program as recorded on the hard drive, a millisecond after it's been recorded. It might look as if you're pausing the action during a live broadcast, but you're merely pausing the read head on the hard disk; the write head continues to record the real live program as it continues in real-time.

How Media Center Works with HDTV

1 Windows Media Center is designed to work with the new high-definition television (HDTV) standard. Media Center can play back and record HDTV broadcasts—as long as your PC is equipped with an HDTV tuner.

ATSC1
ATSC2
NTSC1
NTSC2

2 Media Center supports up to two high-definition ATSC tuners, as well as two standard definition NTSC tuners. This lets you record one HDTV program while you watch another—or record multiple programs at the same time.

3 HDTV contains considerably more picture information than does standard definition television, which results in a much sharper, more realistic picture. A standard definition picture is composed of the equivalent of approximately 300,000 pixels. HDTV in the 1080i format contains more than 2 million pixels—more than six times the amount of picture information than in a standard definition picture.

307,200 pixels

2,073,600 pixels

720p

720

i1280

1080i

i1920

1080

1080

i1920

1080p

4 There are actually several different HDTV standards, all supported by Windows Vista and Media Center. The 720p format has a resolution of 720 x 1280 pixels, with progressive scanning. The 1080i format has a higher resolution of 1080 x 1920 pixels, but with interlaced scanning. The 1080p format also has a 1080 x 1920 resolution, but with the superior progressive scanning. Both 720p and 1080i formats are used for HDTV broadcasts today; the 1080p format is used in next-generation Blu-ray and HD DVD discs.

4:3

SDTV   HDTV

16:9

5 HDTV is more than just a sharper picture. The HDTV standard also includes digital audio and video transmission for superior fidelity to the original source, a 16:9 aspect ratio widescreen display, and Dolby Digital 5.1-channel surround. All these elements work together with the increased picture resolution to provide a complete home theater experience.

How CableCARD Works

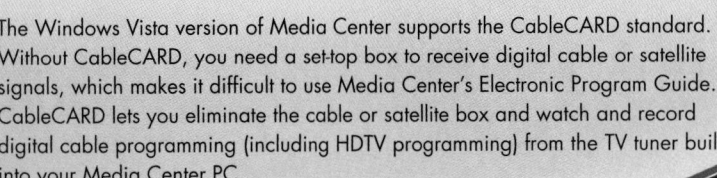

1 The Windows Vista version of Media Center supports the CableCARD standard. Without CableCARD, you need a set-top box to receive digital cable or satellite signals, which makes it difficult to use Media Center's Electronic Program Guide. CableCARD lets you eliminate the cable or satellite box and watch and record digital cable programming (including HDTV programming) from the TV tuner built into your Media Center PC.

2 The CableCARD itself is a small PCMCIA type II flash memory card. It is supplied by your cable or satellite company; each device (TV tuner or Media Center PC) is assigned its own unique CableCARD.

1582VYw52kLOR6890176

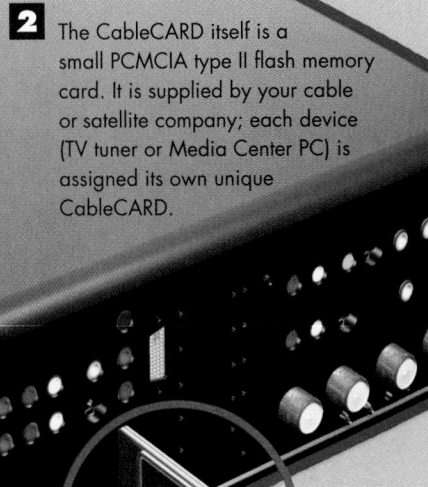

3 Both your Media Center PC and your CableCARD have unique identification keys. These keys must be registered with your cable or satellite company for the CableCARD to work with your PC. They enable the cable or satellite company to provide secure programming tied to your individual subscription to cable services—and prevent you from receiving programming and services to which you haven't subscribed.

Qu1452J6eri57c

Two-Way CableCARDS?

The current generation of CableCARDs are one-way devices—that is, they receive and decode data streams downloaded to your Media Center PC, but cannot send data back upstream to the cable company. This means that today's Media Center PCs cannot display your cable company's interactive program guide (they display media Center's EPG, instead) or provide pay-per-view or video on demand programming. Next-generation CableCARDs will offer this two-way functionality and the associated interactive services.

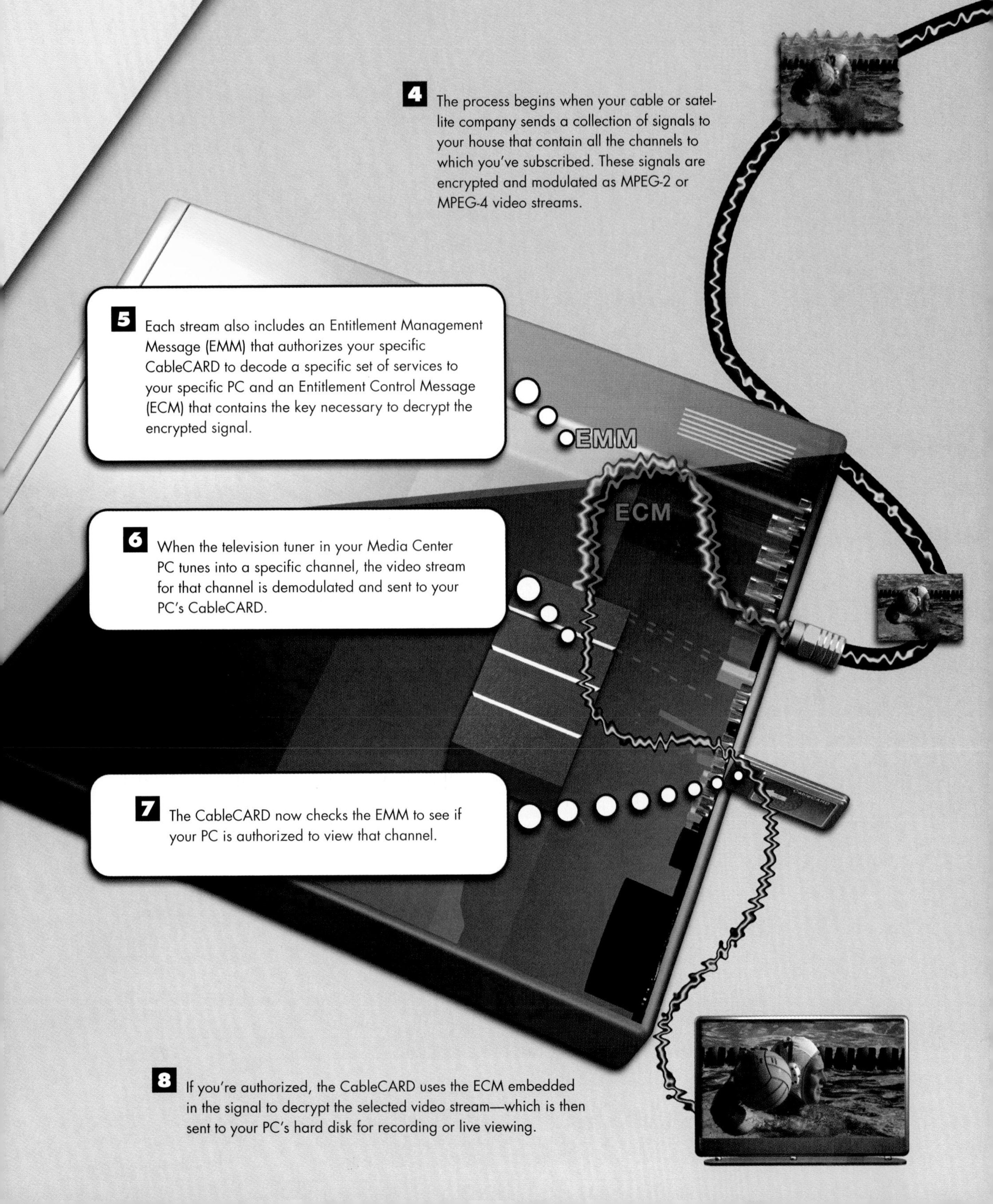

4 The process begins when your cable or satellite company sends a collection of signals to your house that contain all the channels to which you've subscribed. These signals are encrypted and modulated as MPEG-2 or MPEG-4 video streams.

5 Each stream also includes an Entitlement Management Message (EMM) that authorizes your specific CableCARD to decode a specific set of services to your specific PC and an Entitlement Control Message (ECM) that contains the key necessary to decrypt the encrypted signal.

EMM

ECM

6 When the television tuner in your Media Center PC tunes into a specific channel, the video stream for that channel is demodulated and sent to your PC's CableCARD.

7 The CableCARD now checks the EMM to see if your PC is authorized to view that channel.

8 If you're authorized, the CableCARD uses the ECM embedded in the signal to decrypt the selected video stream—which is then sent to your PC's hard disk for recording or live viewing.

How a Media Center PC Interfaces with Your Home Theater System

1 A typical Media Center PC includes one or more built-in TV tuners, as well as the means to reproduce multi-channel audio. It is designed to be connected to your home theater picture, so you can watch video programming and listen to audio recordings.

2 You begin by connecting a television signal (over the air, cable, or satellite) to the tuner input of the Media Center PC.

3 To view video programming, you must connect your Media Center PC to your television display. You can use either component video, DVI, or HDMI cables to make this connection.

4 To listen to stereo audio, you can connect a traditional left/right RCA audio cable from the audio outputs on the back of your Media Center PC to the corresponding inputs on your audio/video receiver.

5 To listen to multi-channel surround sound, you must connect either a digital optical or coaxial cable between your Media Center PC and your A/V receiver.

6 Your A/V receiver is then connected to your individual stereo or surround sound speakers.

7 You use your PC's remote control to control all the entertainment provided by your Media Center PC—listening to CDs and digital audio, viewing live or recorded television programs, or watching movies on DVD.

How Media Center Extenders Work

1 Not everyone wants to put a PC in the living room. Instead, you can use a Media Center Extender to connect to your main desktop PC and feed audio and video programming to your living room PC.

2 Media Center Extenders come in many shapes and sizes. For many users, Microsoft's Xbox 360 videogame console is the perfect Media Center Extender—it not only plays the latest videogames, but it also connects to your home network to play back music, videos, and television programming.

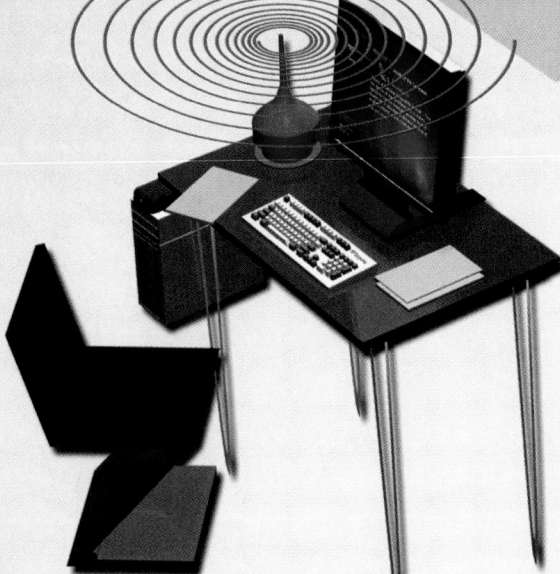

3 A Media Center Extender connects to your home network, via either Ethernet or a wireless network adapter.

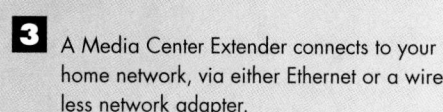

4 Using your home network, the Media Center Extender accesses all the music, video, and photo files stored on your main desktop PC. (The main PC must be running Windows Media Center to connect to Extender.)

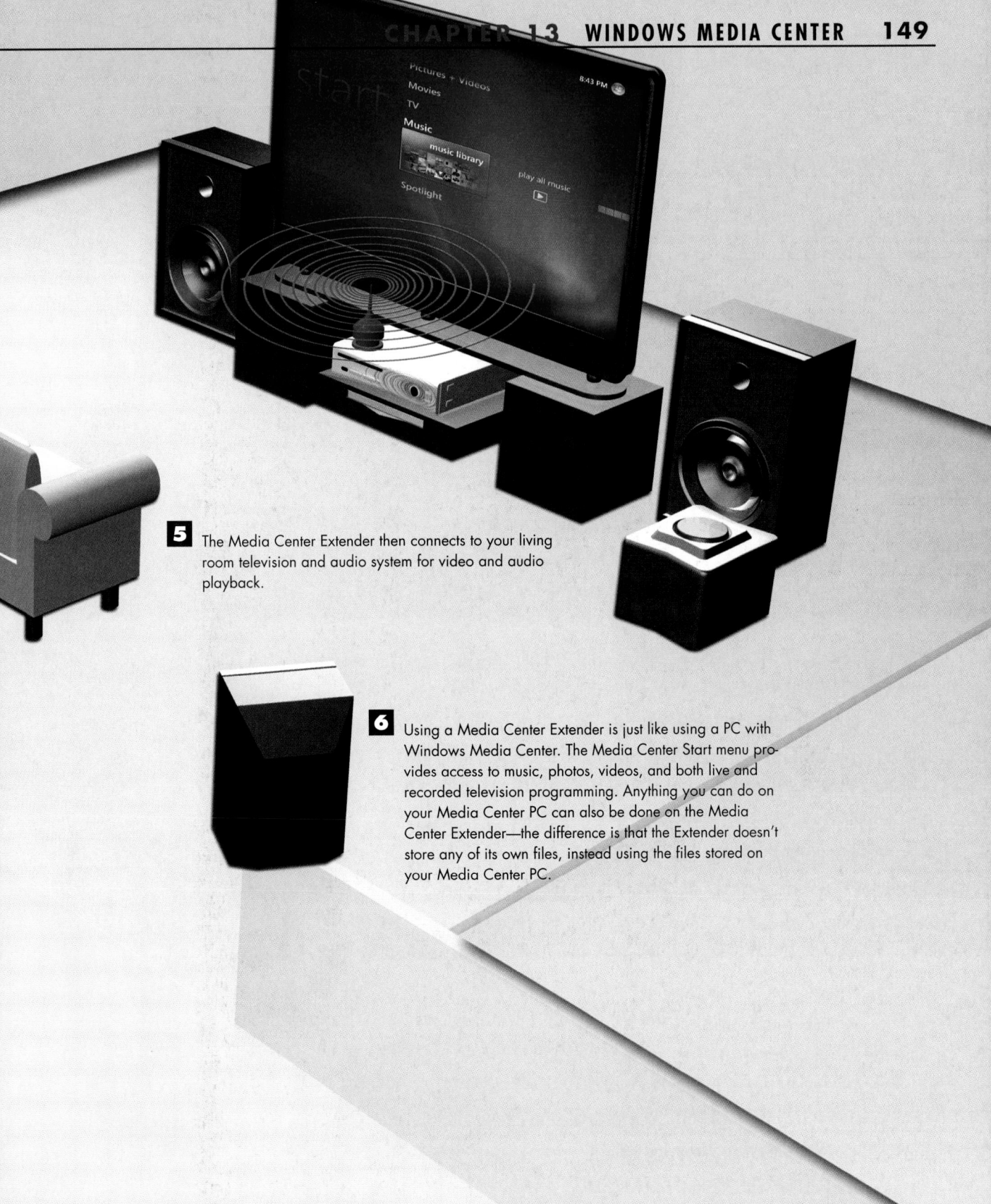

5 The Media Center Extender then connects to your living room television and audio system for video and audio playback.

6 Using a Media Center Extender is just like using a PC with Windows Media Center. The Media Center Start menu provides access to music, photos, videos, and both live and recorded television programming. Anything you can do on your Media Center PC can also be done on the Media Center Extender—the difference is that the Extender doesn't store any of its own files, instead using the files stored on your Media Center PC.

CHAPTER

14

Digital Music

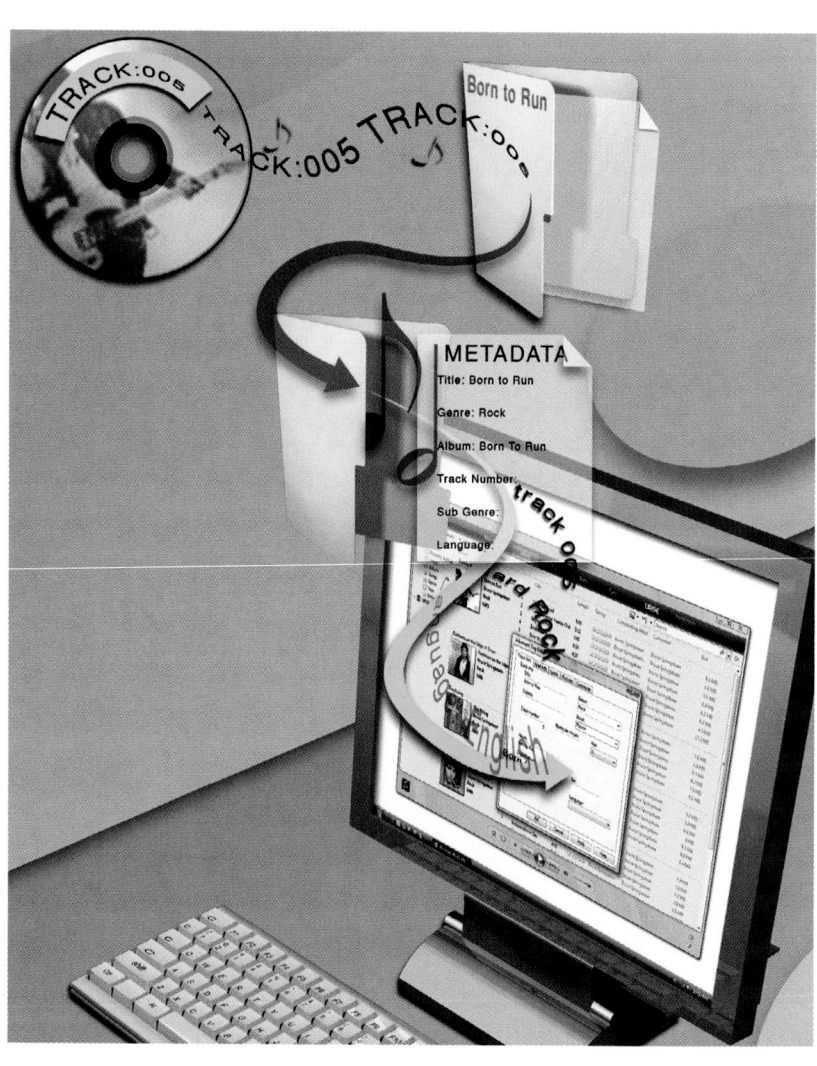

CHANCES are, you already use your computer to listen to music. Maybe you play CDs from your PC's CD drive. Maybe you download songs from the Internet. Maybe you rip songs from your own CDs and then use your computer to transfer them to a portable music player. Maybe you do all of this, and a little more.

Because so many people use their PCs to listen to digital music, Microsoft has included a full-featured music player/manager program in the last several versions of Windows. With Windows Vista, this program—Windows Media Player—gets an extreme makeover, for the better.

Windows Media Player 11 does pretty much everything previous versions did, but it does it all a whole lot better and easier. The program's interface has been completely redesigned, using a series of easily understandable tabs to access various functions. Want to play music stored in your library? Then click the Library tab. Want to rip music from a CD? Click the Rip tab. Want to synchronize the music on your PC with your portable music player? Click the Sync tab. You get the idea.

Everything you need to do, digital music-wise, you can do with Windows Media Player. You can play CDs (and DVDs), rip CD tracks to your hard disk, burn CDs from music stored on your hard disk, play back music you've ripped or downloaded from the Internet, or even copy music to your portable music player.

In addition, Windows Media Player 11 includes access to a new online music service called Urge, with which Microsoft has partnered with music giant MTV. Urge offers music for purchase (99 cents for most songs) and a monthly subscription service called Urge All Access to Go. For $14.95/month, you get access to millions of songs, more than 500 playlists, and 130 or more Internet radio stations. And you access all of this—the music you purchase and the music you "rent" from the monthly service—from the Urge tab in Windows Media Player.

If you've used previous versions of Windows Media Player, WMP 11 will look familiar to you—but also quite a bit different. It pays to check out what's what and what's where in this new version; WMP 11 is a major improvement over WMP 10, and a key feature in Windows Vista.

How Digital Audio Works

1 All digital recordings—starting in the recording studio—are made by creating digital samples of the original sound. An analog-to-digital converter (ADC) "listens" to the original analog signal and takes a digital snapshot of the music at a particular point in time. The length of that snapshot (measured in bits) and the number of snapshots per second (called the sampling rate) determine the quality of the reproduction. The more samples per second, the more accurate the resulting digital "picture" of the original music.

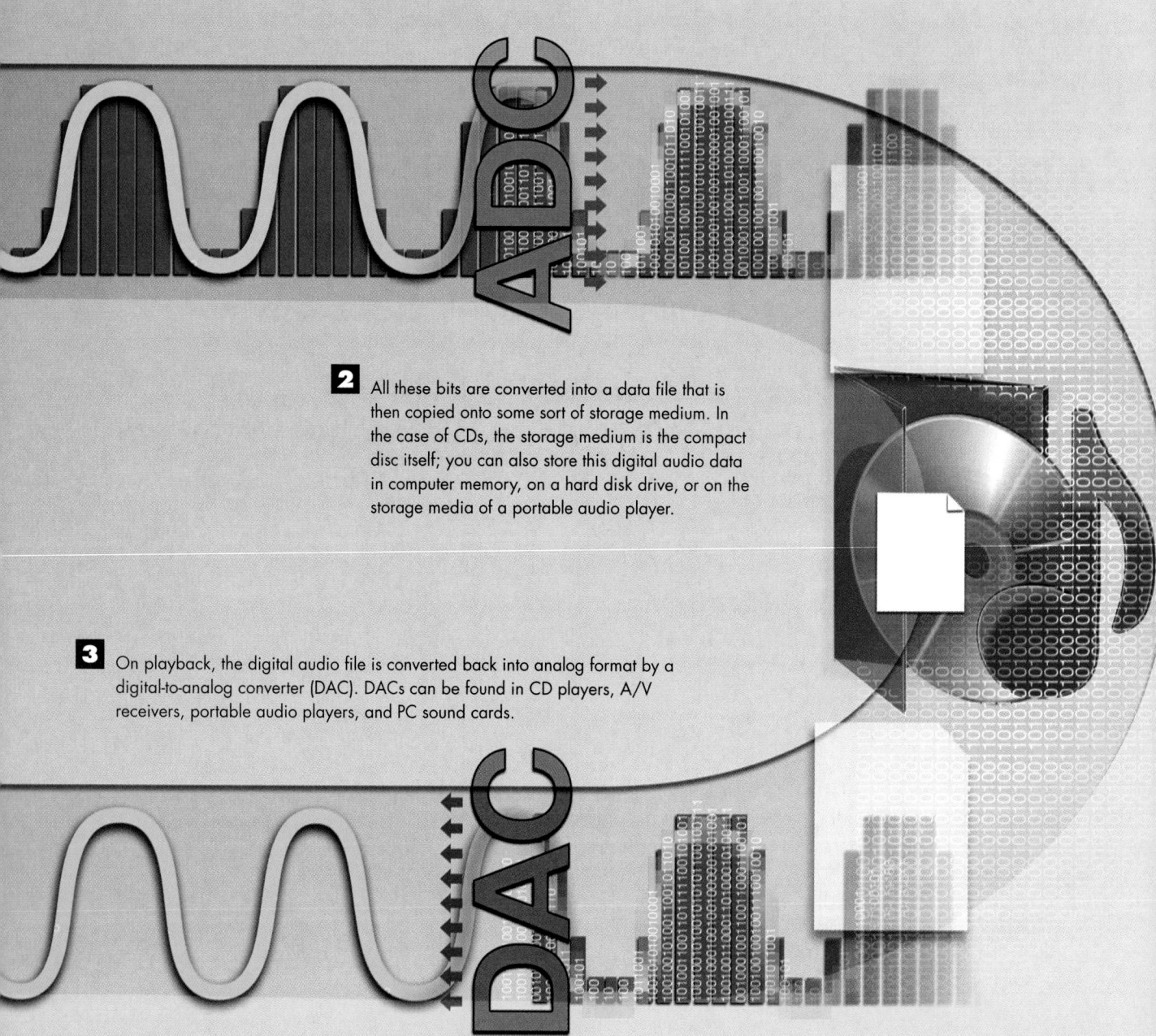

2 All these bits are converted into a data file that is then copied onto some sort of storage medium. In the case of CDs, the storage medium is the compact disc itself; you can also store this digital audio data in computer memory, on a hard disk drive, or on the storage media of a portable audio player.

3 On playback, the digital audio file is converted back into analog format by a digital-to-analog converter (DAC). DACs can be found in CD players, A/V receivers, portable audio players, and PC sound cards.

4 When you copy a digital audio file, you can either copy the file exactly or you can use some sort of compression to reduce the otherwise-huge file sizes. (A typical three-minute song recorded at 44.1KHz takes up 32MB.) The best audio fidelity comes from using a noncompressed file format, such as WAV.

5 Lossy compression works by sampling the original file and removing those ranges of sounds that the average listener can't hear, based on accepted psychoacoustic models. You control the sound quality and the size of the resulting file by selecting different sampling rates for the data. The lower the sampling rate, the smaller the file size—and the lower the sound quality. Popular file formats that use lossy compression include MP3, AAC, and Microsoft's WMA (Windows Media Audio) format.

6 If you want to create a high-fidelity digital archive, a better solution is to use a lossless compression format. These formats work similar to ZIP compression; redundant bits are taken out to create the compressed file, which is then uncompressed for playback. The resulting file has exact fidelity to the original, while still being stored in a smaller-sized file (although larger than lossy files). Microsoft's lossless audio format is called WMA Lossless.

Bit Rate

When you multiply the sampling rate by the sample size and the number of channels (two for stereo), you end up with a **bit rate**. For example, compact discs sample music 44,100 times per second, for a 44.1kHz sampling rate; each sample is 16 bits long. Multiply 44,100 × 16 × 2 and you get a bit rate of 1,400,000 bits per second—or 1,400Kbps.

How Windows Stores Digital Music Files

1 When you copy music from a CD or download songs from the Internet, that music is stored on your hard disk in the form of digital audio files. By default, Windows stores digital audio in the WMA (Windows Media Audio) format, although Vista supports all audio file types.

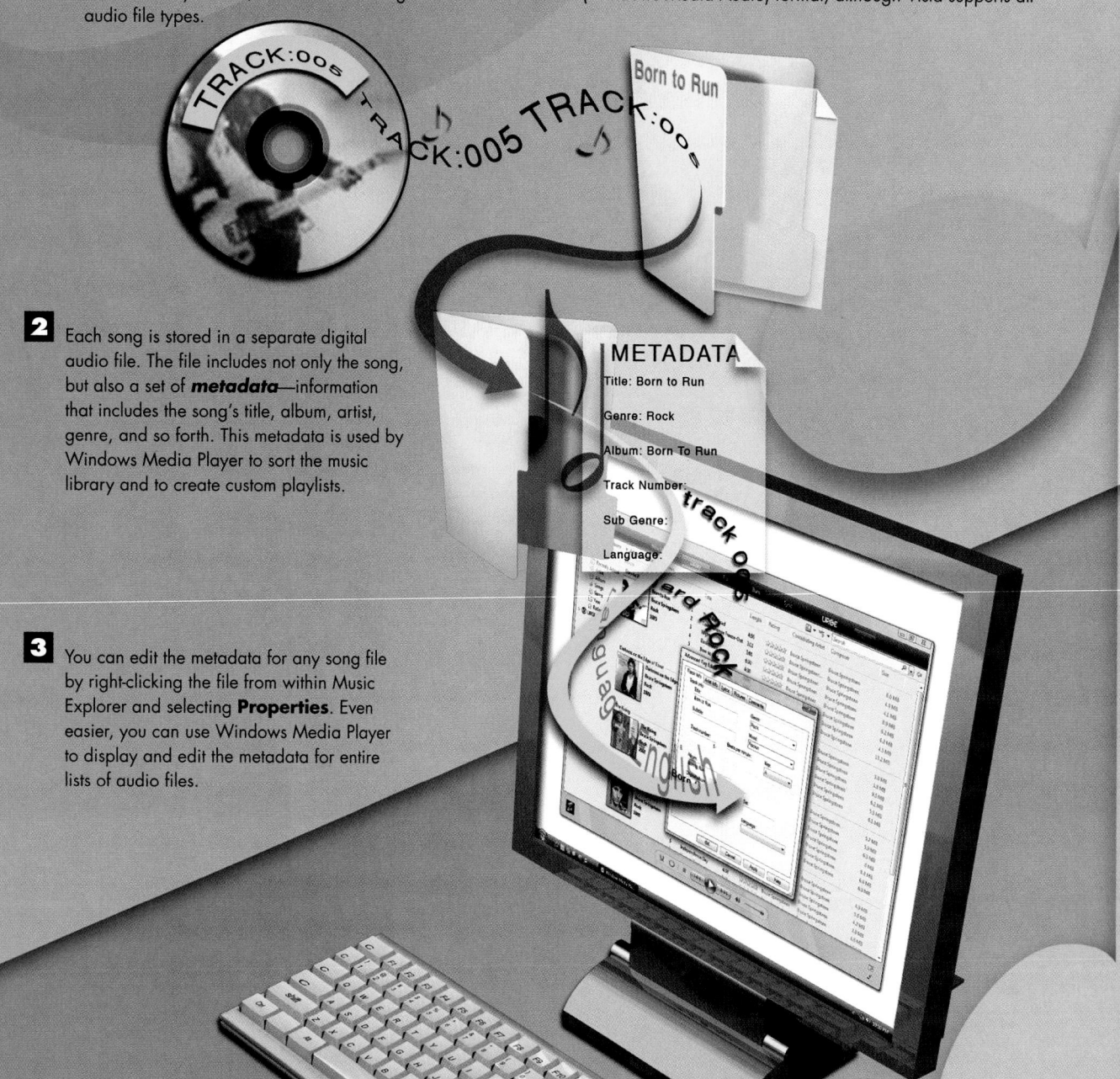

2 Each song is stored in a separate digital audio file. The file includes not only the song, but also a set of *metadata*—information that includes the song's title, album, artist, genre, and so forth. This metadata is used by Windows Media Player to sort the music library and to create custom playlists.

3 You can edit the metadata for any song file by right-clicking the file from within Music Explorer and selecting **Properties**. Even easier, you can use Windows Media Player to display and edit the metadata for entire lists of audio files.

METADATA

Title: Born to Run

Genre: Rock

Album: Born To Run

Track Number:

Sub Genre:

Language:

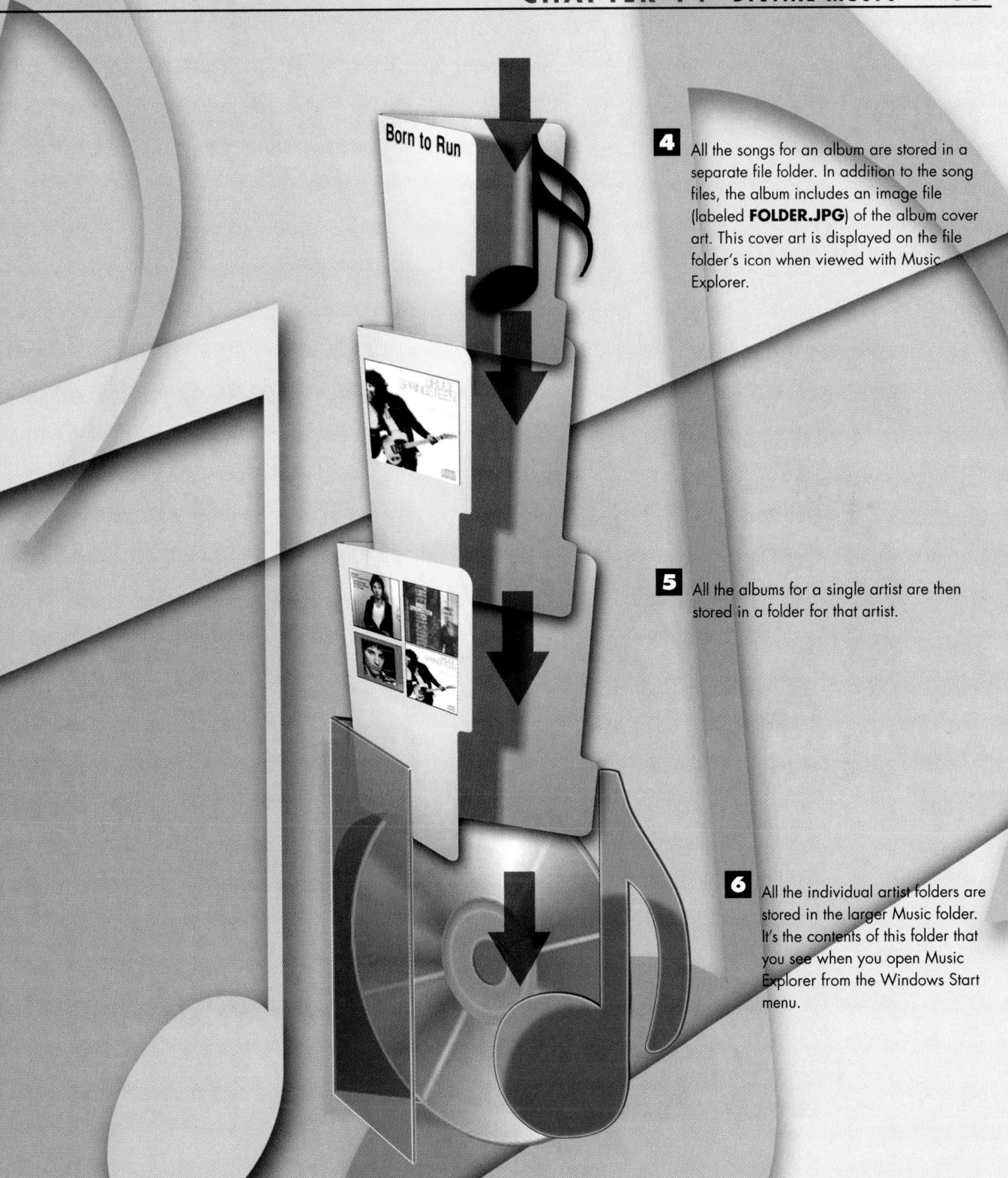

4 All the songs for an album are stored in a separate file folder. In addition to the song files, the album includes an image file (labeled **FOLDER.JPG**) of the album cover art. This cover art is displayed on the file folder's icon when viewed with Music Explorer.

5 All the albums for a single artist are then stored in a folder for that artist.

6 All the individual artist folders are stored in the larger Music folder. It's the contents of this folder that you see when you open Music Explorer from the Windows Start menu.

Born to Run

How Windows Media Player 11 Plays Digital Music Files

1 Windows Media Player assigns different functions to different tabs. For example, if you want to rip music from a CD to your PC's hard drive, you select the Rip tab.

2 All the digital music on your PC is accessed via WMP's Library tab. You can view your library by artist, album, songs, genre, year, rating, contributing artist, composer, parental rating, or recently added files.

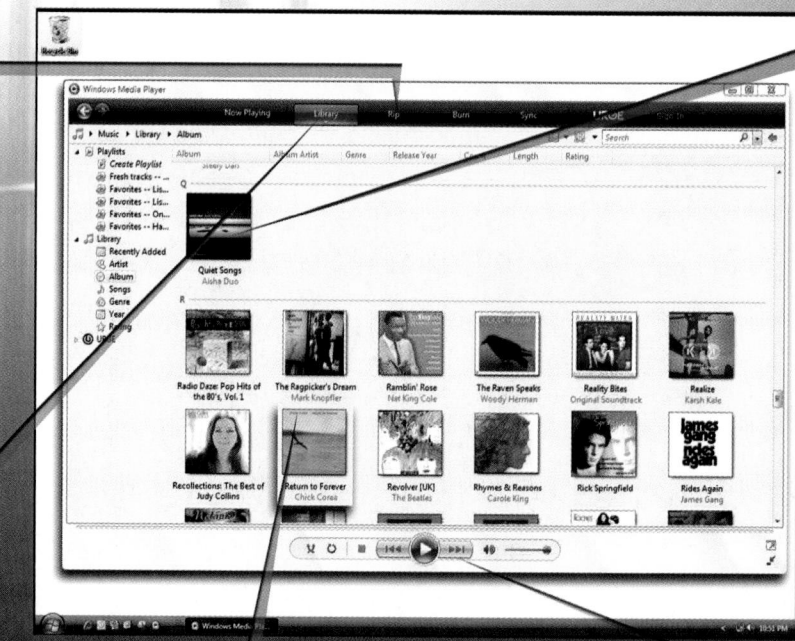

3 The music displayed in the WMP Library resides on your hard disk, typically in the Music folder—although the Library can include files stored in other folders. The list of songs links to the individual audio files stored on your hard disk; when you delete a file from your hard drive, its entry is deleted from the Library.

4 By default, Windows Media Player displays your music by album, complete with the original album art. Double-click an album cover to view the individual tracks for that album.

5 Each song in the Library is displayed with key information about the track, as stored in the audio file's metadata. This information includes the song title, length, rating, contributing artist, composer, genre, release year, and more. You can sort the songs in your Library by any of these criteria.

6 To play a song or album, all you have to do is double-click it. The audio from the selected file is sent to your PC's audio card, and then to your speakers. You control the music playback with the transport controls at the bottom of the WMP window; you can pause, rewind, fast forward, and stop playback at any time.

How Playlists Work

1 By default, the music stored on your PC is organized by album and artist. However, Windows Media Player lets you organize your music however you like, by creating custom **playlists**.

2 A playlist is simply a list of individual songs, assembled from any album or artist. A playlist can be as short as two songs or as long as all the songs on your PC.

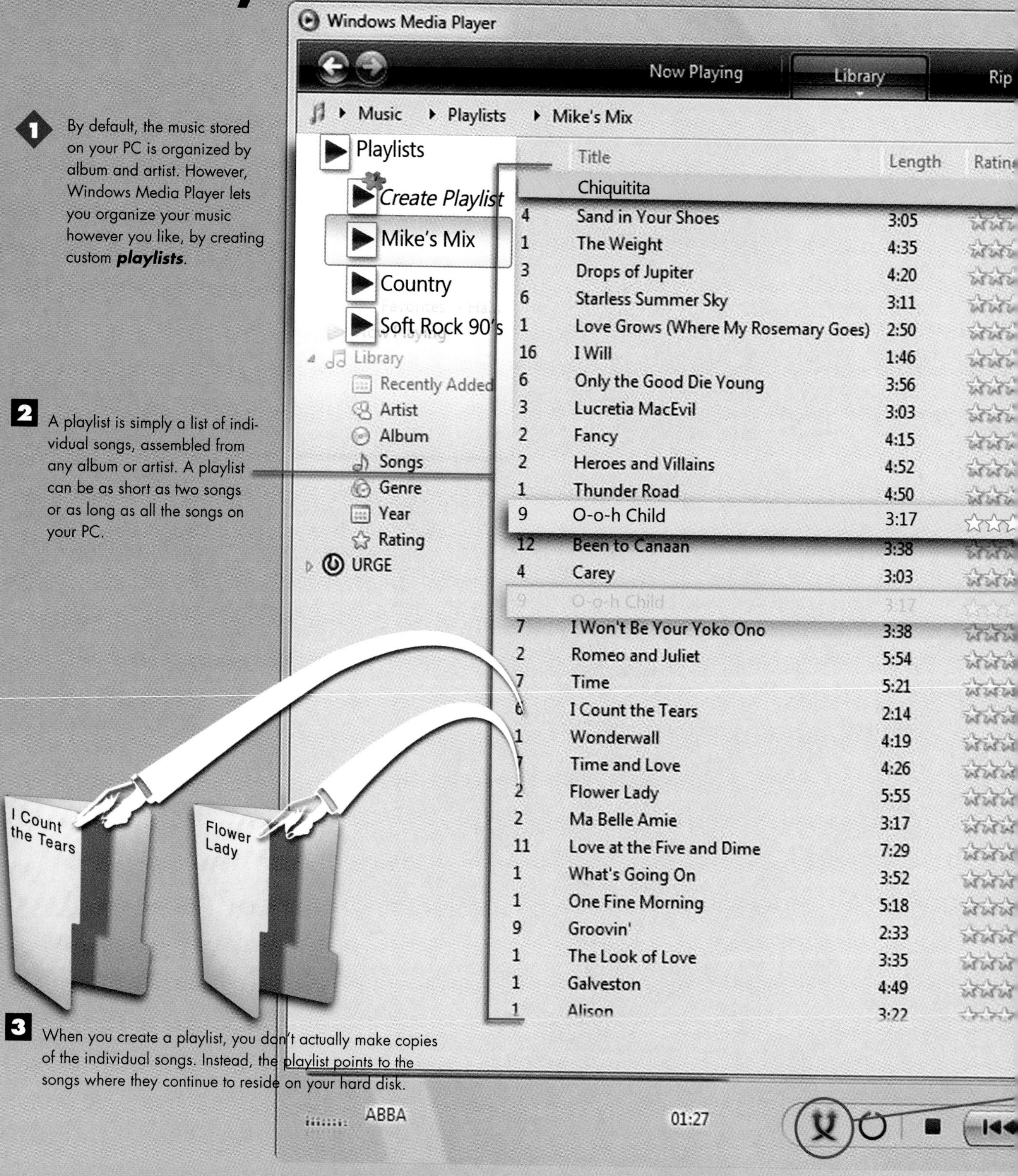

Windows Media Player

Now Playing | Library | Rip

♫ ▸ Music ▸ Playlists ▸ Mike's Mix

▶ Playlists
  ▶ *Create Playlist*
  ▶ Mike's Mix
  ▶ Country
  ▶ Soft Rock 90's
▲ ♫ Library
  ▦ Recently Added
  ♨ Artist
  ☉ Album
  ♪ Songs
  ◎ Genre
  ▦ Year
  ☆ Rating
▷ Ⓤ URGE

	Title	Length	Rating
	Chiquitita		
4	Sand in Your Shoes	3:05	⭐⭐⭐
1	The Weight	4:35	⭐⭐⭐
3	Drops of Jupiter	4:20	⭐⭐
6	Starless Summer Sky	3:11	⭐⭐
1	Love Grows (Where My Rosemary Goes)	2:50	⭐⭐
16	I Will	1:46	⭐⭐
6	Only the Good Die Young	3:56	⭐⭐
3	Lucretia MacEvil	3:03	⭐⭐
2	Fancy	4:15	⭐⭐
2	Heroes and Villains	4:52	⭐⭐
1	Thunder Road	4:50	
9	O-o-h Child	3:17	⭐⭐
12	Been to Canaan	3:38	⭐⭐
4	Carey	3:03	⭐⭐
9	O-o-h Child	3:17	⭐
7	I Won't Be Your Yoko Ono	3:38	⭐⭐
2	Romeo and Juliet	5:54	⭐⭐
7	Time	5:21	⭐
6	I Count the Tears	2:14	⭐⭐
1	Wonderwall	4:19	⭐⭐
7	Time and Love	4:26	⭐⭐
2	Flower Lady	5:55	⭐⭐
2	Ma Belle Amie	3:17	⭐⭐
11	Love at the Five and Dime	7:29	⭐⭐
1	What's Going On	3:52	⭐⭐
1	One Fine Morning	5:18	⭐⭐
9	Groovin'	2:33	⭐⭐
1	The Look of Love	3:35	⭐⭐
1	Galveston	4:49	⭐⭐
1	Alison	3:22	⭐⭐

I Count the Tears

Flower Lady

3 When you create a playlist, you don't actually make copies of the individual songs. Instead, the playlist points to the songs where they continue to reside on your hard disk.

⋮⋮⋮ ABBA   01:27   Ⓨ ◯ ▮ ◀◀

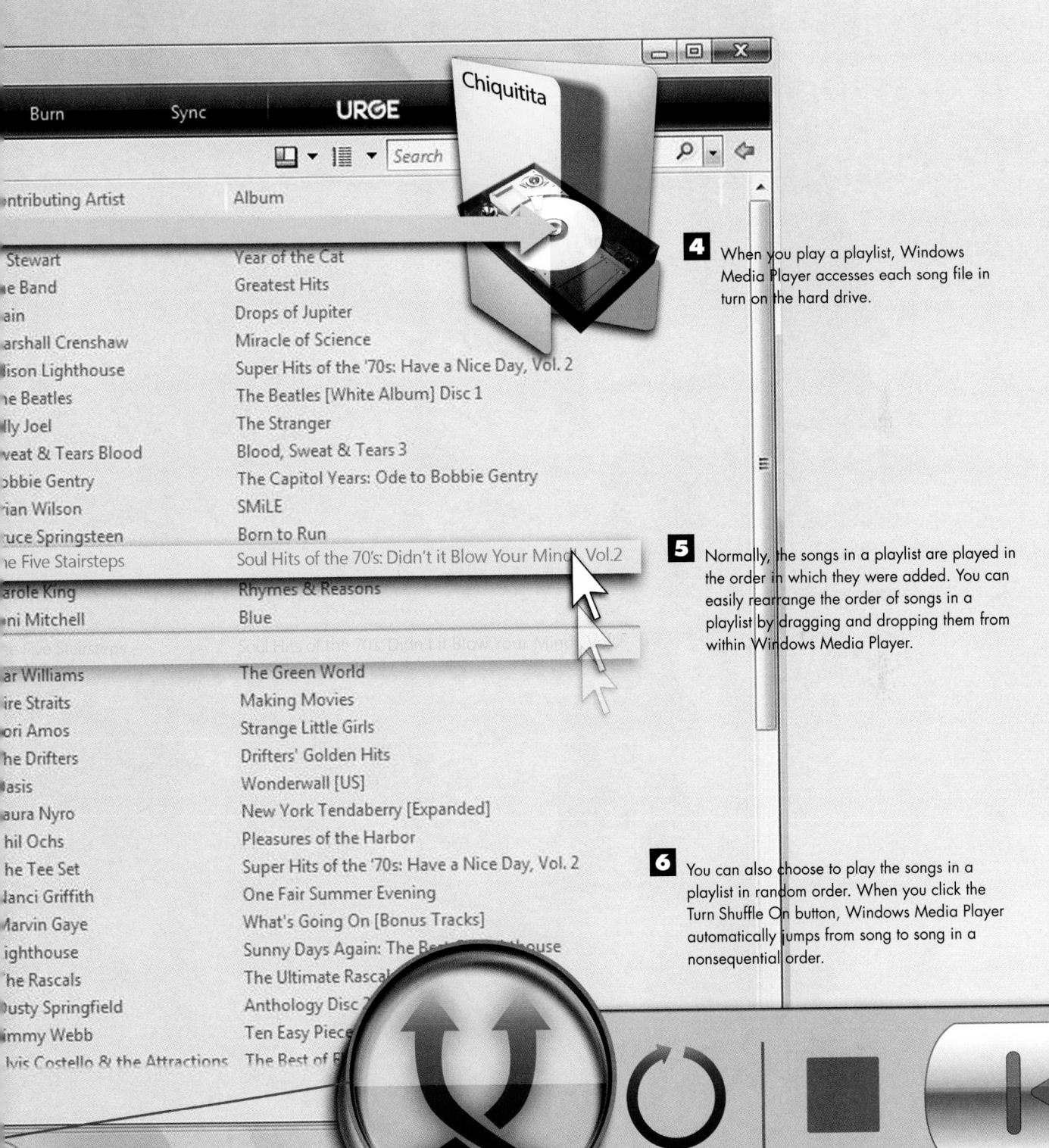

Chiquitita

ntributing Artist | Album

Stewart | Year of the Cat
e Band | Greatest Hits
ain | Drops of Jupiter
arshall Crenshaw | Miracle of Science
lison Lighthouse | Super Hits of the '70s: Have a Nice Day, Vol. 2
he Beatles | The Beatles [White Album] Disc 1
lly Joel | The Stranger
veat & Tears Blood | Blood, Sweat & Tears 3
obbie Gentry | The Capitol Years: Ode to Bobbie Gentry
rian Wilson | SMiLE
ruce Springsteen | Born to Run
he Five Stairsteps | Soul Hits of the 70's: Didn't it Blow Your Mind, Vol.2
arole King | Rhymes & Reasons
ni Mitchell | Blue

ar Williams | The Green World
ire Straits | Making Movies
ori Amos | Strange Little Girls
he Drifters | Drifters' Golden Hits
asis | Wonderwall [US]
aura Nyro | New York Tendaberry [Expanded]
hil Ochs | Pleasures of the Harbor
he Tee Set | Super Hits of the '70s: Have a Nice Day, Vol. 2
Nanci Griffith | One Fair Summer Evening
Marvin Gaye | What's Going On [Bonus Tracks]
ighthouse | Sunny Days Again: The Best of Lighthouse
he Rascals | The Ultimate Rascals
Dusty Springfield | Anthology Disc
Jimmy Webb | Ten Easy Pieces
lvis Costello & the Attractions | The Best of

4 When you play a playlist, Windows Media Player accesses each song file in turn on the hard drive.

5 Normally, the songs in a playlist are played in the order in which they were added. You can easily rearrange the order of songs in a playlist by dragging and dropping them from within Windows Media Player.

6 You can also choose to play the songs in a playlist in random order. When you click the Turn Shuffle On button, Windows Media Player automatically jumps from song to song in a nonsequential order.

How Music is Transferred from Your PC to a Portable Music Player

1 Windows Media Player helps you manage all the music (as well as movies and pictures) you have stored on your portable music player. When you want to transfer new items to your music player, you use WMP's Sync tab.

Sync
▼

2 When you connect your portable music player to your PC, it appears in the right-hand pane of the Sync tab. Most music players connect to your PC via USB.

3 If your portable music player has a large-enough storage capacity, your entire music library will be automatically copied to your music player.

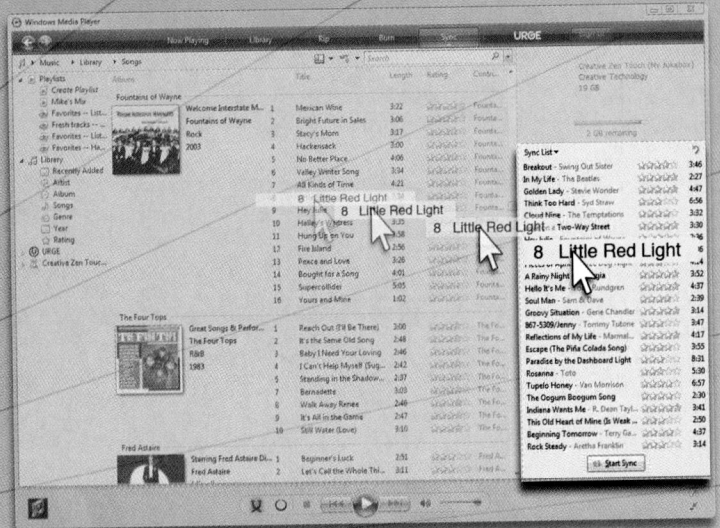

4 If your portable music player has less than 4GB storage capacity or if your entire music library won't fit on the device, you can manually choose which songs to transfer to the player. Simply drag the songs, albums, or playlists you want to copy from the List pane to the Sync List.

5 To copy the items in the Sync List to your portable music player, click the Start Sync button.

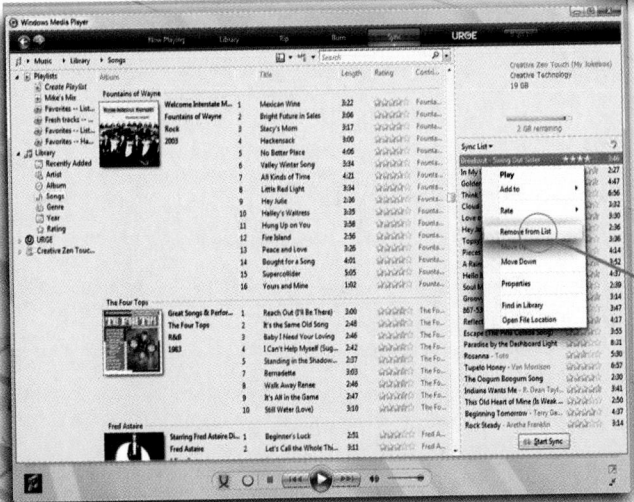

6 To remove a song from your portable music player, right-click the item in WMP's Sync List and select **Remove from List**. WMP will then locate that file on your portable music player and delete it.

Remove from list

How Digital Music Is Copied from CD to Your PC

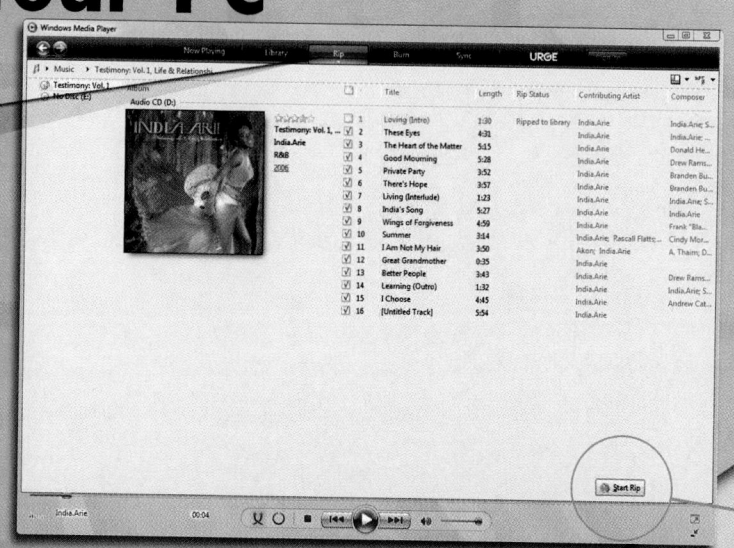

1 When you want to store your music digitally or transfer music to a portable music player, you need to copy that music from a compact disc to your computer's hard drive. This process is called *ripping* and is managed by Windows Media Player.

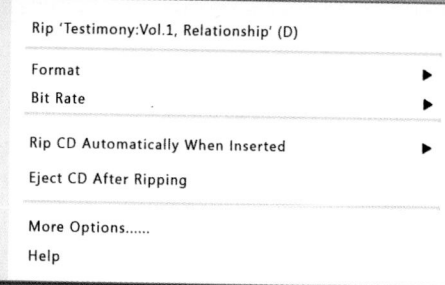

Rip 'Testimony:Vol.1, Relationship' (D)

Format ▶
Bit Rate ▶

Rip CD Automatically When Inserted ▶
Eject CD After Ripping

More Options......
Help

2 Before you rip a CD, you have to select the file type and quality you want for your ripped music files. You do this by clicking the down arrow beneath the Rip tab and selecting both **Format** (file type) and **Bit Rate** (audio quality).

Format	▶	✓ Windows Media Audio
Bit Rate		Windows Media Audio Pro
		Windows Media Audio (Variable Bit Rate)
		Windows Media Audio Lossless
		MP3
		WAV (Lossless)

3 The **Format** you select determines what type of audio file is created. For most users, the Windows Media Audio (WMA) format is good, although you might want to go with Windows Media Audio Lossless for the highest sound quality or the MP3 format for almost-universal compatibility with all portable music players.

Bit Rate ▶

| 48 Kbps (Smallest Size) |
| 64 Kbps |
| 96 Kbps |
| ✓ 128 Kbps (Default) |
| 160 Kbps |
| 192 Kbps (Best Quality) |

4 The **Bit Rate** you select determines the quality and the file size of the audio files you create. Files created at a higher bit rate sound better, but are larger. Files created at a lower bit rate don't sound quite as good, but they take up less disc space.

5 Once you've set the Format and Bit Rate, you begin the ripping process by inserting a music CD into your PC's CD drive.

 Start Rip

6 Once the CD is inserted, select the Rip tab in Windows Media Player, check those tracks you want to copy, and then click the Start Rip button.

7 Windows Media Player now extracts the selected tracks from the CD and converts them from their original CD Audio format to the file format you selected. During this process, the tracks are sampled at the bit rate you selected.

Love Song

WMA

8 The converted files are now written to your PC's hard disk and added to the Windows Media Player Library. Each track is stored as a separate audio file, in a folder named for the CD you copied. The CD folder is stored in a larger folder named for the CD's artist, which itself is stored in the Music folder on your hard disk.

How Windows Plays CDs and DVDs with HotStart

1 If you have a notebook PC, you can use your PC as a portable music or DVD player, thanks to Windows Vista's HotStart technology. HotStart lets PC manufacturers include a special button that launches Windows Media Player for music or movie playback, even if your computer is in sleep mode or powered completely off.

2 Using HotStart uses less power than running a full instance of Windows Vista, which helps to conserve your notebook's battery life. HotStart is also faster than powering on your PC, loading Windows, and then launching the program manually. With HotStart, WMP launches within seconds, so you can quickly listen to a CD, watch a DVD, or listen to digital music stored on your PC's hard drive.

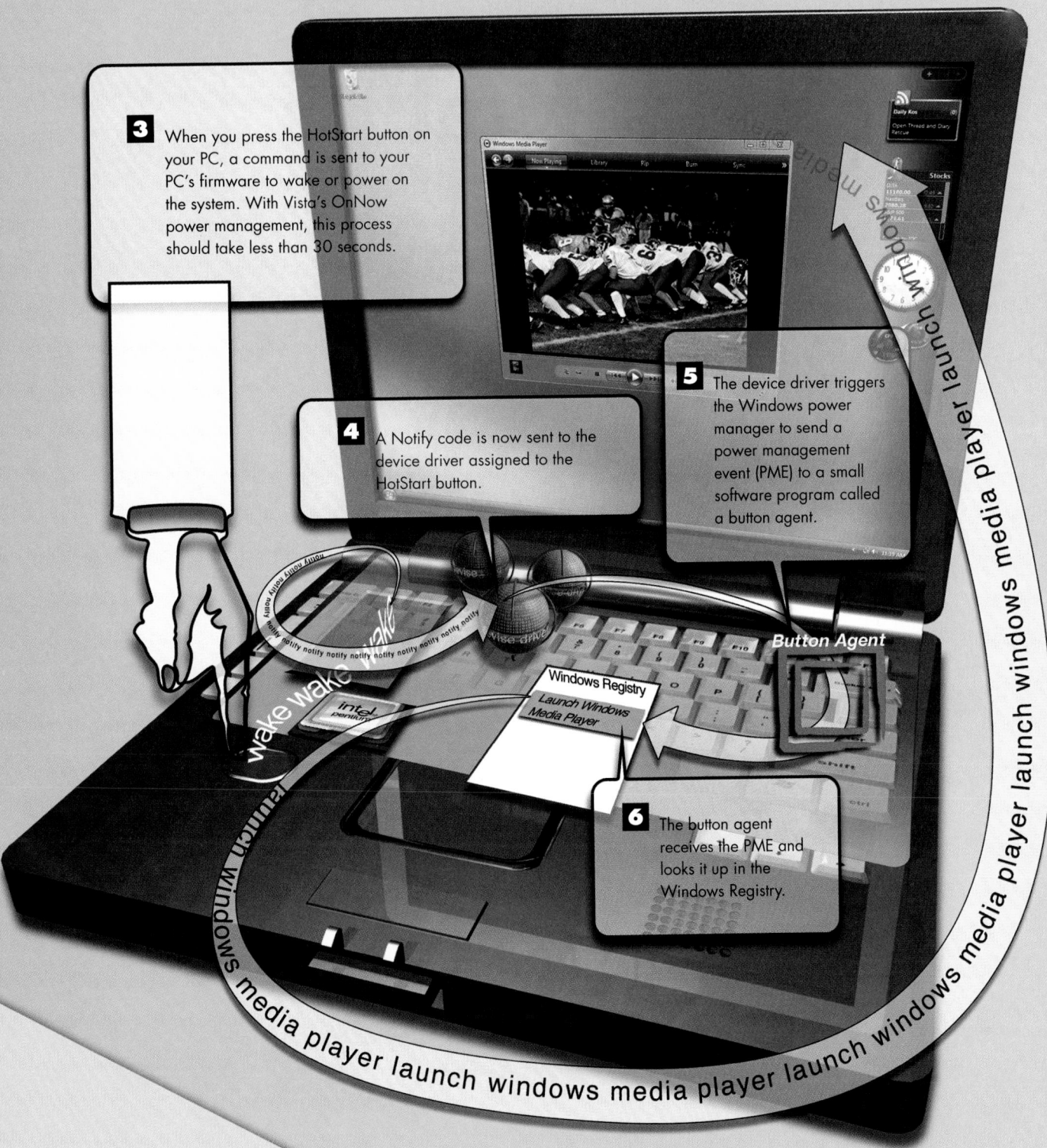

3 When you press the HotStart button on your PC, a command is sent to your PC's firmware to wake or power on the system. With Vista's OnNow power management, this process should take less than 30 seconds.

4 A Notify code is now sent to the device driver assigned to the HotStart button.

5 The device driver triggers the Windows power manager to send a power management event (PME) to a small software program called a button agent.

Button Agent

Windows Registry

Launch Windows Media Player

6 The button agent receives the PME and looks it up in the Windows Registry.

7 Based on the information stored in the Registry, the button agent then starts the associated application—in most cases, Windows Media Player.

15

Digital Images

EVERYBODY and their neighbor has a digital camera. Digital cameras are great for taking candid photos, as well as more professional portraits and the like.

It doesn't matter which type of digital camera you have; the photos you take are all saved in some sort of digital image format. There are a variety of image formats; the most popular of which is the JPEG format used by most point-and-shoot digital cameras. JPEG images are also ubiquitous on the Internet; the images you see on just about any web page are probably in the JPEG format.

JPEG and other digital images can be edited in any photo editing program. It's easy to make a digital photo lighter or darker, crop out unwanted elements, remove the occasional case of red eye, and so forth.

Up until now, you had to purchase a third-party photo editing program, which could cost you $100 or more. In Windows Vista, however, photo editing is built into the operating system, in the form of the new Windows Photo Gallery application. Windows Photo Gallery not only offers essential photo editing tools, it also serves to manage all the digital photos stored on your PC. For most users, Windows Photo Gallery will be all you need to edit and manage your digital photos. It's a great program and a great money saver.

Windows Vista also introduces a new digital image format, designed to compete with and perhaps replace JPEG files. Microsoft's new Windows Media Photo (WMPhoto) format promises better quality pictures at smaller file sizes than what JPEG currently delivers. While WMPhoto isn't yet widely adopted (it's brand-new, after all), expect it to make a big impact in the digital photography market—and it's fully supported in Windows Vista and Windows Photo Gallery.

How Different Digital Image Formats Compare

1 One digital image isn't the same as the next. Images (photographs, drawings, and the like) can be saved in one of several different file formats. Each format is slightly different from the next and has its own advantages and disadvantages.

2 One of the primary differences between image formats is the type of compression used. Some image formats don't compress the image at all; every single pixel of the original image is retained in the image file. Unfortunately, this results in very large file sizes. To reduce file size, most image formats use some sort of compression, which squeezes the data that composes the image. *Lossless compression* works by finding more efficient ways to represent an image, without losing any image data. *Lossy compression* is more efficient, but works by removing some (hopefully less important) data from the image; lossy files suffer from some degradation in image quality.

3 The other differentiating factor between image formats is the number of colors that can be reproduced. Obviously, the more colors, the more true-to-life the image. Some image formats can only reproduce 256 colors; others can reproduce 16 million colors or more. This type of color reproduction is typically measured in terms of bit-depth—an image with 256 colors has 8-bit color, whereas an image with 16 million colors has 24-bit color.

Format	File Extension	Number of Colors	Compression	File Size	Supports Transparency	Best Used For...	Comments
...w	Varies by camera manufacturer	16 million+	Lossless	Large	No	Photographs, printing	The digital equivalent of a film negative; must be converted to another format for use.
...gged ...age ...e Format	TIFF or TIF	16 million+	Lossless	Large	No	Digital photographs, printing	Offers the best fidelity for printed photos; files are too large to be used on the web or sent via email
...rtable ...twork ...aphics	PNG	16 million+	Lossless	Small	Yes	Web graphics, line art	Intended as a replacement for the GIF, JPEG, and TIFF formats, but not yet widely adopted
...indows ...edia ...oto (aka ...MPhoto)	WDP	16 million	Lossy	Small	Yes	Digital photographs, web graphics	Microsoft's new graphics file format, included in Windows Vista; intended as a replacement for the JPEG format
...int ...otographic ...xperts ...roup	JPEG or JPG	16 million	Lossy	Small	No	Digital photographs, web graphics	The most-used image format today
...raphics ...terchange ...ormat	GIF	256	Lossy	Small	Yes	Web graphics, line art, other "flat" images	Supports multiple-image animations; not ideal for photographic images
...indows ...tmap	BMP	16 million+	None	Large	No	Windows system graphics	Used primarily for graphics within the Windows operating system

How the Windows Media Photo Format Works

 1 Windows Vista includes support for a brand-new image format. Windows Media Photo (also called WMPhoto) was developed by Microsoft to eventually replace the JPEG file format. WMPhoto files have the .WDP extension.

2 For maximum compatibility, WMPhoto provides native support for a variety of color formats, including RGB, CMYK, n-channel, and monochrome, along with multiple fixed and floating point numerical representation. This provides a wide range of compression options for different types of photos.

CMYK VS RGB

3 WMPhoto uses a variable compression ratio of up to 25:1, compared to the 6:1 compression ratio used by JPEG and other similar formats. This higher compression is combined with a sophisticated non-arithmetic entropy encoding scheme, that uses symbols instead of numbers, to create files that are just half the size of similar JPEG images, at higher perceived quality.

4 The WMPhoto format enables various image processing operations on the compressed image data; other formats first need to decompress the data to perform these operations. This means that you can automatically rotate, flip, crop, and reduce the resolution of WMPhoto images without first going through a decode/re-encode process. The result is much faster image operations: almost instantaneous in some instances.

5 The image data in a WMPhoto file is wrapped in a container that also includes key metadata. Each WMPhoto file begins with an 8-byte file header that points to an Image File Directory (IFD). The IFD contains important information about the photo, including the make and model of the camera used to take the photo; the date and time the photo was taken; the aperture, shutter speed, focal length, and film speed settings; and other metadata stored in the EXIF (Exchangeable Image File) format.

6 The WMPhoto container also accommodates the storage of an alternate view of an image. This is typically used to include a thumbnail or reduced resolution preview that can be accessed from photo viewing or editing programs—or in Windows Vista file Explorers.

How Windows Photo Gallery Works

1 Windows Vista includes a new application for viewing, managing, and editing digital photos. Windows Photo Gallery performs many of the same functions found in expensive photo editing programs, but is included free with Windows Vista.

2 Windows Photo Gallery imports all the digital photos stored on your hard disk. The photos remain in their original locations (typically in the Photos folder), but are pointed to from within the Photo Gallery program. All imported photos are displayed as thumbnail images within the Gallery.

3 When you import photos into the Photo Gallery, you can add descriptive keywords to each photo. You can then use these keywords to sort and search for specific photos, thus making it easier to organize your photo library.

KEYWORDS

vacation,africa,rhino
animals,hunting,2005
anniversary trip,
textures,

4 Windows Photo Gallery includes basic photo editing tools. You can use these tools to crop and rotate your photos, adjust brightness and contrast levels, change color and tint, and even remove red eye.

5 Whenever you make a change to a photo within Photo Gallery, a new photo file is created. Your original photo is left untouched on your hard disk, so you always revert back to the original image.

6 Windows Photo Gallery also features a photo email wizard that helps you resize your photos to send via email. The program also lets you burn your images to CD or DVD for easier distribution.

CHAPTER 16

Digital Video and Movies

WHEN you talk about digital media in Windows Vista, you immediately think of digital music and digital photos. But Vista also handles digital video, in two separate but related applications—one old and one new.

The old application is Windows Movie Maker, which has been significantly enhanced for Windows Vista. This most recent version of WMM sports a spiffy new interface, a bunch of new video effects and transitions, and some much-requested new features—including the ability to edit recorded TV programs and burn your edited movies to DVD. Quite frankly, it's amazing what you can do with Windows Move Maker; the editing functions and special effects rival those used by television stations and movie studios. With Windows Movie Maker, you can create true professional-quality movies and videos, and you don't have to spend a dime to do it. Just as with previous versions, Windows Movie Maker is included free with Windows Vista.

The new application is one that has long been requested by Windows users. Windows DVD Maker lets you burn your own DVDs from within Windows, without the need for an expensive third-party program. In reality, Windows DVD Maker is more like a fancy wizard, but it does what it needs to do. You can burn just about any type of media file to DVD—movies, music, even digital photos. And you get to choose how the resulting DVD looks, in the form of menus and backgrounds. Windows DVD Maker even adds chapter stops to your movies, automatically.

The addition of Windows DVD Maker completes Windows' suite of digital media applications. With Windows Vista, you get Windows Media Player for digital music; Windows Photo Gallery for digital photos; Windows Movie Maker for digital movies; and Windows DVD Maker to burn all you digital media files to DVD. It's a full-featured suite, with all the programs quite easy to use—and completely free. Microsoft doesn't give them a collective name, but if it were up to me, I'd call them the Windows Digital Media Suite. Put together, the new and enhanced applications in this suite could very well justify the upgrade from Windows XP to Windows Vista.

How Digital Video Works

1 Digital video is a method of representing the infinite variations of an analog video signal as a limited quantity of binary numbers. The conversion of an analog video signal into a digital signal is accomplished via an analog-to-digital converter (ADC). The ADC samples the original analog video at designated intervals and effectively slices the signal into consecutive discrete segments, thus creating a stream of digital bits.

2 The digital video signal is processed through a video *codec*, which is a software module that encodes the digital data stream into a data file. Popular video codecs include MPEG-1, used for some lower-quality online video; MPEG-2, used in DVDs and most digital television broadcasts; MPEG-4, used in some newer broadcast systems and in next-generation HD DVD and Blu-ray discs; and Microsoft's Windows Media Video (WMV), used in a variety of applications up to and including high-definition programming.

3 The encoding process involves some form of lossy compression. By selectively removing duplicative information from consecutive frames of the video, the resulting file size is reduced while the quality of the video is only slightly degraded.

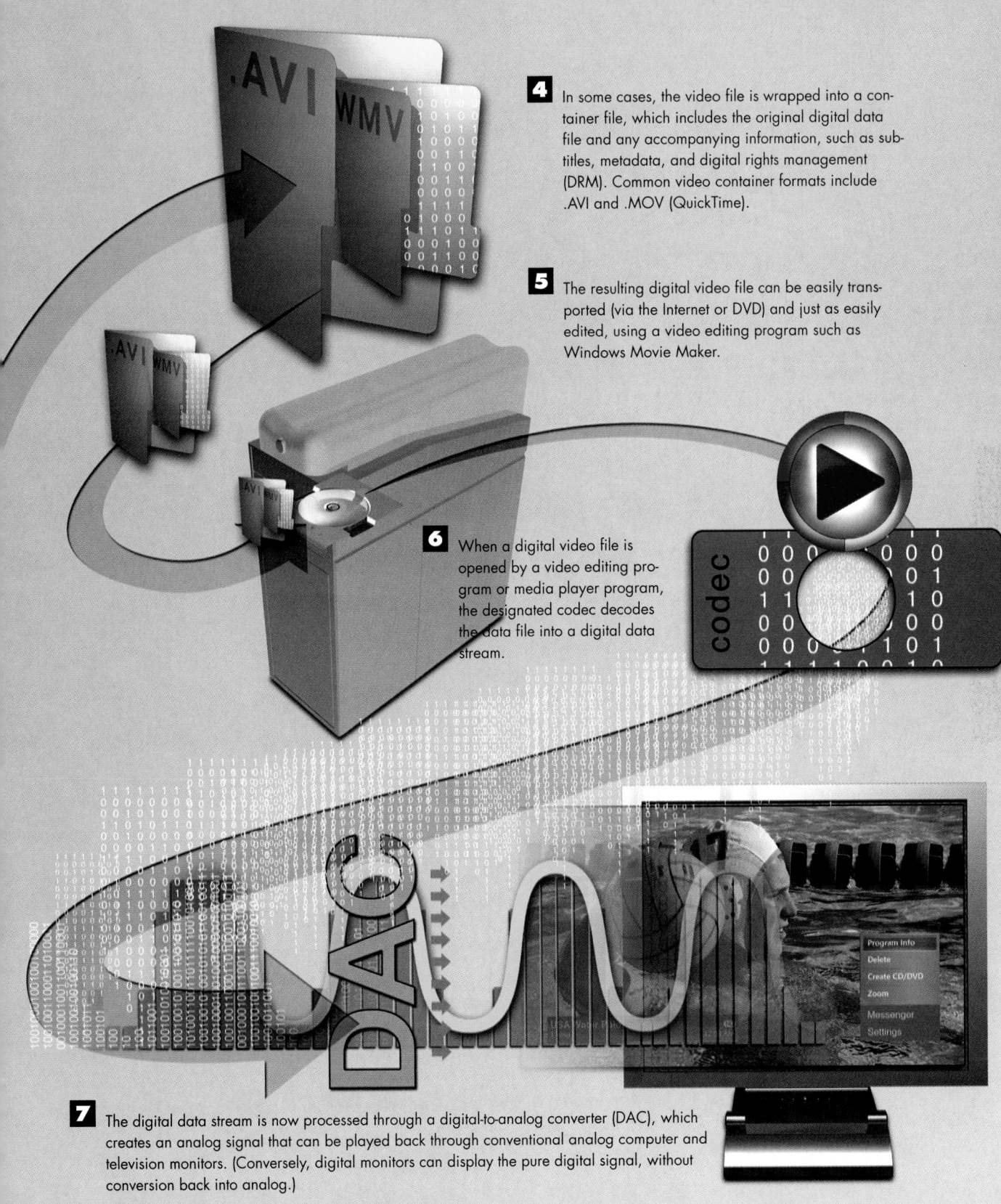

4 In some cases, the video file is wrapped into a container file, which includes the original digital data file and any accompanying information, such as subtitles, metadata, and digital rights management (DRM). Common video container formats include .AVI and .MOV (QuickTime).

5 The resulting digital video file can be easily transported (via the Internet or DVD) and just as easily edited, using a video editing program such as Windows Movie Maker.

6 When a digital video file is opened by a video editing program or media player program, the designated codec decodes the data file into a digital data stream.

7 The digital data stream is now processed through a digital-to-analog converter (DAC), which creates an analog signal that can be played back through conventional analog computer and television monitors. (Conversely, digital monitors can display the pure digital signal, without conversion back into analog.)

How Windows Movie Maker Works

1 Windows Movie Maker (WMM) is an application that lets you import and edit your home movies. The version of WMM in Windows Vista features an improved interface and additional transitions and special effects. You can also use this version of WMM to edit television programs you record in Windows Vista.

2 Windows Movie Maker can open and edit any format digital video file. You can also use WMM with a video capture card or device to import analog video from older camcorders or VHS tapes; WMM can also import digital still photos and music files to create multimedia presentations.

3 You begin your editing by breaking your movie into specific scenes, using the storyboard in the Window Movie Maker window.

Windows Movie Maker HD

Windows Movie Maker HD, included in Windows Vista Home Premium and Ultimate editions, adds support for high-definition video. This lets you utilize a high-def camcorder to create and edit HDTV-compatible videos.

4 Windows Movie Maker lets you add transitions between scenes, by dragging and dropping a transition effect onto a specific scene clip. Transitions include dissolves, fades, wipes, reveals, and the like.

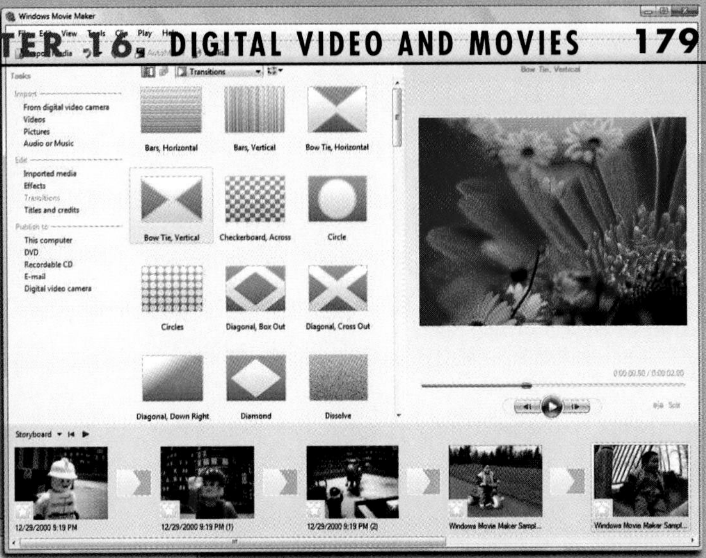

5 You can process your video by adding a variety of special effects. For example, you can make your video look like an old film, convert it to black and white, pixelate the picture, or speed up or slow down the video.

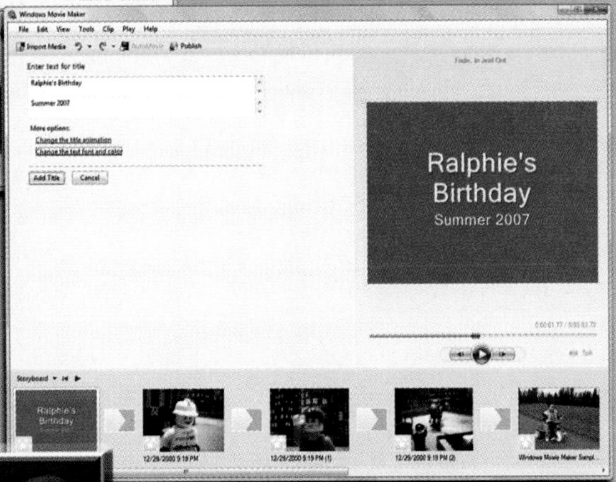

6 Another useful feature is the ability to add titles and credits to your videos.

7 When you're done editing, Windows Movie Maker lets you burn your completed movie to a blank DVD —or share your movie via email or the Web.

How Windows DVD Maker Works

1 Windows DVD Maker lets you burn your home movies and other video files to blank DVD discs, which you can then distribute to friends and family.

2 When you launch Windows DVD Maker, the program automatically generates a list of scenes within your video and creates a chapter stop for each new scene.

chapter stop

chapter stop

3 Windows DVD Maker lets you select from a variety of styles for your DVD's menus and background screens.

4 At the click of the Burn button, Windows DVD Maker adds the selected menus, backgrounds, and chapter stops to your original video files. The resulting files are converted to MPEG-2 format and temporarily stored on your PC's hard disk. (This step is called the *DVD authoring process*.)

5 Once the DVD is authored, Windows DVD Maker copies the authored files and file structure to a blank DVD. (This step is called the *DVD burning process*.)

6 The resulting DVD can be played back in any consumer DVD player.

P   A   R   T

5

NETWORKING AND THE INTERNET

THE so-called personal computer isn't so personal anymore. Rare is the PC that is not somehow connected to another computer, either via a local computer network or the Internet—the largest computer network of them all. In fact, it's difficult to use Windows Vista if you're not connected to the Internet; the registration process takes place online, and Windows needs access to the Internet to download essential system updates.

What most users don't realize is that the operating system's networking and Internet functions are related—and, in many cases, they're the same functions. That's because connecting to the Internet is a form of networking, using many of the same protocols and technologies. So when Microsoft upgrades its networking protocols (which it has in Windows Vista), it also improves its Internet capabilities.

The core technology behind both networking and Internetworking is called TCP/IP, for Transmission Control Protocol/Internet Protocol. In the old days of personal computing (pre-Windows 95, if you can remember back that far), users had to manually install and configure a TCP/IP stack before they could connect to the Internet. Since Windows 95, however, TCP/IP technology has been built into the operating system, no installation or configuration necessary.

What's new in Windows Vista is an updated TCP/IP stack, called (appropriately enough) the Next Generation TCP/IP stack. This new TCP/IP stack supports Internet Protocol version 6 (IPv6), which is the technology that manages your computer's connection to the Internet. What you get from this new version of TCP/IP is easier and more reliable networking connections, both on a local network and when you're connecting to your Internet service provider (ISP).

You'll notice the Next Generation TCP/IP stack at work the next time you have to set up a network connection or connect to a wireless Internet hotspot. Unlike in past versions of Windows, where establishing a new connection was somewhat tedious and often tenuous, Windows Vista networking is smooth as silk and steady as a rock. You'll experience fewer (if any) dropped connections, and find it much easier to identify and connect with a Wi-Fi hotspot while roaming. And, thanks to Vista's new network management utilities, it's easier than ever to do what you need to do, network-wise; little or no technical expertise is necessary.

Once you're connected to the Internet, you'll find some of Vista's most notable improvements, chief of which is the new Internet Explorer 7 (IE7) web browser. IE7 dramatically enhances the browsing experience, adding such useful features as tabbed browsing, an integrated RSS feed reader, and a web search box right in the browser window. Of these features, perhaps the most impressive is tabbed browsing, which lets you open multiple web pages simultaneously within the same browser window. This is a real boon if you browse to a lot of different websites on a regular basis, or like to switch back and forth between two or more web pages.

IE7 is also more secure and more solid than previous versions of the browser. Microsoft realized that a large number of computer attacks come via the browser, and worked hard to plug the most notable security holes and "harden" the browsing experience. This has resulted in a slew of new security-related features in IE7, including protected-mode operation, an integrated pop-up blocker, and an anti-phishing filter. Combine all these features with the

Windows Defender anti-spyware utility, and you have an operating system that's far less susceptible to both annoying intrusions and dangerous attacks.

If you use the Internet a lot when you're on the road, you'll appreciate the way Vista connects to Wi-Fi hotspots. Everything you need to identify and connect to a wireless network is right up front in the new Connect to a Network dialog box; all available hotspots are automatically listed, and connecting is as easy as clicking a network icon.

For home wireless networks, Vista helps to make your network more secure by offering four different types of wireless security. Depending on what's built into your wireless router and adapters, Vista supports WEP-64, WEP-128, WPA, and the new WPA2 wireless security protocols. And, as with all things networking in Vista, this security is easy to set up and easy to manage.

All these networking and Internetworking features combine to create an operating system that's optimized for communicating with other computers. Microsoft recognizes that a large part of the time you spend with your PC is spent either online or connected to a local area network; Windows Vista ensures that this connected time is both hassle-free and secure.

CHAPTER

17

Windows Vista and the Internet

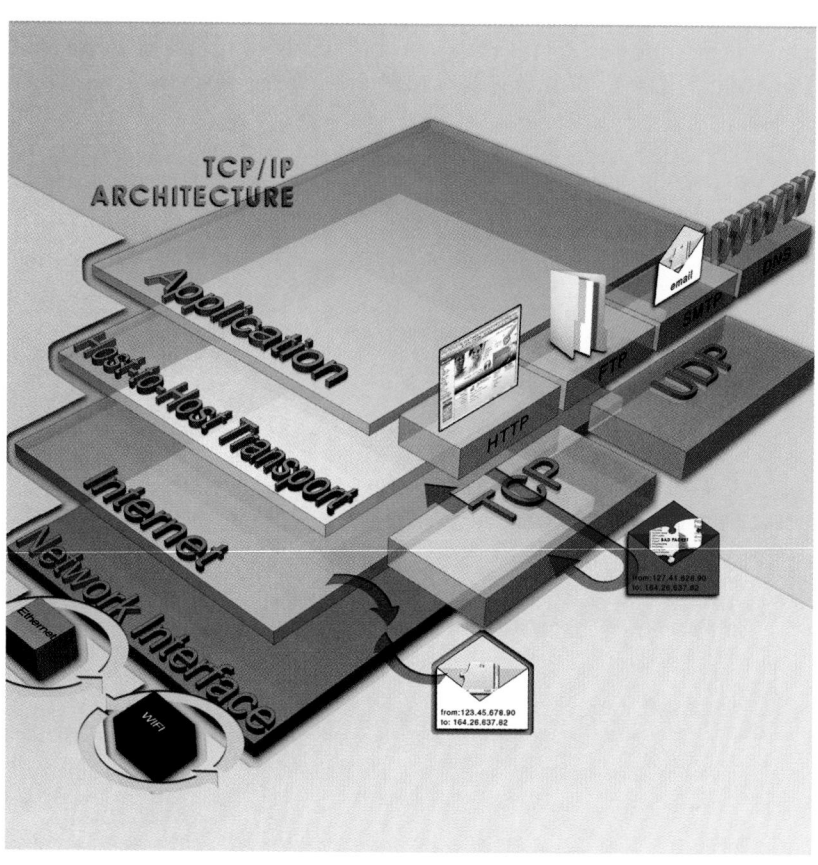

SOME of the most noticeable changes in Windows Vista concern how you connect to and use the Internet. It makes sense for Microsoft to focus on its Internet-related features, as the typical user is spending an increasing amount of time online, both on the Web and sending and receiving email.

The new features start with a new way to connect to the Internet, via a new Next Generation TCP/IP stack. This is a complete redesign of the operating system's TCP/IP functionality for Internet Protocol version 6 (IPv6), which is the underlying technology behind Windows' Internet connection. IPv6 is the latest version of the Internet layer of the TCP/IP protocol suite, which, believe it or not, was first designed in the late 1970s. (It was time for an overhaul!) IPv6 increases the address space for Internet devices, provides more efficient routing of data packets, and ensures more effective protection against address and port scanning attacks. In short, IPv6 makes your Internet connections more stable and more secure.

The whole TCP/IP thing happens behind-the-scenes, of course. More visible are the changes in Vista's core Internet applications. For example, Internet Explorer 7 enhances the web browsing experience by adding tabbed browsing, inline browser search, integrated RSS newsfeeds, and protection against phishing sites. It's the most significant upgrade to Internet Explorer in years, and it makes your browsing more efficient and enjoyable.

On the email front, Vista has replaced Outlook Express with Windows Mail. While Windows Mail looks pretty much like Outlook Express, it's a completely different application under the hood. In addition to a few new features, such as Instant Search and anti-phishing technology, Windows Mail stores your email messages in a much different fashion than did the older application. Each email message is stored as a separate file on your hard disk, which reduces the risk of data loss.

Windows Vista also includes a new Internet-related application, called Windows Calendar, that helps you manage all your schedules and tasks—both private and public. You can create multiple calendars for different activities, and share your calendars with others over the Internet. It's a great idea, especially if you have a lot of public activities (like Little League games) that a lot of different people need to keep track of.

How Windows Connects to the Internet

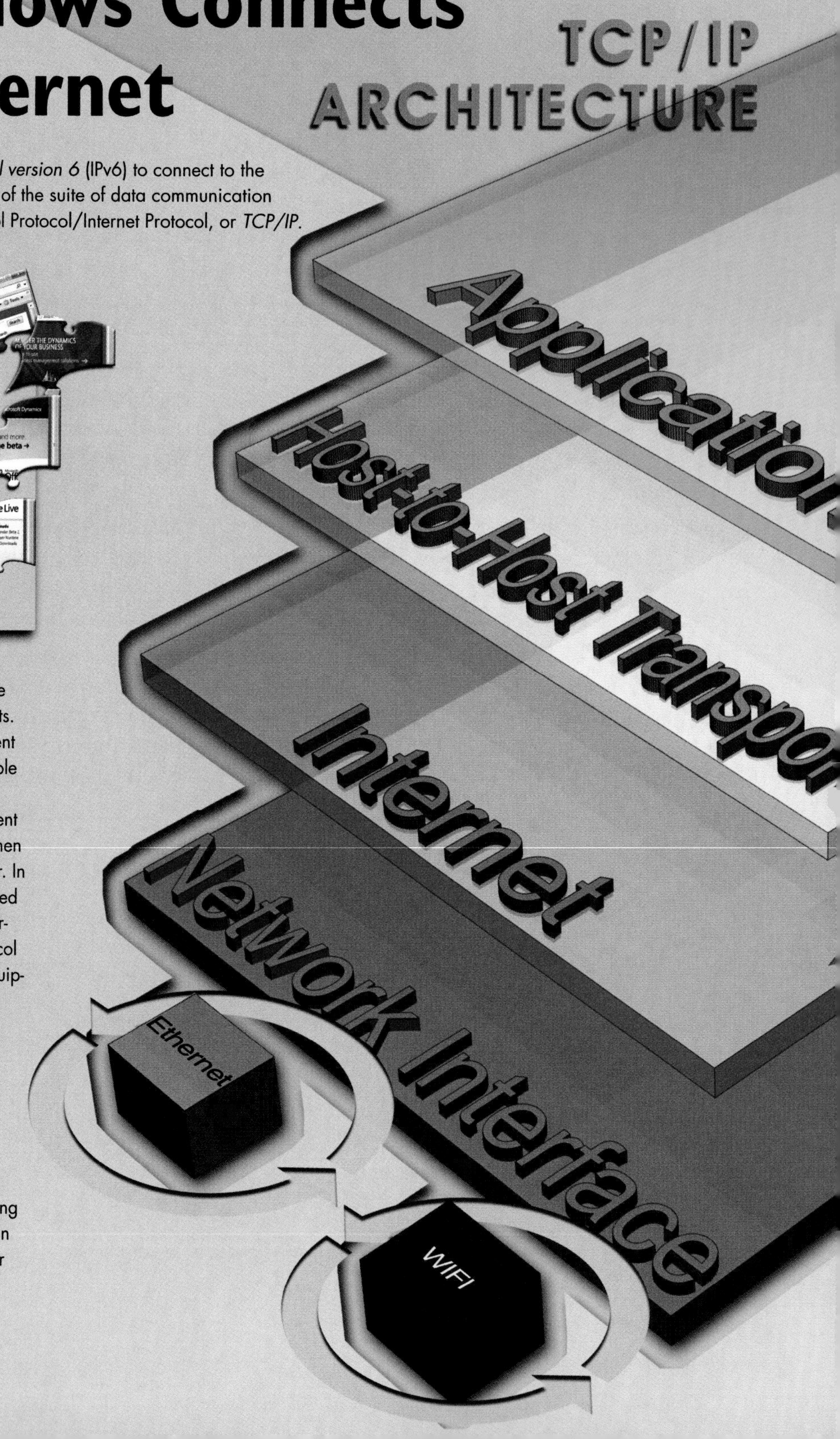

TCP/IP ARCHITECTURE

1 Windows Vista uses *Internet Protocol version 6* (IPv6) to connect to the Internet. The Internet Protocol is part of the suite of data communication protocols called Transmission Control Protocol/Internet Protocol, or *TCP/IP*.

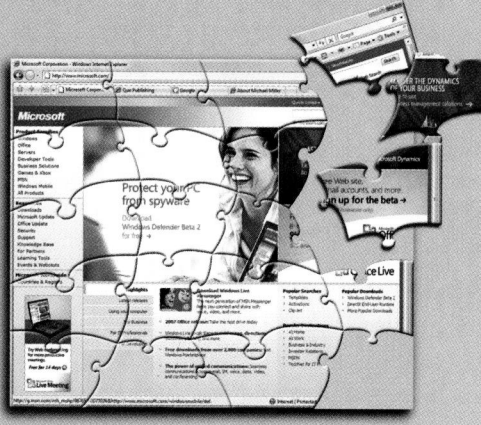

2 The *Internet Layer* is responsible for the addressing and routing of data packets. All web pages and email messages sent over the Internet are broken into multiple data packets for easier transmission. These packets are then sent independent of each other over the Internet—and then reassembled at the receiving computer. In Windows Vista, this process is managed by either the older Internet Protocol version 4 (IPv4) or the new Internet Protocol version 6 (IPv6), depending on the equipment installed on your system.

3 The *Network Interface Layer*, which is hidden from users, is tasked with moving data to and from a physical network. In most Windows Vista systems, this layer interfaces with an Ethernet or Wi-Fi network.

Application

Host-to-Host Transport

Internet

Network Interface

Ethernet

WIFI

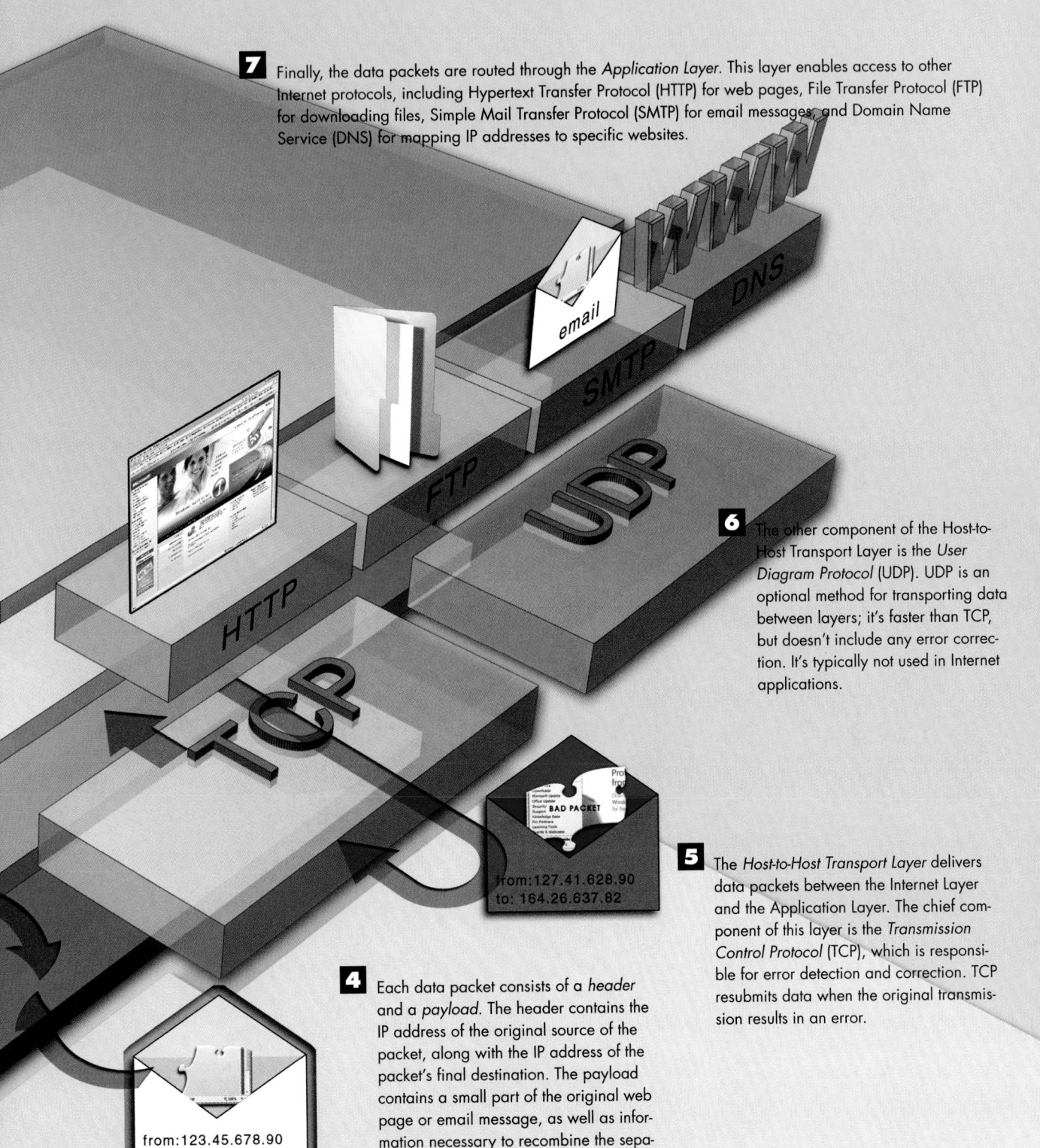

7 Finally, the data packets are routed through the *Application Layer*. This layer enables access to other Internet protocols, including Hypertext Transfer Protocol (HTTP) for web pages, File Transfer Protocol (FTP) for downloading files, Simple Mail Transfer Protocol (SMTP) for email messages, and Domain Name Service (DNS) for mapping IP addresses to specific websites.

6 The other component of the Host-to-Host Transport Layer is the *User Diagram Protocol* (UDP). UDP is an optional method for transporting data between layers; it's faster than TCP, but doesn't include any error correction. It's typically not used in Internet applications.

5 The *Host-to-Host Transport Layer* delivers data packets between the Internet Layer and the Application Layer. The chief component of this layer is the *Transmission Control Protocol* (TCP), which is responsible for error detection and correction. TCP resubmits data when the original transmission results in an error.

4 Each data packet consists of a *header* and a *payload*. The header contains the IP address of the original source of the packet, along with the IP address of the packet's final destination. The payload contains a small part of the original web page or email message, as well as information necessary to recombine the separate packets when received.

How Internet Explorer 7 Works

1 Internet Explorer 7 is the newest version of Microsoft's web browser. The most noticeable change in Internet Explorer 7 is the browser's redesigned interface. All functions are combined on two slim tool-bars at the top of the window, resulting in a streamlined look and less screen space used for navigation functions.

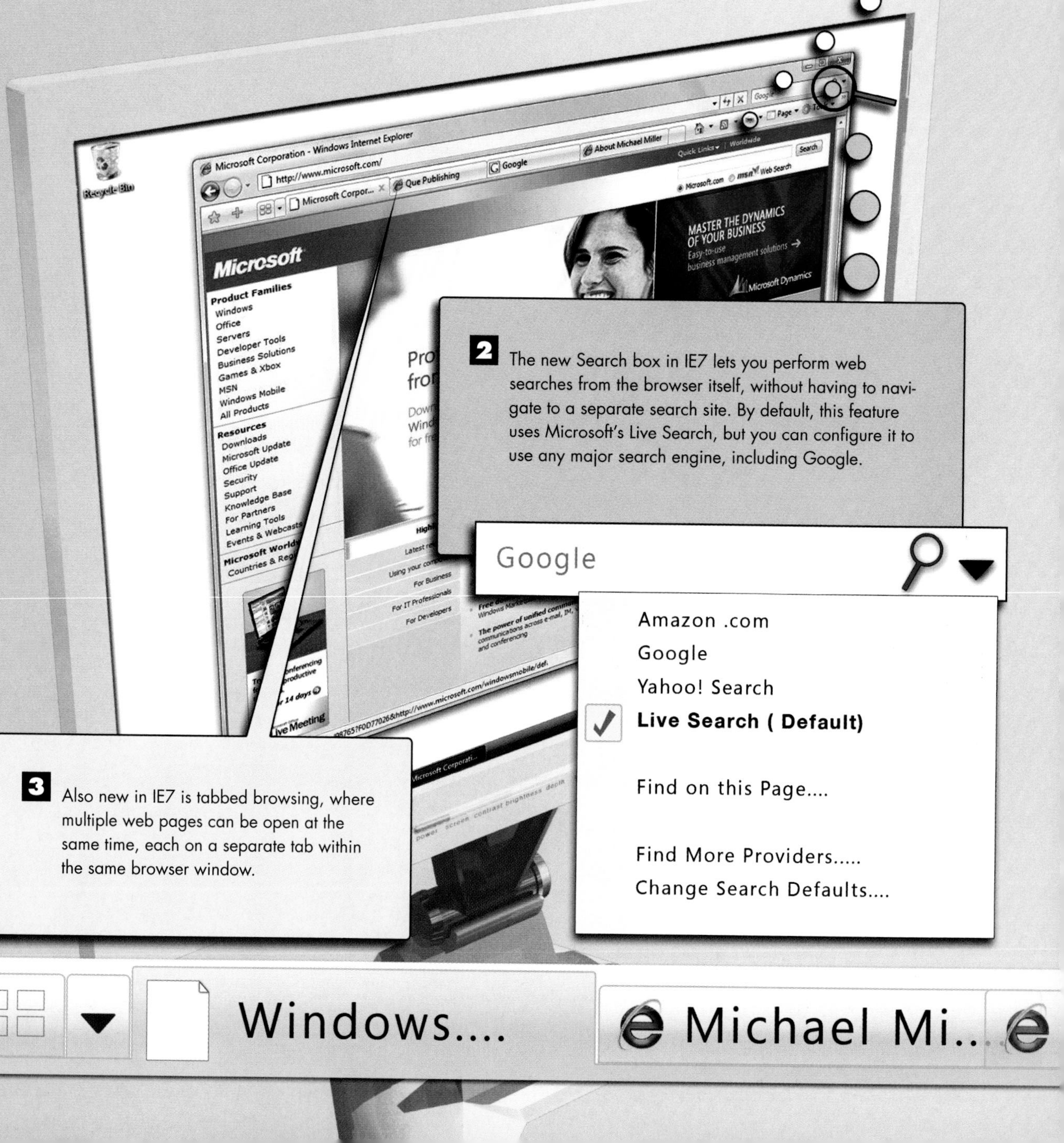

2 The new Search box in IE7 lets you perform web searches from the browser itself, without having to navigate to a separate search site. By default, this feature uses Microsoft's Live Search, but you can configure it to use any major search engine, including Google.

Google

Amazon .com
Google
Yahoo! Search
✓ **Live Search (Default)**

Find on this Page....

Find More Providers.....
Change Search Defaults....

3 Also new in IE7 is tabbed browsing, where multiple web pages can be open at the same time, each on a separate tab within the same browser window.

 Windows.... Michael Mi..

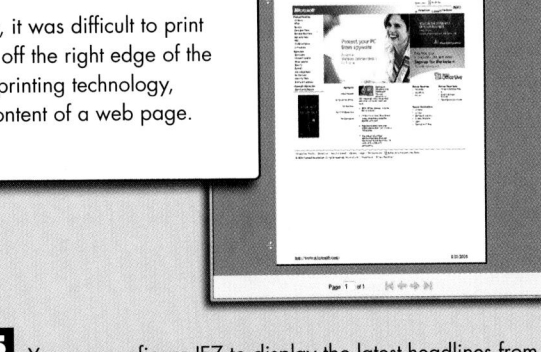

4 In previous versions of Internet Explorer, it was difficult to print wide web pages; they tended to bleed off the right edge of the paper. IE7 uses scalable "shrink to fit" printing technology, which makes it easier to print the full content of a web page.

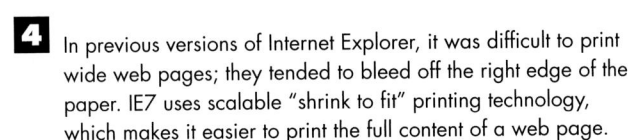

5 You can configure IE7 to display the latest headlines from your favorite RSS newsfeeds. When a new feed is available, the Feeds button illuminates; you can then read the RSS feed directly in the browser window.

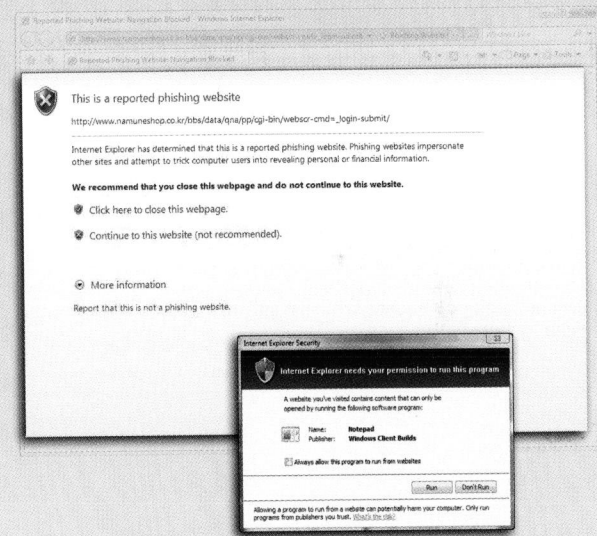

6 To protect you from accidentally entering information on fraudulent websites, IE7 incorporates anti-phishing technology. The Microsoft Phishing Filter automatically connects to an online service that contains a huge database of suspicious websites and alerts you if you attempt to go to one of these sites.

7 To increase security, Internet Explorer 7 runs in *Protected Mode*. This mode prevents malicious websites or programs from modifying system files and settings without your explicit approval, thus protecting you from viruses, spyware, and computer attacks.

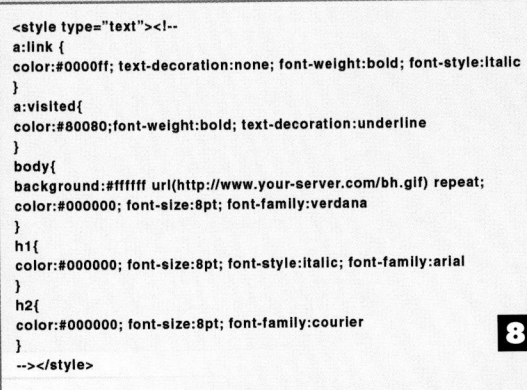

```
<style type="text"><!--
a:link {
color:#0000ff; text-decoration:none; font-weight:bold; font-style:italic
}
a:visited{
color:#80080;font-weight:bold; text-decoration:underline
}
body{
background:#ffffff url(http://www.your-server.com/bh.gif) repeat;
color:#000000; font-size:8pt; font-family:verdana
}
h1{
color:#000000; font-size:8pt; font-style:italic; font-family:arial
}
h2{
color:#000000; font-size:8pt; font-family:courier
}
--></style>
```

8 Finally, IE7 incorporates support for the latest design standards used to create feature-rich websites, including improved support for cascading style sheets (CSS) and transparent PNG graphics files. The result is more accurate web page reproduction, with fewer positioning and display problems.

e Publish....

How Tabbed Browsing Works

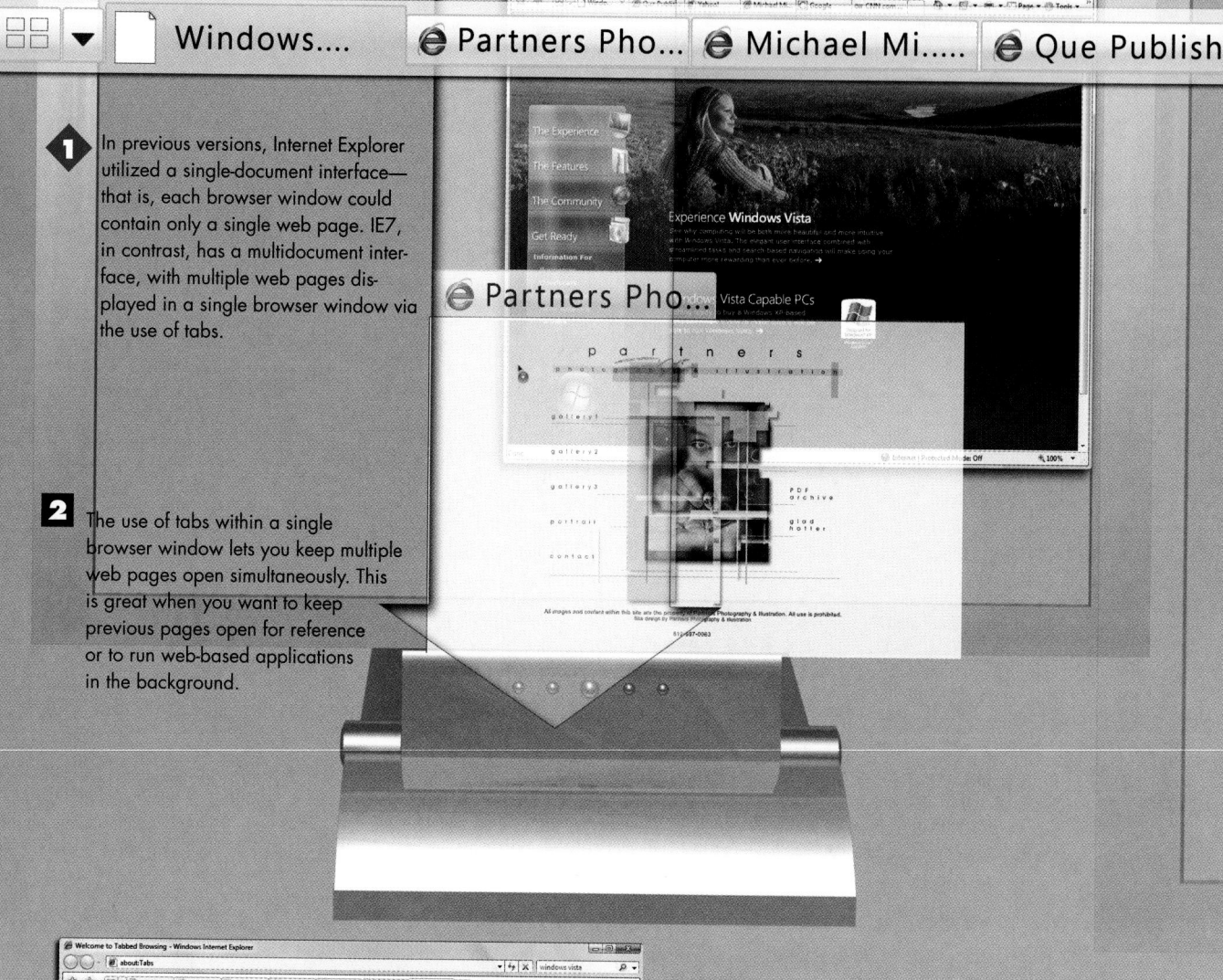

1 In previous versions, Internet Explorer utilized a single-document interface—that is, each browser window could contain only a single web page. IE7, in contrast, has a multidocument interface, with multiple web pages displayed in a single browser window via the use of tabs.

2 The use of tabs within a single browser window lets you keep multiple web pages open simultaneously. This is great when you want to keep previous pages open for reference or to run web-based applications in the background.

3 To open a web page on a new tab, just click the next (empty) tab and enter a URL. You can also choose to open a link within a page in a new tab, by right-clicking the link and selecting Open in New Tab.

4 You switch between tabs by clicking a tab with your mouse, or by pressing Ctrl+Tab on your keyboard. You can also reorder your tabs by dragging and dropping them into a new position.

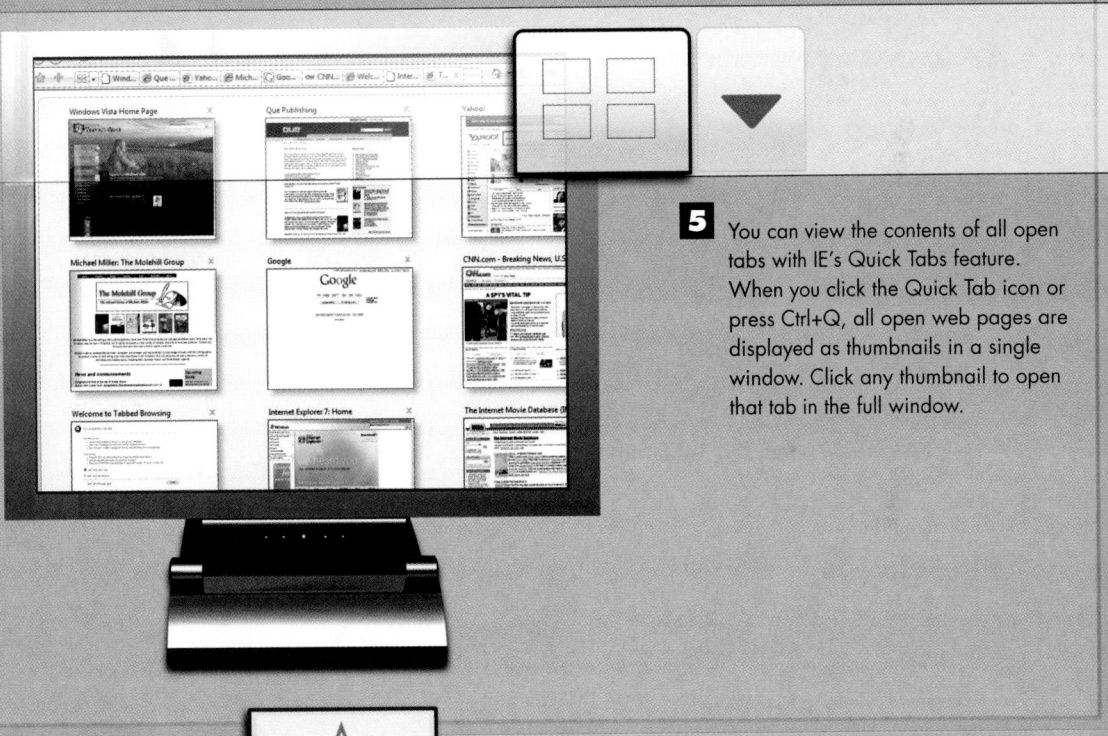

5 You can view the contents of all open tabs with IE's Quick Tabs feature. When you click the Quick Tab icon or press Ctrl+Q, all open web pages are displayed as thumbnails in a single window. Click any thumbnail to open that tab in the full window.

6 You can also save a specific collection of web pages by creating a *Tab Group*. Simply open the pages you want to save, in a series of tabs, and then save this Tab Group in your Favorites list. You can then select a single Favorites entry to open all the web pages you selected, in the series of tabs you saved.

How Internet Explorer Stops Pop-Ups

1 If you're an active Web surfer, you've no doubt been subjected to annoying pop-up windows when you visit certain websites. To eliminate these pesky pop-ups, Internet Explorer 7 includes a built-in Pop-up Blocker. This feature, which is enabled by default, blocks the automatic opening of unwanted pop-up windows.

2 The Pop-up Blocker works by changing the behavior of selected application programming interfaces (APIs) that are inserted via script code into a web page's underlying HTML. For example, the **window.open** command in a script is typically used to open a new pop-up window. When the Pop-up Blocker encounters this command in the code for a web page, it changes the function of the command so that a "null" value is returned. This results in nothing happening when the command is invoked—thus blocking the pop-up.

3 When a site tries to open a pop-up window that is blocked by Internet Explorer, a notification appears in the Information Bar of the browser window. If you click the notification, you can choose to temporarily or permanently allow pop-ups from this site.

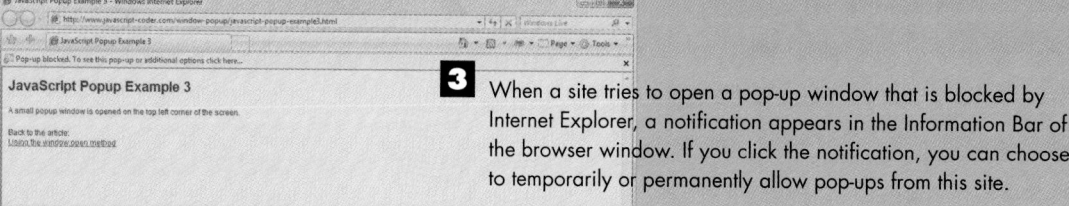

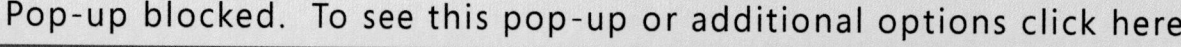

Pop-up blocked. To see this pop-up or additional options click here

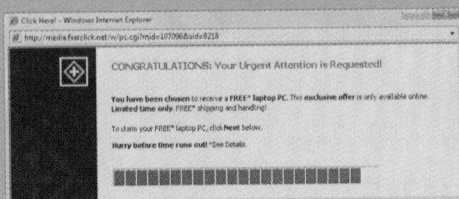

http://media.fastclick.net/w/pc.cgi?mid=10

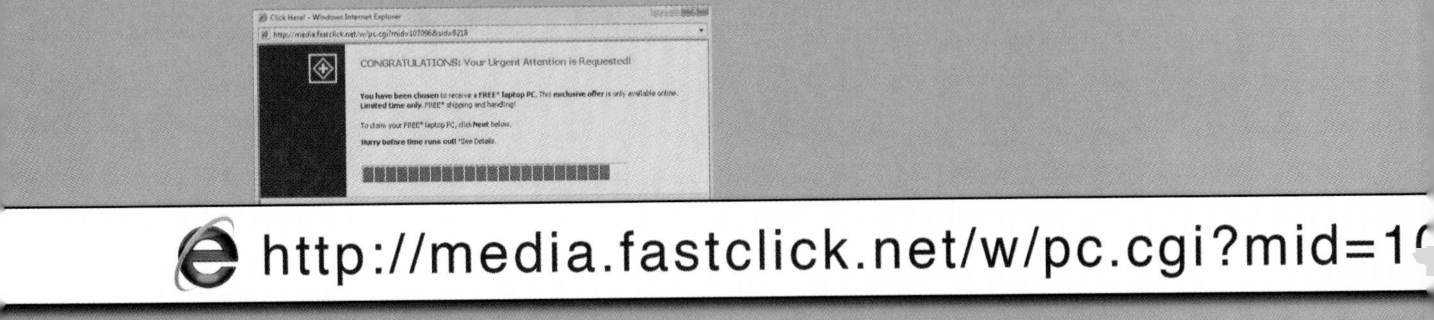

4 If you choose to allow pop-ups, some sites design their pop-up windows to look like legitimate system messages. IE7 helps to expose these tricks by overriding the original page code to display a read-only Address Bar in every pop-up window. When you see the Address Bar, you'll know that the pop-up is not a system message—and that you can ignore it.

5 The Pop-up Blocker also works to reign in unruly windows that are otherwise opened normally. Windows that would be opened outside the viewable screen are positioned into the viewable desktop area, and Windows that would be larger than the viewable screen are resized to fit within the desktop.

How Internet Explorer Reads RSS Feeds

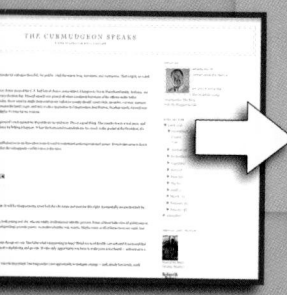

1 Real Simple Syndication (RSS) is a technology used to syndicate, or distribute, content from blogs, news sites, and other websites with constantly updated content. The RSS information for a site is stored in a single XML-format file on the website. When new content is posted to the site, that information is added to the RSS file. RSS newsreader programs and RSS aggregator websites periodically check the RSS files on selected websites and notify the user when new content is available. (Users of these programs and services must *subscribe* to a given feed for the program or service to automatically check that feed's content.)

2 With Windows Vista and Internet Explorer 7, you can easily subscribe to and read RSS feeds directly in the web browser. To subscribe to the feed for a given website, navigate to the site and then click the Feeds button on the Internet Explorer 7 toolbar. This displays an RSS-friendly version of the current page; click the Subscribe to This Feed to add the subscription.

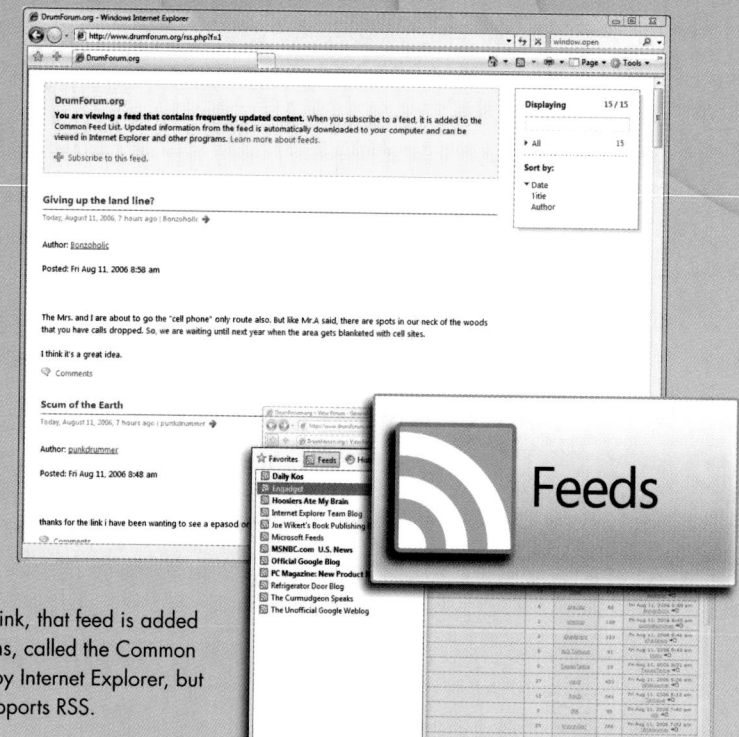

3 When you click the Subscribe to This Feed link, that feed is added to a systemwide list of your RSS subscriptions, called the Common Feed List. This list can be accessed not just by Internet Explorer, but by any application or online service that supports RSS.

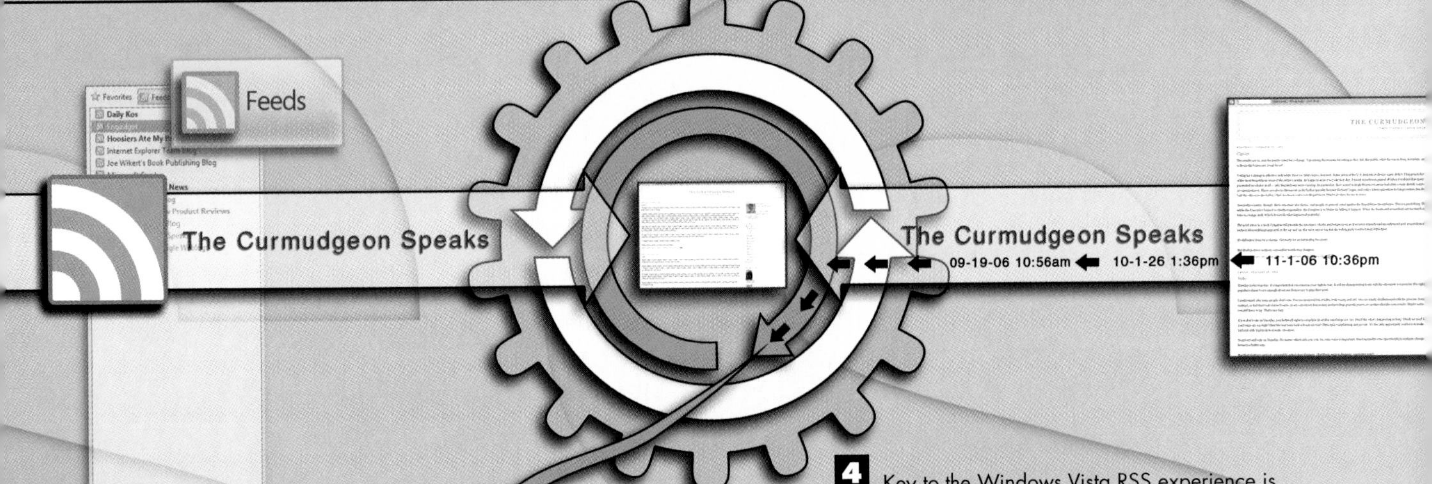

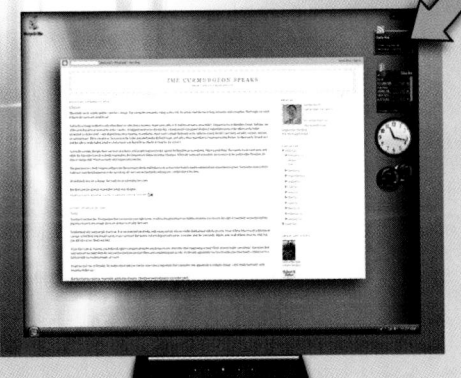

4 Key to the Windows Vista RSS experience is the RSS Platform Sync Engine. This is a service that runs in the background and automatically downloads new RSS content from each of your subscribed feeds.

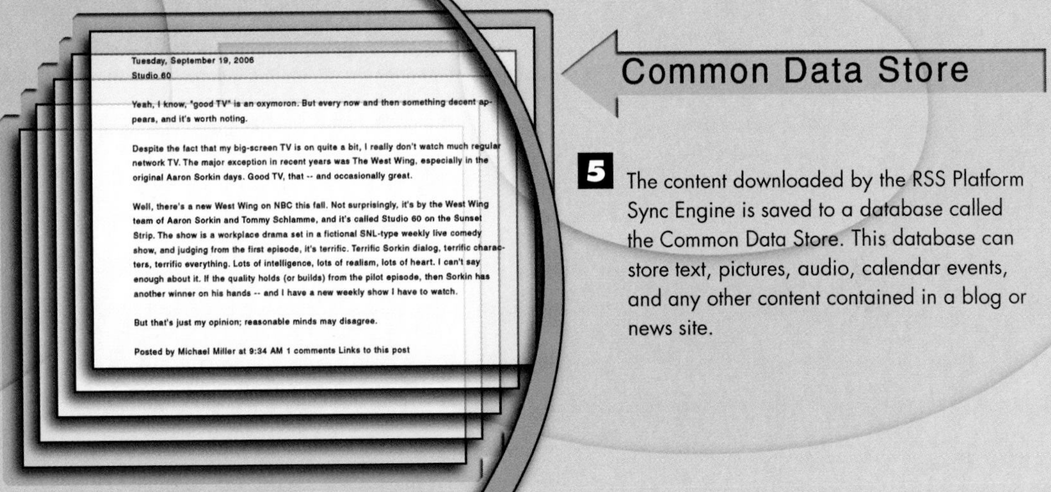

Common Data Store

5 The content downloaded by the RSS Platform Sync Engine is saved to a database called the Common Data Store. This database can store text, pictures, audio, calendar events, and any other content contained in a blog or news site.

6 When you click the link for a subscribed RSS feed from within Internet Explorer, the most recent content for that feed is retrieved from the Common Data Store and displayed in your web browser.

How Internet Explorer Search Works

1 Internet Explorer 7 adds a Toolbar Search Box to the main toolbar, to the right of the Address box. This lets you perform web searches without having to first navigate to a separate search site.

2 To conduct a search, enter your query into the Search box and click the Go button (or press the Enter key on your keyboard).

3 Your query is now sent over the Internet to the selected search provider.

OpenSearch

IE7 also supports the OpenSearch technology for sharing search results. Search engines that support OpenSearch produce search results that are syndicated via RSS, just like blog entries and other newsfeeds. Any site that supports OpenSearch can be specified as the search provider for the Toolbar Search Box.

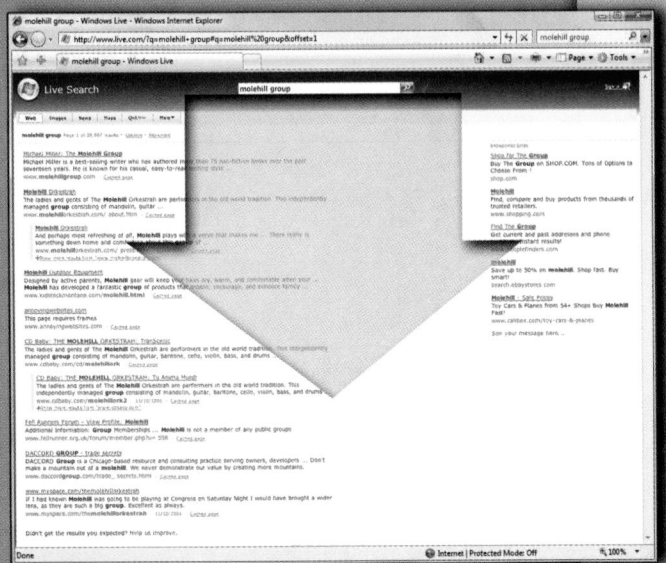

4 The search site receives the query, searches their own previously compiled index of web pages, and returns a page of search results, which is displayed in the Internet Explorer window.

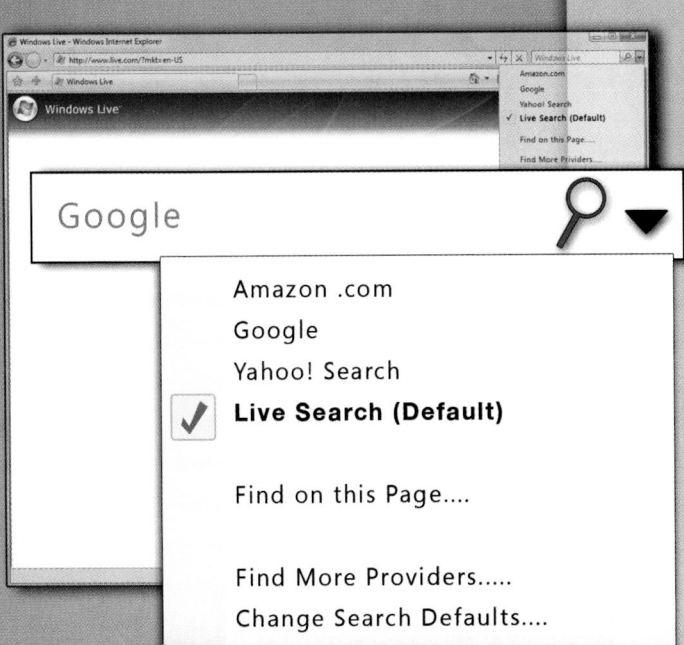

5 For the default search provider, IE7 uses Windows Live Search—or the search provider you specified in the autosearch settings for Internet Explorer.

6 You can change search providers by clicking the down arrow next to the Search box and selecting a search engine from the list. The next time you initiate a search, your query will be sent to the selected search engine.

How Windows Mail Works

1 In Windows Vista, the Outlook Express email application has morphed into Windows Mail. Windows Mail looks and acts much like Outlook Express, but with the Aero interface look and feel.

2 Windows Mail adds an Instant Search box so that you can quickly search for and find specific email messages.

search 🔍

3 Also new is the inclusion of Vista's anti-phishing technology. When you receive a potentially fraudulent message (with a link that leads to a phony website), Windows Mail blocks the links in the email and displays a warning message.

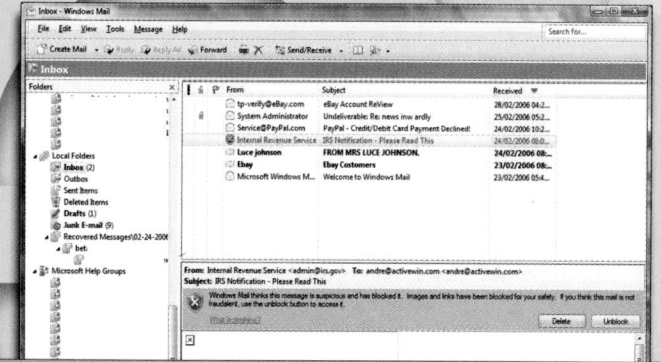

Windows Mail thinks this message is suspicious and has blocked it. Images and links have been blocked for your safety. If you think this mail is not fraudulent, use the unblock button to access it.

What is phishing?

Delete   Unblock

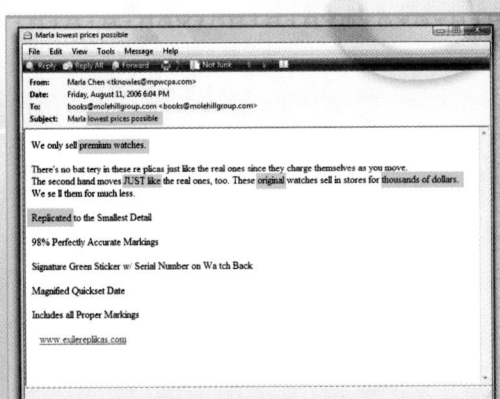

4 To help stop the flood of spam email messages, Windows Mail includes an improved Junk Mail Filter. This new filter uses Bayesian filtering, which analyzes the probability of any given word being included in spam messages, and then applies that analysis to all incoming messages. Emails that include high-probability spam words are automatically routed to the Junk E-mail folder.

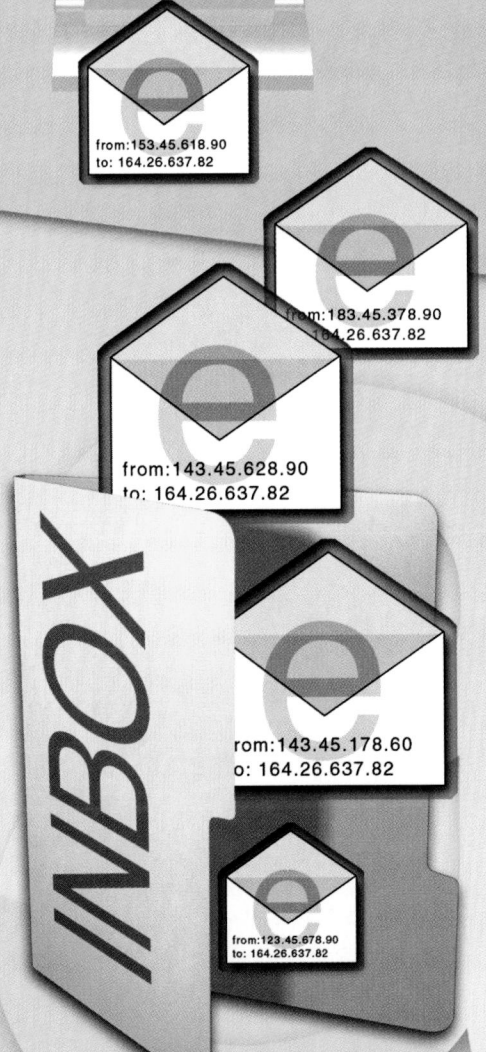

5 In Outlook Express, all email messages within a given folder were stored on your hard disk in a single large database file, which created the opportunity for massive data loss if that file became corrupted. With Windows Mail, individual email messages are stored as separate .EML files in folders on your hard disk, which reduces the risk of data loss. This also lets you view the contents of these email folders from within any Windows Explorer.

How Windows Calendar Works

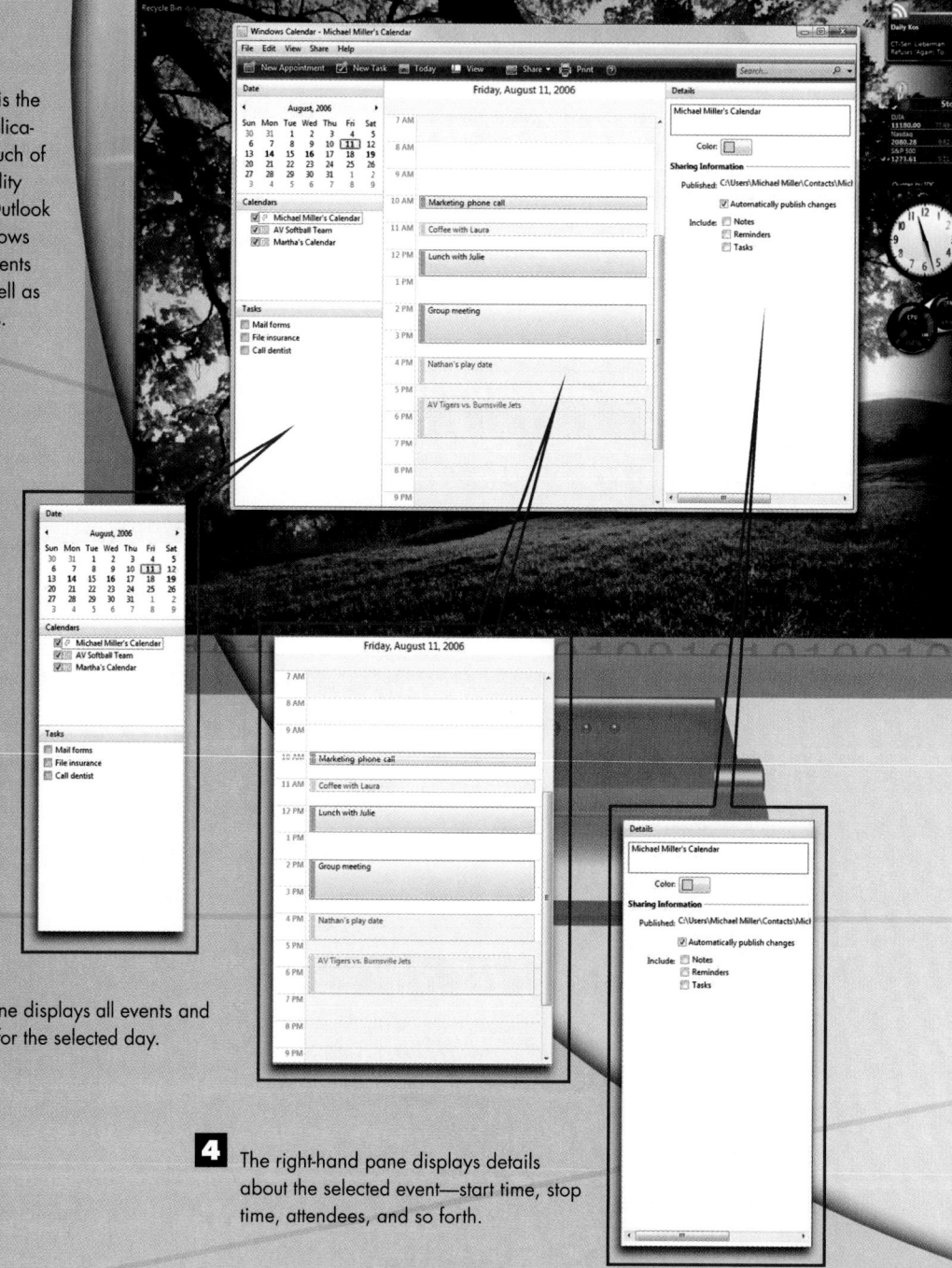

1 New to Windows Vista is the Windows Calendar application, which replicates much of the scheduling functionality found in the Microsoft Outlook program. You use Windows Calendar to schedule events and appointments, as well as to create task (to-do) lists.

2 The left-hand pane displays a monthly calendar, a list of individual calendars you've created, and a list of open tasks.

3 The middle pane displays all events and appointments for the selected day.

4 The right-hand pane displays details about the selected event—start time, stop time, attendees, and so forth.

5 You can create multiple calendars within Windows Calendar. For example, you might create one private calendar with your work appointments and another public calendar with the schedule for your children's soccer team.

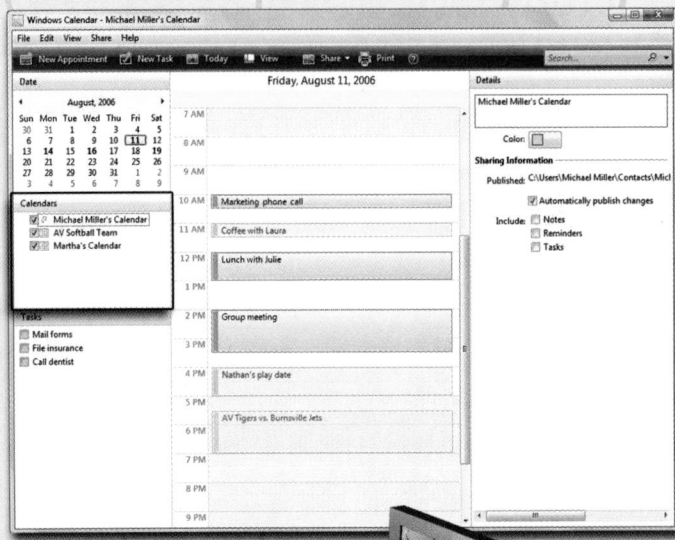

6 You can use Windows Calendar to subscribe to and view other web-based calendars. Windows Calendar supports the iCalendar format, which lets it share calendars and appointments with other compatible calendar applications and websites.

upload

7 Windows Calendar also lets you publish your calendars to the Web. These shared calendars can be viewed or (optionally) edited by any user with which you share the calendars' URLs. You can send email invitations to anyone with whom you want to share your web-based calendars.

CHAPTER

18

Windows Vista Networks

A COMPUTER network is, quite simply, two or more computers connected to each other. When the computers are connected, they can send electronic signals back and forth. This lets them communicate with each other or share things. The computers on a network can share files—that is, one computer can access the files stored on another computer. They can share printers by sending their print requests over the network to the PC that is physically connected to the printer. They can share a single Internet connection, especially a fast cable or DSL broadband connection. They can even share software applications. (Think multiple-player games here.)

Physically, you can choose to set up either a wired (Ethernet) or wireless (Wi-Fi) network. A wired network transmits data faster, but is more of a hassle to set up—you have a lot of Ethernet cables to run. A wireless network doesn't force you to run a lot of cables, but also isn't as fast or as secure as a wired network.

That said, the most common type of home network today is the wireless kind. Once you have your wireless router and adapters connected, Windows Vista makes it easy to create the network on your computers, and then manage all network communications. It even facilitates the implementation of wireless security, to prevent outsiders from tapping into your network or Internet connection.

If you're running a large corporate network, you'll appreciate Vista's new Network Access Protection (NAP) feature. NAP monitors all the computers connected to the network, looking for those that are most susceptible to viruses and other malware. If an "unhealthy" computer is found, NAP prevents it from fully connecting to the network—and can even automatically update the computer's security functions, if desired.

Finally, it's worth repeating that Vista includes the Next Generation TCP/IP stack, which makes for more secure and more solid network connections. If you've ever experienced a flaky network connection, or had a computer that wasn't always recognized by the network, you'll appreciate how Vista's Next Generation TCP/IP eliminates these pesky network connection problems. Vista is, for both IT professionals and casual home users, a much better networking solution than Windows XP or previous versions of the operating system.

How Networking Works
in Windows Vista

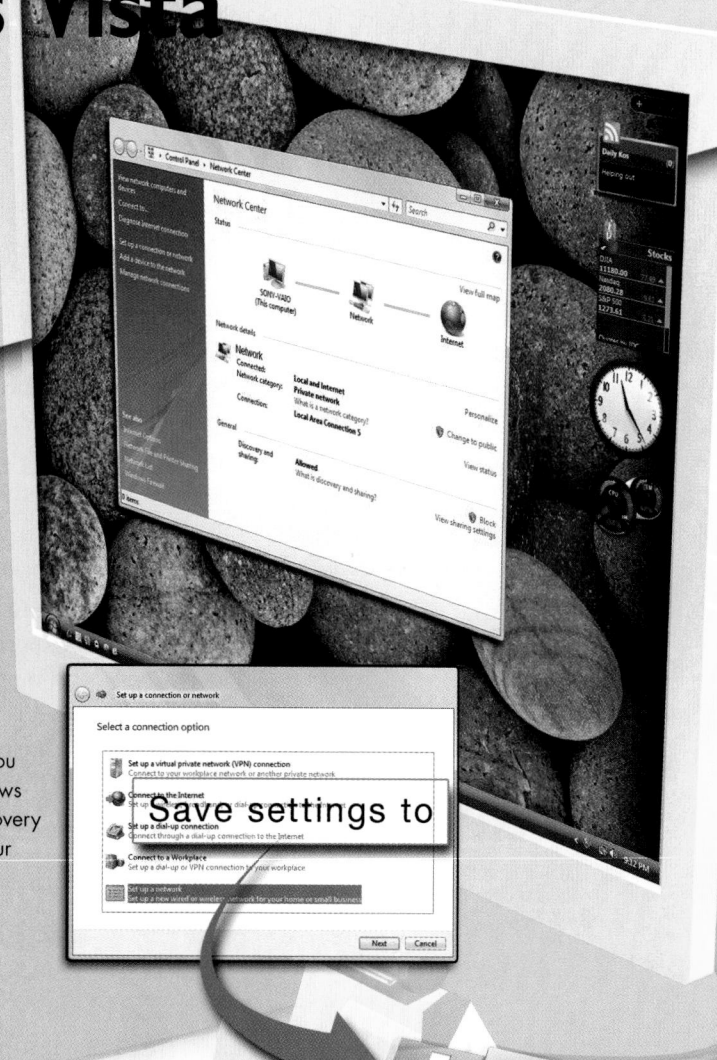

1 Some of the most significant changes in Windows Vista involve network-related functions. In Windows Vista, all networking activities are managed from the **Network Center**. From here, you can navigate to any computer on your network, set up a new network, diagnose network-related problems, and otherwise manage your Windows networks.

2 To set up your network in Windows Vista, you use the **Network Setup Wizard**. Windows Vista incorporates Link Layer Topology Discovery (LLTD) technology to automatically detect your wireless router.

3 New to Vista is **Windows Connect Now** (WCN) technology, which lets you save the network settings from your main computer to a USB flash drive. You can then insert the USB drive into any other computer on your network, and it automatically reads the data and configures itself as necessary to work with your new network.

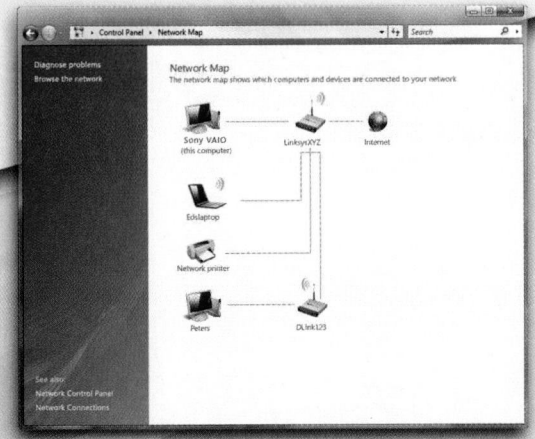

4 Once your network is set up, you can view a graphical map of all the computers and devices on your network in the **Network Map** window.

5 To view the current status of your network—whether it's connected, the connection speed, current activity, and so forth—click the View Status link in Network Center. This opens the **Status** window for the network, with appropriate data displayed. From here, you can click the **Diagnose** button to troubleshoot any network problems.

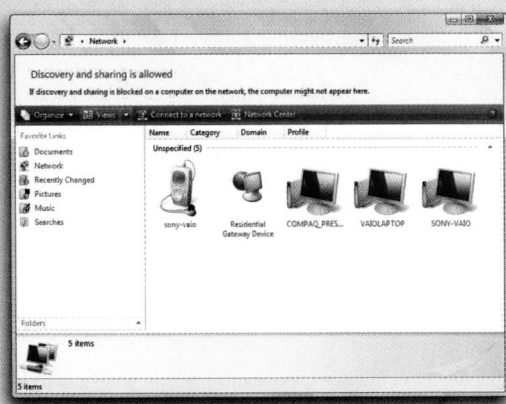

6 Instead of the My Network Places window found in Windows XP, Vista displays all your networked computers in the new **Network Explorer**. To see a shared drive or folder on a particular network PC, simply double-click that PC's icon.

How to Set Up a Wireless Network

1 To share a broadband Internet connection, the broadband modem must be connected to the wireless router via an Ethernet cable. Once this connection is made, all computers on the network can connect to the Internet through the modem.

2 The central point of a wireless network is the wireless router. Data is sent from every computer connected to the network to the router, which then routes the data to the appropriate computer or network device. All network communications must pass through the router; no data is sent directly from computer to computer.

3 Each computer connected to the network is equipped with a wireless network adapter. The adapter broadcasts data from the computer to the network router, and back again. Desktop computers typically use external wireless adapters that connect to the computer via USB.

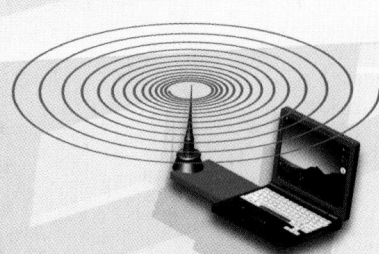

4 Most notebook computers today have built-in wireless adapters. No external adapters are necessary.

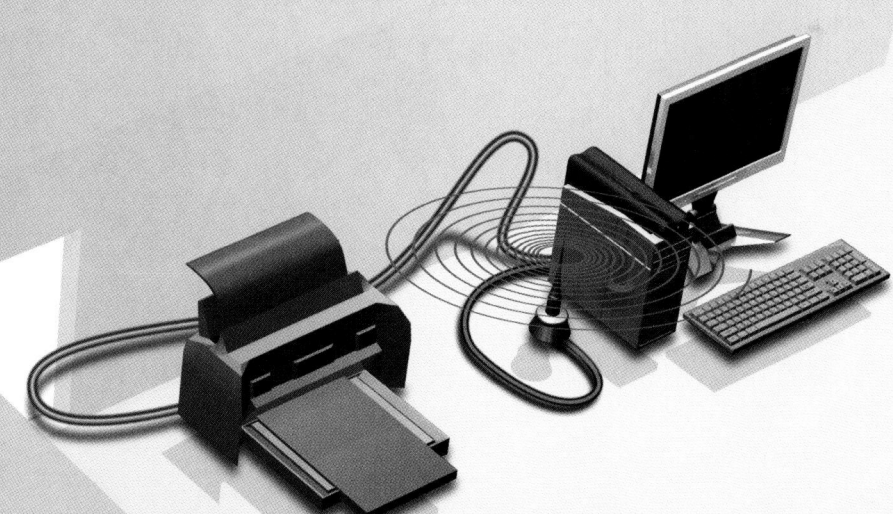

5 In addition, various peripherals can be shared among all the computers connected to a network. For example, a single printer connected to one of the network computers can be shared by all the other computers on the network. To do this, print sharing must be enabled on the host computer, via Vista's Network and Sharing Center.

How Network Access Protection Works

1 Computer viruses are often introduced to private networks by infected mobile or remote computers. Network Access Protection (NAP) is a policy enforcement platform built into Windows Vista that helps protect the security of a corporate computer network by blocking the introduction of these viruses.

2 NAP works by detecting and reporting the "health status" of all computers connected to the network. The health status includes whether the computer has the latest Windows updates installed, whether the computer's virus signatures are up-to-date, the status of the computer's security settings, and so on.

3 Once detected, the computer's health status is transmitted to the NAP enforcement service installed on the network policy server (NPS). The health status of the computer is then validated against the health policies defined by the network administrator.

4 If the computer's health is satisfactory, the network policy server instructs the network's health certificate server to issue a health certificate to the computer. This health certificate is used to validate the computer to other clients on the network.

Health Status

✓ Windows Updates Installed?
✓ Virus Signatures up-to-date?
✓ Security Settings Configured?

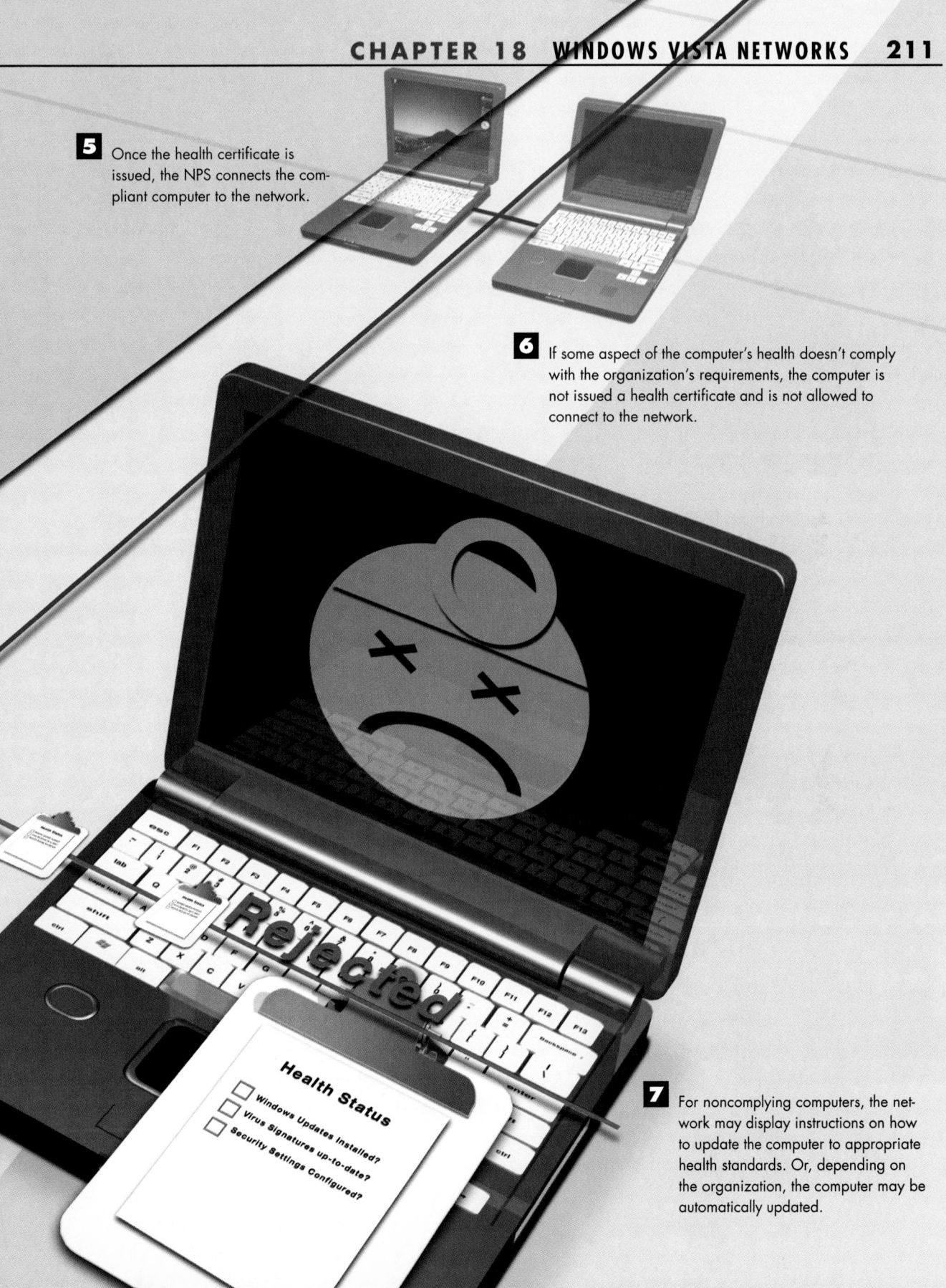

5 Once the health certificate is issued, the NPS connects the compliant computer to the network.

6 If some aspect of the computer's health doesn't comply with the organization's requirements, the computer is not issued a health certificate and is not allowed to connect to the network.

7 For noncomplying computers, the network may display instructions on how to update the computer to appropriate health standards. Or, depending on the organization, the computer may be automatically updated.

Rejected

Health Status

☐ Windows Updates Installed?
☐ Virus Signatures up-to-date?
☐ Security Settings Configured?

How Windows Detects and Connects to a Wi-Fi Hotspot

1. When you're on the road with your notebook PC, Windows Vista makes it easy to connect to any nearby Wi-Fi wireless hotspot. All that your notebook needs is a built-in or add-on Wi-Fi wireless adapter, and for that adapter to be enabled.

2. A public Wi-Fi hotspot continuously broadcasts its Service Set Identifier (SSID), or network name, over the 2.4 GHz radio frequency band.

3. When your computer is in range of a Wi-Fi hotspot, Vista's Link Layer Topology Discovery (LLTD) technology automatically detects the network and notes the SSID being broadcast.

coffeehouse hotspot

coffeehouse hotspot detected

coffeehouse hotspot

coffeehouse hotspot

SSID

SSID

4 To connect to the Wi-Fi hotspot, you first have to open Vista's Connect to a Network dialog box. You open this dialog box by clicking the wireless connection icon in the Windows System Tray, or by selecting **Start > Connect To**.

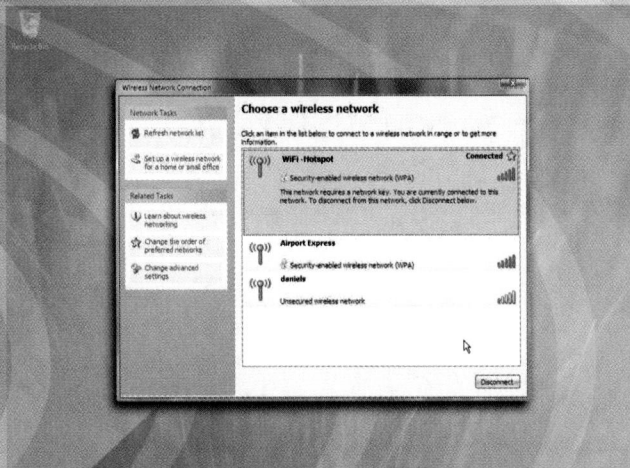

5 The Connect to a Network dialog box lists the SSIDs of all wireless networks detected by LLTD. Select the Wi-Fi hotspot or wireless network you wish to connect to, and then click the **Connect** button.

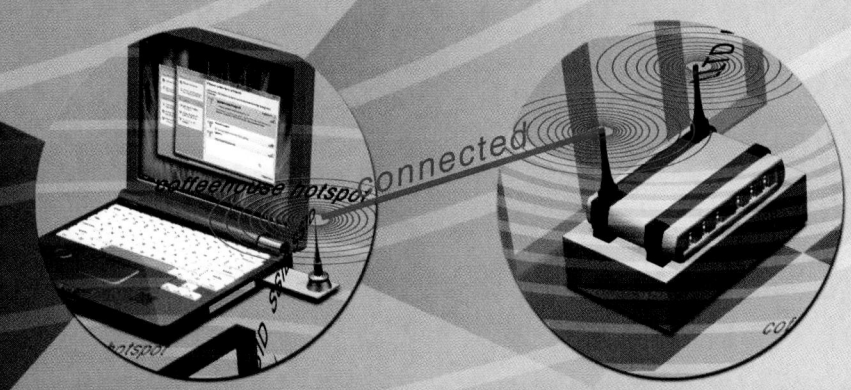

6 Windows now makes a formal connection to the Wi-Fi hotspot, essentially joining the existing wireless network as a temporary user.

How Wireless Security Works

1 To keep outsiders from tapping into your wireless network, Windows Vista lets you add wireless security to your network. This is done by assigning a fairly complex encryption code, called a *network key*, to all the PCs in your network. In order to access the network, a computer must know the code.

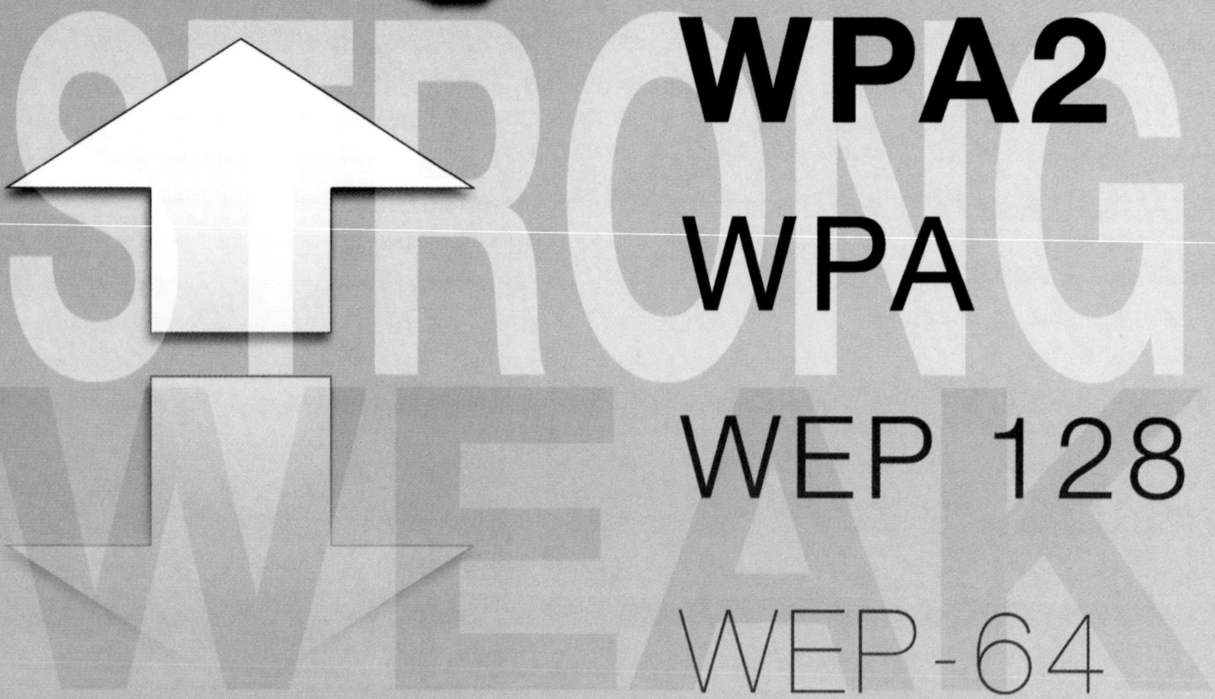

WPA2

WPA

WEP 128

WEP-64

2 Four primary types of wireless security are available today: **WEP (Wired Equivalent Privacy) 64-bit**, **WEP 128-bit**, **WPA (Wi-Fi Protected Access)**, and **WPA2**—the strongest type of encryption currently available.

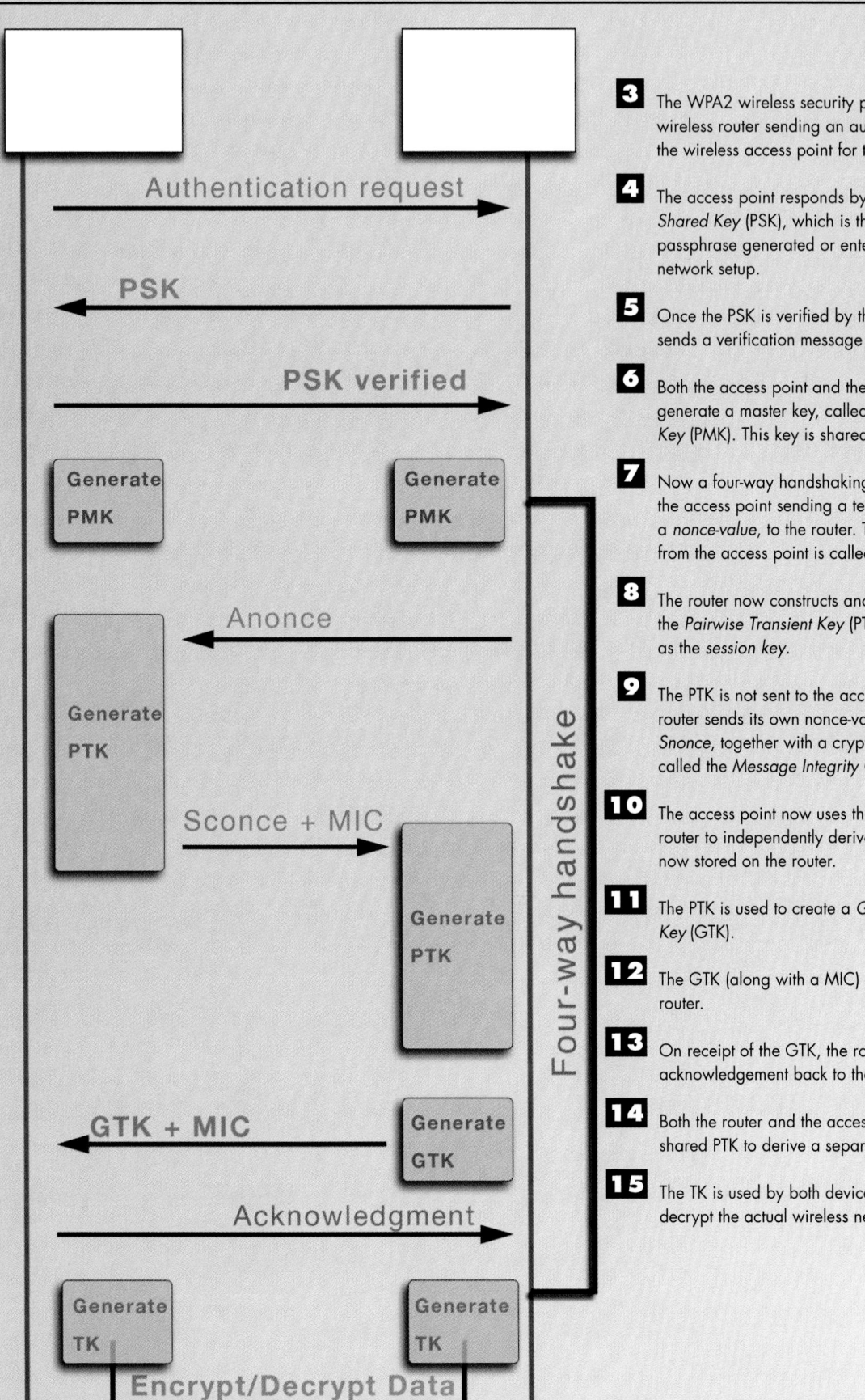

Authentication request

PSK

PSK verified

Generate PMK

Generate PMK

Anonce

Generate PTK

Sconce + MIC

Generate PTK

Four-way handshake

GTK + MIC

Generate GTK

Acknowledgment

Generate TK

Generate TK

Encrypt/Decrypt Data

3 The WPA2 wireless security process begins with the wireless router sending an authentication request to the wireless access point for the remote computer.

4 The access point responds by sending the *Pre-Shared Key* (PSK), which is the encrypted passphrase generated or entered during the initial network setup.

5 Once the PSK is verified by the router, the router sends a verification message to the access point.

6 Both the access point and the router use the PSK to generate a master key, called the *Pairwise Master Key* (PMK). This key is shared by both devices.

7 Now a four-way handshaking process begins, with the access point sending a temporary value, called a *nonce-value*, to the router. The nonce-value sent from the access point is called the *ANonce*.

8 The router now constructs another secret key, called the *Pairwise Transient Key* (PTK), otherwise known as the *session key*.

9 The PTK is not sent to the access point. Instead, the router sends its own nonce-value, called the *Snonce*, together with a cryptographic checksum called the *Message Integrity Code* (MIC).

10 The access point now uses the Snonce sent from the router to independently derive the same PTK that is now stored on the router.

11 The PTK is used to create a *Group Temporary Key* (GTK).

12 The GTK (along with a MIC) is sent back to the router.

13 On receipt of the GTK, the router sends an acknowledgement back to the access point.

14 Both the router and the access point now use the shared PTK to derive a separate *Temporal Key* (TK).

15 The TK is used by both devices to encrypt and decrypt the actual wireless network traffic.

How File Sharing Works

1 By default, most of the files and folders stored on your hard disk are private—they can't be shared by other users on your network. If you want other users to view or edit a document on your computer, you must enable file sharing for that particular file. There are two ways to do this.

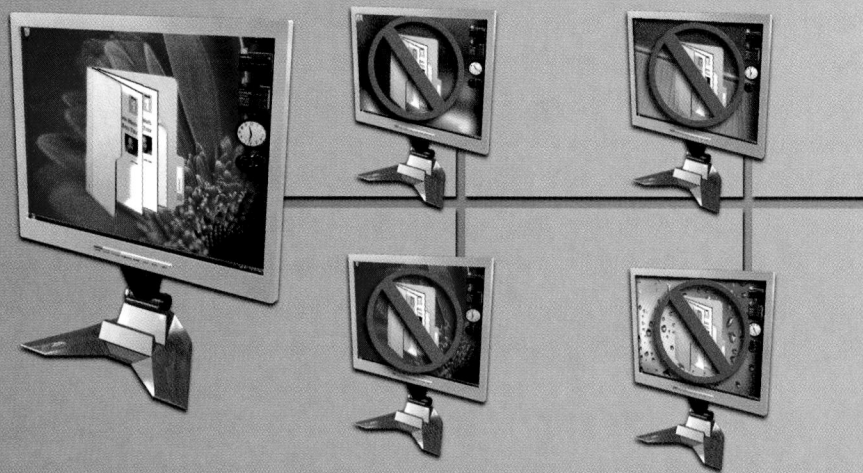

2 If you want to share a single document, the easiest way to proceed is to save that document to the Public folder on your hard disk. This folder is, by default, accessible to every user on this computer, as well as every user on the network.

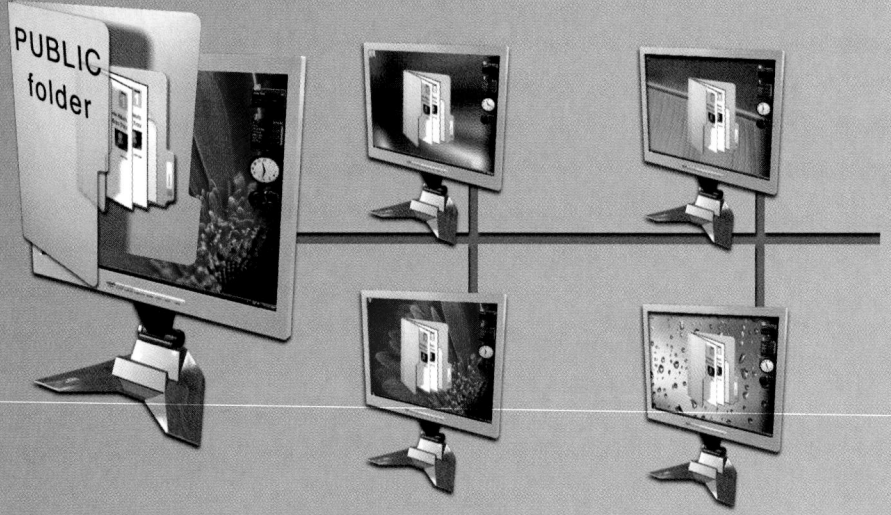

READ ONLY

3 You can configure the Public folder in three ways. First, you can allow other users to only open but not edit documents in the Public folder.

4 Second, you can allow users to both view and edit documents in the Public folder.

5 Finally, you can disable the file sharing feature so that documents in the Public folder are not accessible to users other than yourself.

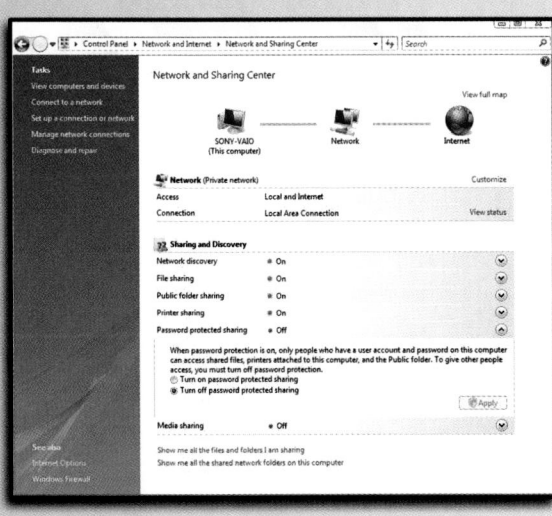

6 You configure file and printer sharing from the Network and Sharing Center window. From here you can also choose to enable password-protected sharing, which requires other users to enter a password before accessing files in the Public folder.

How Windows Meeting
Space Works

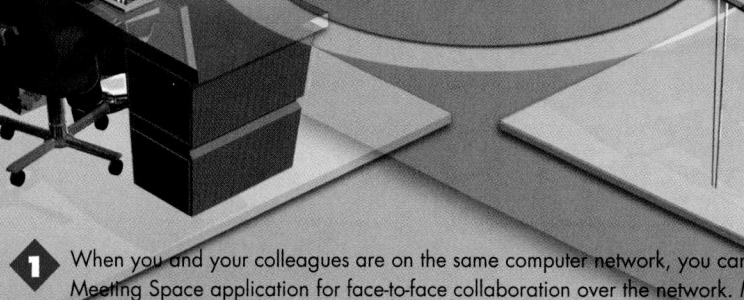

1 When you and your colleagues are on the same computer network, you can use the Windows Meeting Space application for face-to-face collaboration over the network. Meeting Space lets as many as 10 people collaborate in real-time; you can also use Meeting Space to give presentations to users in different locations.

2 Windows Meeting Space is a peer-to-peer application. This means that your data is shared from each PC in the group, not on a central server.

3 To initiate a Meeting Space session, a lead user designates which users he wants in the session. Those users can then log in to the session using the Sessions Near Me feature. Sessions Near Me automatically locates other live Meeting Space sessions on the current network, or occurring on any private ad hoc wireless networks.

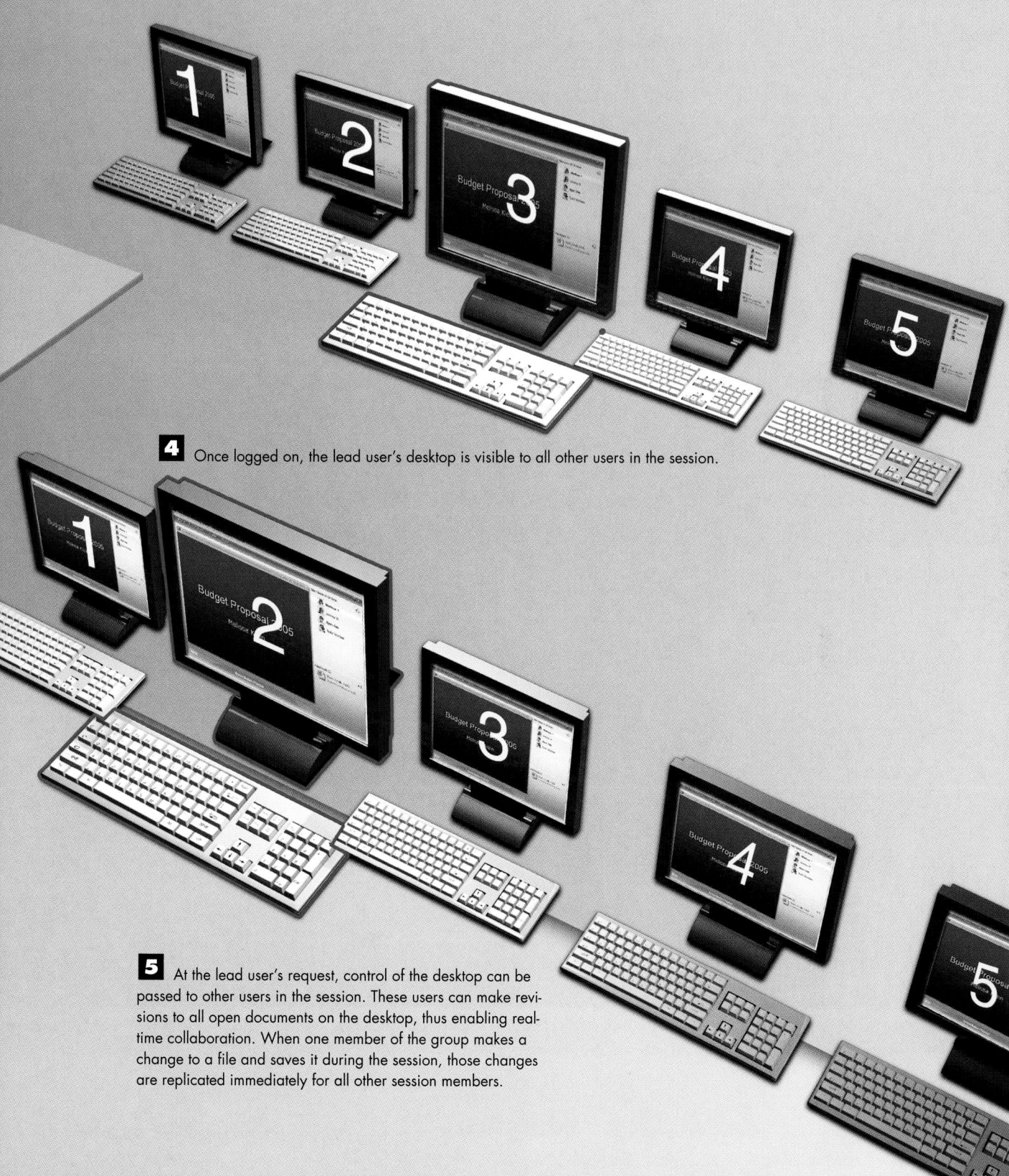

4 Once logged on, the lead user's desktop is visible to all other users in the session.

5 At the lead user's request, control of the desktop can be passed to other users in the session. These users can make revisions to all open documents on the desktop, thus enabling real-time collaboration. When one member of the group makes a change to a file and saves it during the session, those changes are replicated immediately for all other session members.

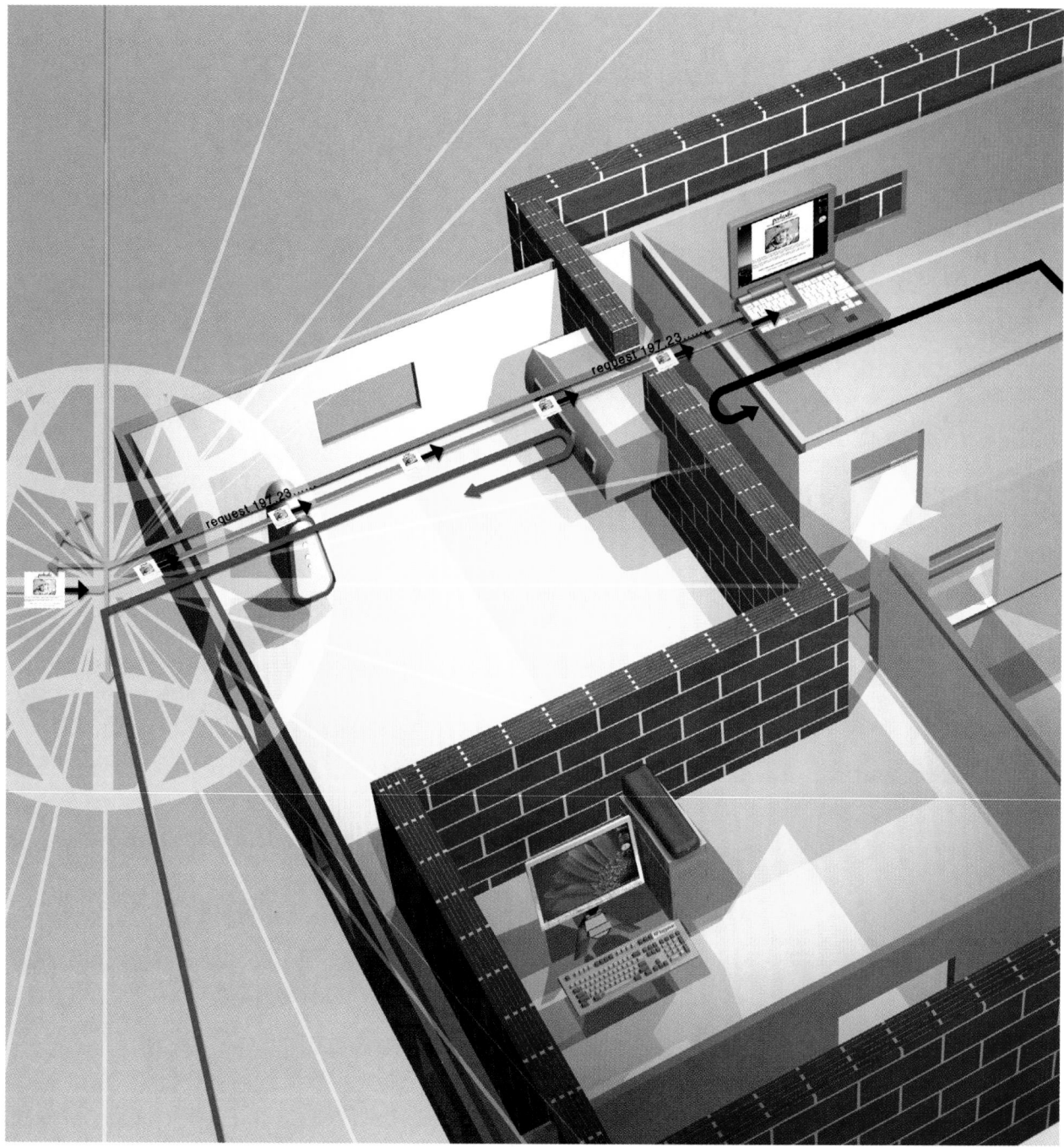

P A R T

SECURITY AND MAINTENANCE

DON'T you just hate housekeeping? Even though you know it's necessary, having to dust the furniture, sweep the carpets, and wash the windows is a real pain in the posterior. But you do it anyway because you always like living in a clean house.

You also like living in a secure house, which is why you close the windows and lock the doors whenever you leave. You may even invest in a high-tech alarm system so that you're even better protected against intruders and thieves.

When it comes to both housekeeping and security, an operating system is like a house. You have to perform periodic housekeeping duties to keep your system "clean" and in good working condition. And you have to engage in various security-related practices, to keep outsiders from breaking in and damaging or stealing your data. It's the computer equivalent of sweeping your carpets and locking your doors.

Fortunately, Microsoft includes a lot of built-in utilities and technologies to make it easier to perform these housekeeping and security tasks. In fact, many of these utilities are activated by default and run in the background when you're doing your day-to-day tasks. As most users will attest, it's easier to perform maintenance and maintain security when you don't have to think much about it.

Some of the biggest changes in Windows Vista revolve around computer security. Not only do you get the tried-and-true (and somewhat improved) Windows Firewall, to protect your system from outside attack, you also have a new anti-phishing filter, new service hardening and protected mode technologies, new User Account Control protection, and—for corporate users—drive encryption technology to protect data stored on portable PCs. The goal is to make your system more secure without requiring more work on your part.

On the maintenance front, Vista includes some familiar utilities, some new utilities, and some familiar utilities with new features. For example, the familiar Disk Defragmenter utility now works full time, in the background, so you don't have to manually activate a defragmentation session. And Vista resurrects the old Microsoft Backup utility with a bevy of new features, including (in some editions) the capability of creating a mirror image of your entire hard disk.

One of my favorite Windows utilities, and one that's not as well-known as it should be, is System Restore—which remains relatively unchanged in Vista. What's great about System Restore is that it lets you return your system to a previous working condition if you happen to run into system problems. If your system starts acting up, just launch System Restore and choose a restore point from before you started having problems. It's like putting your system in a time machine and jumping back in time to when things were still working. It's the easiest solution to computer problems you're likely to find.

Vista expands this time machine approach to individual documents with the new Previous Versions feature. With Previous Versions, all it takes is a few clicks of your mouse to resurrect a previous version of any file you've been working on—even files that you forgot to save. It's like System Restore, but for data files. It's pretty useful.

Then there's the matter of keeping Windows up-to-date, which has become pretty much a full-time job. You see, Windows is like a lot of big government projects—it's never actually finished, and it often needs to be fixed.

In older versions of Windows, Microsoft saved up all its bug fixes, security patches, and driver updates and threw them all into annual "service packs." The problem with the service pack approach is that months can go by before blatant security holes are patched; in today's fast-paced online environment, you need to act as quickly as possible to fix any identified security or operational problem. If you don't act fast, hackers will.

That's why Microsoft introduced Windows Update, an online extension of Windows that works to keep your operating system up-to-date. When Windows Update is activated, it goes online on a regular basis and checks with the main Windows Update website. If updates are available, Windows Update downloads and installs them. In Windows Vista, Windows Update works automatically in the background, without any action required on your part. All you need is an always-on Internet connection, and Windows Update can do its thing—and keep your version of Vista as up-to-date as Microsoft allows.

CHAPTER 19

Windows Vista Security Features

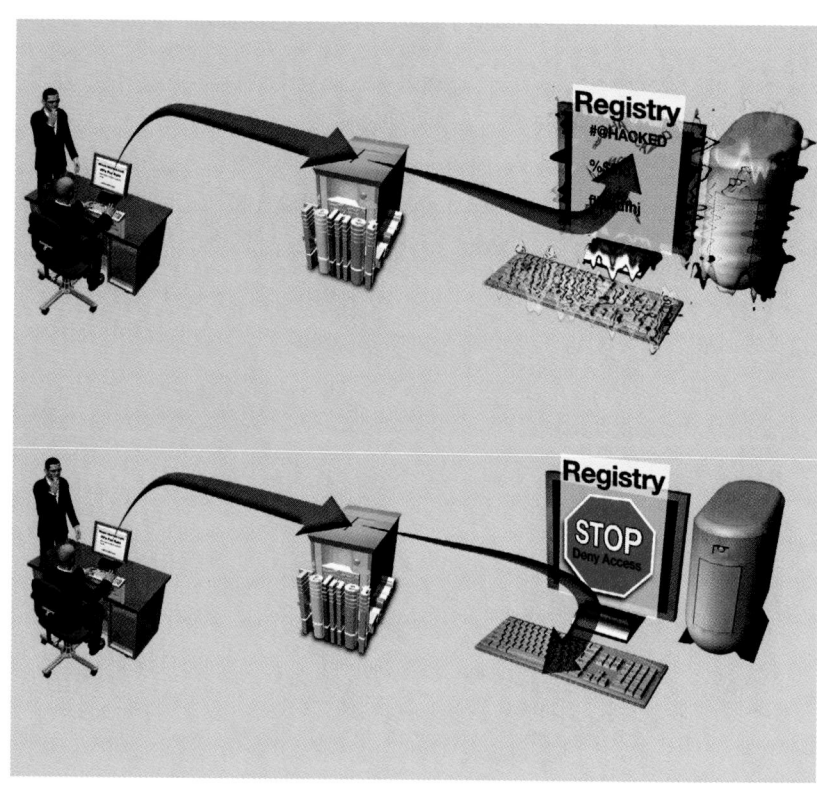

SECURITY is paramount. Keeping your computer—and your personal data—secure and safe from theft or attack is a full-time endeavor.

Unfortunately, the Windows operating system has been a focal point for computer hackers and attackers. Malicious-minded individuals have focused on Windows' weaknesses, working overtime to exploit security holes and system weaknesses. The result has been a flood of security alerts and resulting security patches, all in an attempt to keep the barbarians from breaching the gates.

One of Microsoft's goals with Windows Vista was to dramatically improve the operating system's security. While real-world experience will determine whether Microsoft was successful in this regard, the bevy of new security features in Vista certainly shows how seriously Microsoft has taken this threat.

One of the key security features in Vista is User Account Control (UAC), which is discussed earlier in this book. UAC prevents unauthorized people and processes from taking control of your system and installing and running malicious programs. With UAC, programs no longer automatically have administrator access to the system; this looks to block a large number of software-based exploits.

UAC isn't the only new security feature, however. Windows Service Hardening limits the access privileges of system services; Internet Explorer's Protected Mode isolates suspicious programs in their own private "sandbox"; the Microsoft Phishing Filter protects against fraudulent emails and websites; Windows Defender guards against malicious spyware; and, of course, the Windows Firewall blocks Internet-based intrusions.

And if you've ever worried about someone stealing your notebook PC and accessing all the data stored within, you need to check out Vista's new BitLocker Drive Encryption. BitLocker locks up the data on your notebook's hard drive, so even if a thief tries to hack his way in, your data remains inaccessible. You may lose a laptop, but you won't lose your personal and business data.

How the Windows Firewall Protects Against Attacks

1 The Windows Firewall is a program that acts as a barrier between your computer or network and the Internet. It's like a guard on a door—the firewall lets good visitors in and keeps bad visitors out. In the case of your computer system, good visitors are the normal email communications and web pages you visit; bad visitors are attackers trying to bomb or infiltrate your system.

2 The firewall blocks unwanted inbound traffic via a process called *stateful packet inspection*. This process works by matching incoming traffic with outgoing requests; any data not specifically requested will be automatically blocked. For example, when you want to view a web page, you request that page to be displayed in Internet Explorer. When the web page is sent to your PC, the Windows Firewall allows that data to pass through, since you requested it.

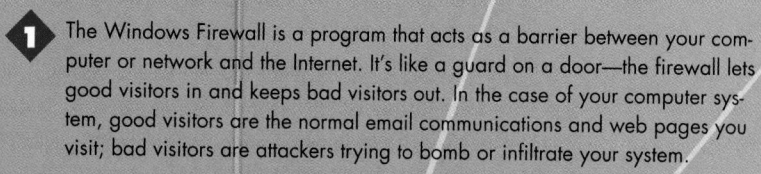

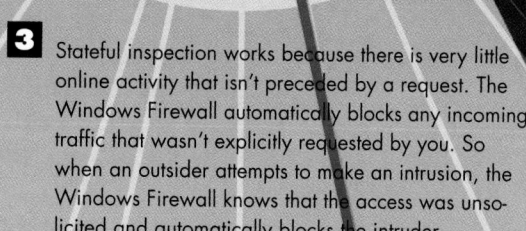

3 Stateful inspection works because there is very little online activity that isn't preceded by a request. The Windows Firewall automatically blocks any incoming traffic that wasn't explicitly requested by you. So when an outsider attempts to make an intrusion, the Windows Firewall knows that the access was unsolicited and automatically blocks the intruder.

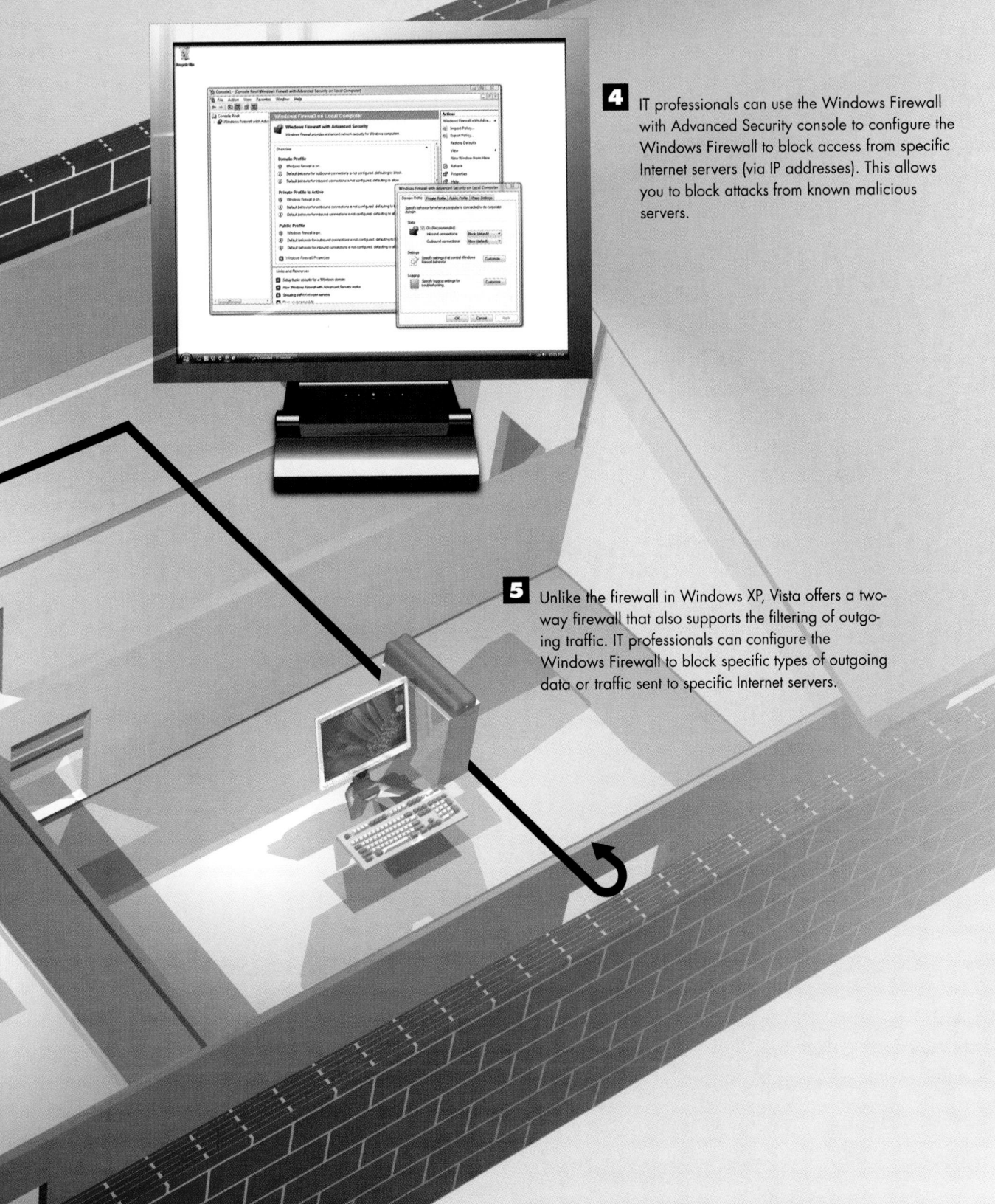

4 IT professionals can use the Windows Firewall with Advanced Security console to configure the Windows Firewall to block access from specific Internet servers (via IP addresses). This allows you to block attacks from known malicious servers.

5 Unlike the firewall in Windows XP, Vista offers a two-way firewall that also supports the filtering of outgoing traffic. IT professionals can configure the Windows Firewall to block specific types of outgoing data or traffic sent to specific Internet servers.

How Windows Service Hardening Limits Damage from Attacks

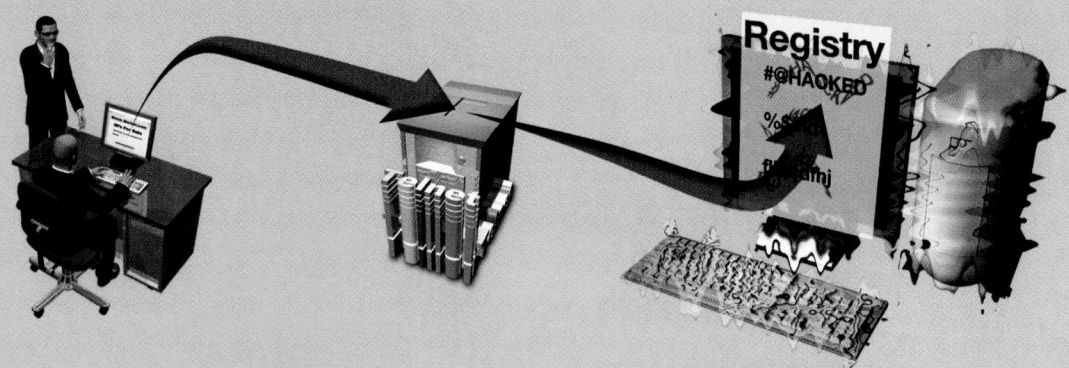

1 In previous versions of Windows, hackers could hijack various Windows services, such as Telnet or SMTP, and use those services to mount an attack on a computer system. That's because most Windows services had full access privileges to all system resources, including the Windows Registry.

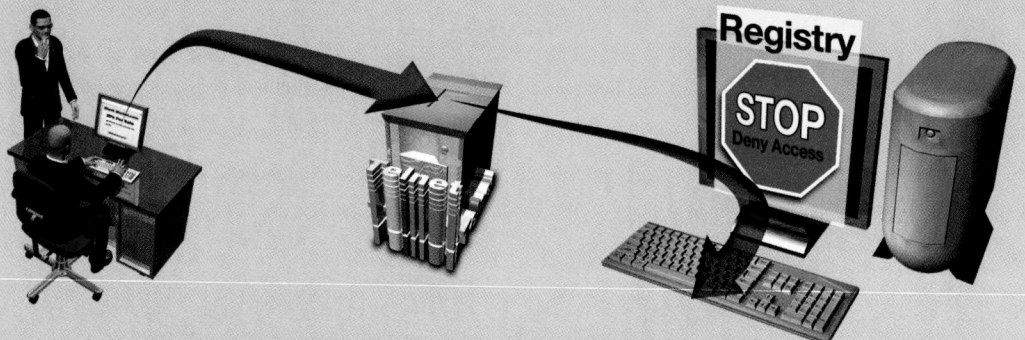

2 In Windows Vista, Windows Service Hardening forces all background processes to run with the lowest-possible privileges necessary to do their jobs—and to run in isolation from each other. Even if a hacker could hijack a service, he couldn't use that service to access essential system resources. The attack would be thwarted.

3 Previously, most system and third-party services ran at the LocalSystem level, which provided access to most processes on the local machine. With Windows Service Hardening, these same services run at the less-privileged LocalService or NetworkService levels, which have less access to other processes.

4 As part of Windows Service Hardening, a service can only access its own specific subset of the Windows Registry. With no access to the full Registry, a service can't overwrite settings that it shouldn't be accessing.

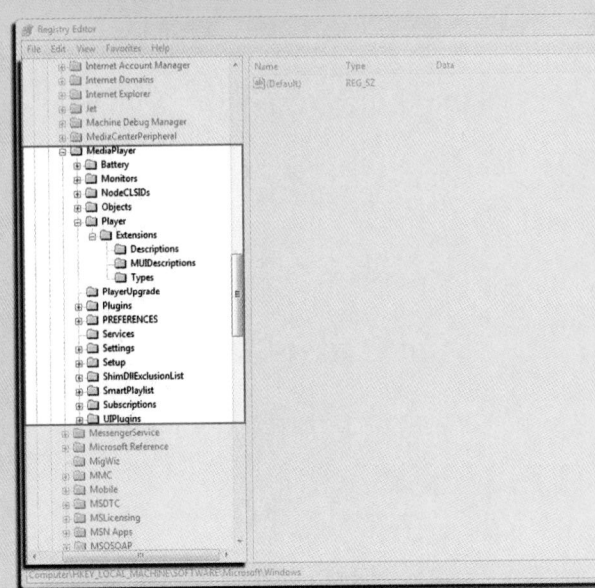

5 Services in Windows Vista are assigned a security identifier (SID), which provides a per-service identity that can be used to limit access to system resources. A Windows service can use an access control list (ACL) to specify which resources it is private to, thus prohibiting unauthorized access to the resource by unlisted services.

6 Services are also assigned a network firewall policy, which prohibits network access outside the normal bounds of the service. This keeps a service from improperly accessing other computers on the network or going online to download malicious code.

How Windows Defender Protects Against Spyware

1 Spyware is a type of computer program that, like a Trojan horse, is typically installed on your system without your consent or knowledge. It runs in the background, hidden from view, and spies on all your computer-related activities. The information collected by a spyware program is typically transmitted over the Internet to a third party, where it can be used in any number of unauthorized ways.

2 To determine whether a program is spyware, Microsoft's researchers check to see if the program runs processes on your computer without notifying you; if it collects or communicates your personal information and behavior without your consent; if it attempts to circumvent or disable the security features on your computer; if it undermines your computer's performances; and if it is recognized by industry professionals as malicious software.

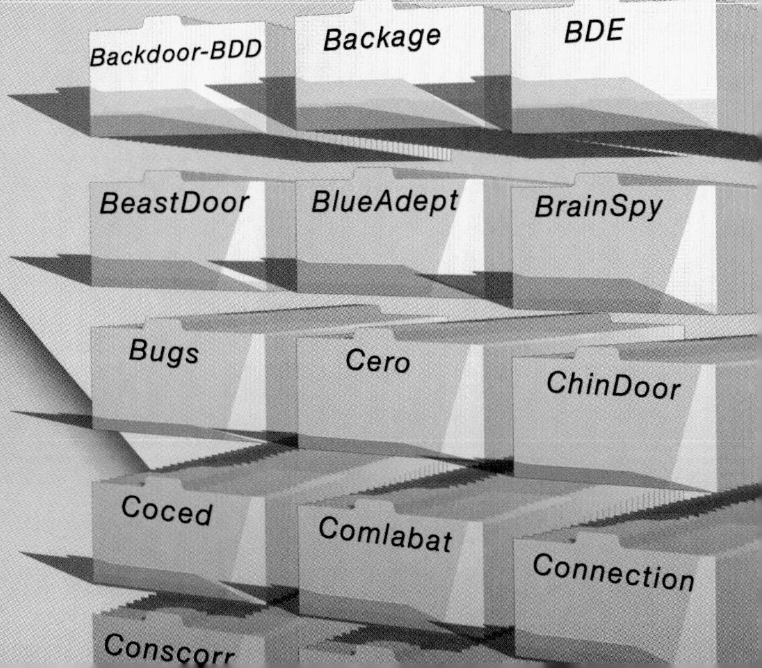

Backdoor-BDD

Backage

BDE

BeastDoor

BlueAdept

BrainSpy

Bugs

Cero

ChinDoor

Coced

Comlabat

Connection

Conscorr

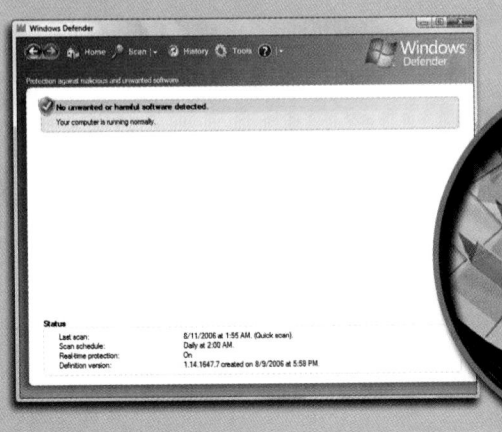

3 To protect against known spyware programs, Windows Vista includes the Windows Defender anti-spyware utility. Windows Defender works by automatically scanning your computer on a periodic basis, comparing the programs installed on your PC with Microsoft's database of spyware programs. If a matching program is found, it is quarantined or deleted.

Spyware, Malware, and Viruses

Spyware is a type of *malware*, or malicious software. Other types of malware include computer viruses and worms, which infect your system and make unwanted changes to program files and documents. A spyware program is not a virus, and is not normally detected by antivirus utilities; nor does Windows Defender detect or protect against computer viruses and worms. This is why you should install a separate antivirus program in addition to the Windows Defender anti-spyware utility.

4 Windows Defender also provides real-time scanning for spyware. The program constantly monitors key Windows system locations, watching for changes that signal the presence of spyware. Defender also checks all files you access against the database of spyware programs. If it detects any sign of spyware, Windows Defender notifies you of the potential problem.

How Windows Protects Against Phishing Scams

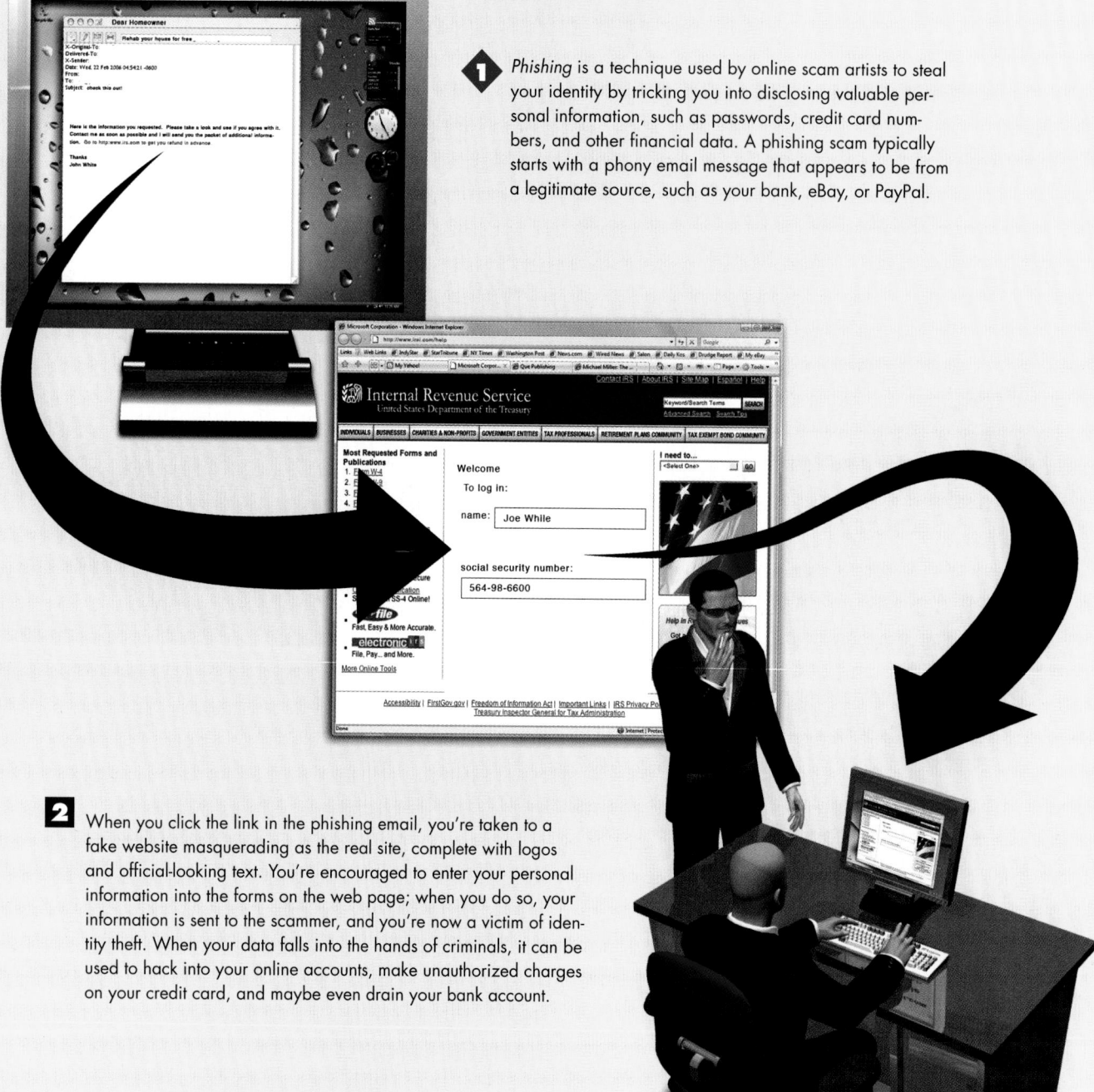

1 *Phishing* is a technique used by online scam artists to steal your identity by tricking you into disclosing valuable personal information, such as passwords, credit card numbers, and other financial data. A phishing scam typically starts with a phony email message that appears to be from a legitimate source, such as your bank, eBay, or PayPal.

2 When you click the link in the phishing email, you're taken to a fake website masquerading as the real site, complete with logos and official-looking text. You're encouraged to enter your personal information into the forms on the web page; when you do so, your information is sent to the scammer, and you're now a victim of identity theft. When your data falls into the hands of criminals, it can be used to hack into your online accounts, make unauthorized charges on your credit card, and maybe even drain your bank account.

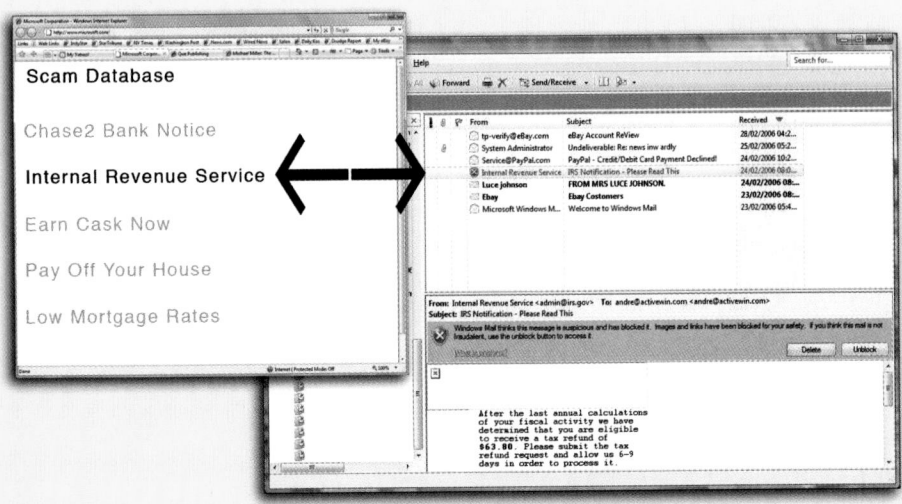

3 To reduce the risk of phishing incidents, Windows Vista includes the Microsoft Phishing Filter, which works within both Windows Mail and Internet Explorer 7. The Phishing Filter compares all the links in your Windows Mail email messages to an online list of known phishing websites. If the link matches a fraudulent site, Windows Mail displays a warning message at the top of the message.

4 If you attempt to click a link to a known phishing site, the Microsoft Phishing Filter blocks access to the site, changes the Address Bar to red, navigates to a neutral page, and displays a warning message. If you attempt to click a link to a site that is not on the list of known fraudulent sites but behaves in a way similar to such sites, the Microsoft Phishing Filter changes the Address Bar to yellow and cautions you of potentially suspicious content.

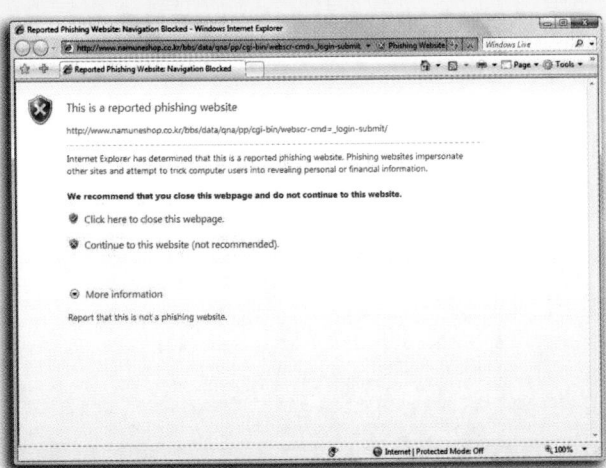

Don't Click the Links

The best defense against phishing schemes is to use common sense and never click links in email messages that ask for your personal information. Instead, go directly to the legitimate site in question, and enter your information there—not through an email link.

How Internet Explorer's Protected Mode Isolates Malicious Code

1 Hackers often use web browsers to deliver malware to your system and cause damage to your PC, in the form of "elevation of privilege" attacks. This is typically done by executing code within a web page that then takes over your browser and accesses critical parts of your system.

2 To block these web-based attacks, Internet Explorer 7 incorporates Protected Mode operation. This mode isolates suspicious programs from other applications and the operating system, thus preventing any destructive program from taking over your browser and initiating an attack.

3 IE7's Protected Mode functions like an isolation sandbox. Any program or code downloaded from the Internet is isolated in its own browser window, which insulates the Windows operating system from the potentially malicious code.

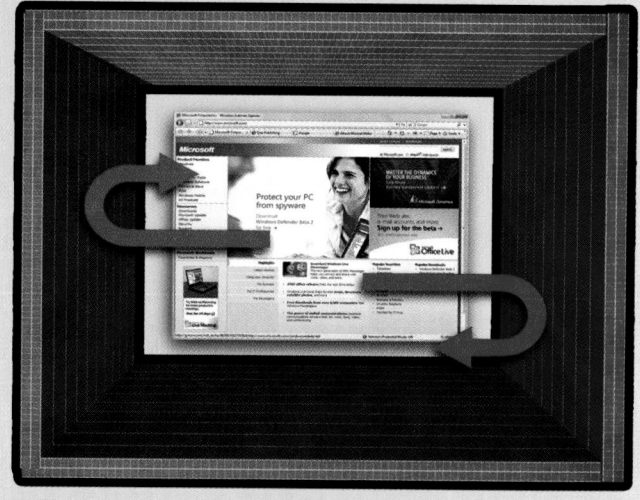

Windows Registry

PROTECTED

4 A program in Protected Mode lacks the permission to modify user or system files and settings. A Protected Mode program is also blocked from writing to the Windows Registry or other processes.

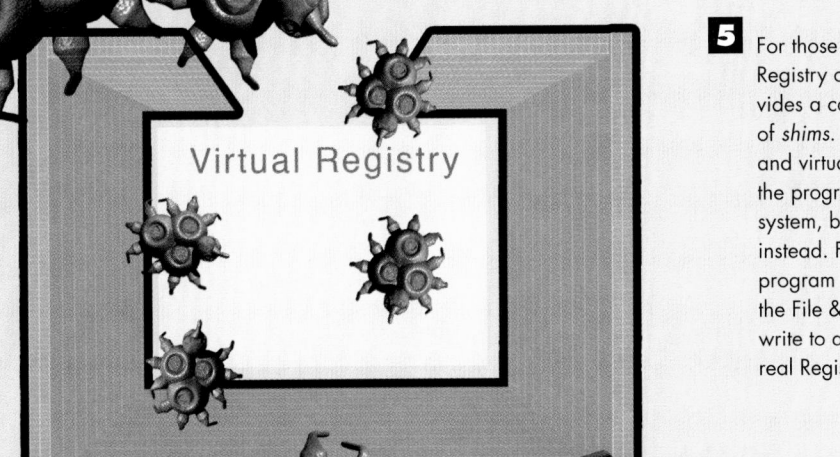

Virtual Registry

BLOCKED

5 For those processes that have to write to the Registry or run an add-on process, Windows provides a compatibility layer consisting of a series of *shims*. These shims intercept system API calls and virtualize the necessary system operations; the program thinks its writing to the Windows system, but it's actually writing to a fake version, instead. For example, when a Protected Mode program needs to write to the Windows Registry, the File & Registry Compat Shim lets the program write to a virtual Registry, without affecting the real Registry.

6 Communications from a Protected mode program to the operating system are mediated via a broker process. This process prohibits any scripted actions or automatic processes from acting without user input—thus preventing automatic downloads of malicious code.

How BitLocker Drive Encryption Protects Your Data

1 What do you do if your laptop PC gets stolen? How do you prevent a thief from using a specialized hacking tool to access all the important data stored on your PC—even those files you've password protected? To protect your data if your PC is stolen, Enterprise and Ultimate editions of Windows Vista feature BitLocker Drive Encryption. This is a technology that encrypts all the data on your PC's hard drive, so no one—not even a technically sophisticated thief—can view it.

2 BitLocker Drive Encryption works by encrypting all user and system files on the hard disk, including the swap and hibernation files. No one can decrypt these files without the proper decryption key, which is automatically generated by the BitLocker utility. By default, BitLocker uses 256-bit encryption, which requires a 96-character key to decrypt—long enough to be almost impossible to hack.

2g3ygr17ad3990572jkMBDS3629F34WWWp8172fajrwppatw771
tywwwg551772MMM-feyyskkt4719932j61ffaauuqo
Start decryption

3 There are three user-selected ways to decrypt a BitLocker encrypted disk. The first is *transparent operation mode*, which requires that your PC include a Trusted Platform Module (TPM) chip. In this mode, the TPM chip performs an integrity check of early boot components when the PC is powered on. If these system boot files appear to be unmolested, BitLocker instructs the TPM chip to release the decryption key, and the files are decrypted. If the boot files have been altered—or if the encrypted drive has been moved to another computer—then the decryption key is not released.

2g3ygr17ad3990572jkMBDS3629F34WWWp8172fajrwppatw771
tywwwg551772MMMahwyskkt4719932j61ffaauuqo
Start decryption

4 The second decryption mode, called the *user authentication mode*, requires the user to either enter a personal identification number (PIN) or insert a USB device that contains the required startup key. Once the PIN or startup key is authenticated, the decryption key is released by the TPM chip and the files are decrypted.

2g3ygr17ad3990572jkMBDS3629F34WWWp8172fajrwppatw771
tywwwg551772MMMahwyskkt4719932j61ffaauuqo
Start decryption

5 The final decryption mode does not require the presence of a TPM chip. With the so-called *USB key mode*, the user simply inserts a USB device that contains a startup key. Once the startup key is authenticated, the BitLocker drive is automatically decrypted. This mode is less secure than the transparent or user authentication modes.

CHAPTER 20

Routine Maintenance

WINDOWS Vista includes several utilities to help you keep your system running smoothly. Some of these utilities are unchanged from Windows XP; others are either new or dramatically improved.

What remains important is that you need to perform periodic maintenance on your system, to keep your system in optimal running condition. What Vista does is automate the running of many of these utilities so that you don't have to run them manually. For example, Disk Defragmenter now runs all the time, in the background, continuously defragmenting your hard disk.

What are the key system utilities in Windows Vista? Here's a quick list:

- **Disk Cleanup**, which identifies and deletes unused files from your hard disk, thus freeing up excess disk space
- **Disk Defragmenter**, which recombines fragmented files on your hard disk, thus making your system run faster
- **Windows Backup and Restore**, which lets you create backup copies of all your data files—or, with the CompletePC Backup option (available with selected versions of Vista), create a mirror image of your entire hard disk, including program and operating system files
- **Previous Versions**, a new "time machine" technology that lets you return to a previous version of any document—even those versions you forgot to save
- **System Restore**, which lets you return your entire system to a previous working condition, in the event of some sort of system problem
- **Windows Update**, which downloads regular updates to the Vista operating system, automatically as necessary

It's important to familiarize yourself with all these maintenance utilities—and to keep your system in tip-top operating condition.

How to Clean Up Your Hard Disk

1 The longer you use your PC, the more cluttered your hard disk becomes—filled with old documents, temporary files, even programs you don't use anymore. All these unnecessary files take up valuable hard disk space, and could even slow down your system.

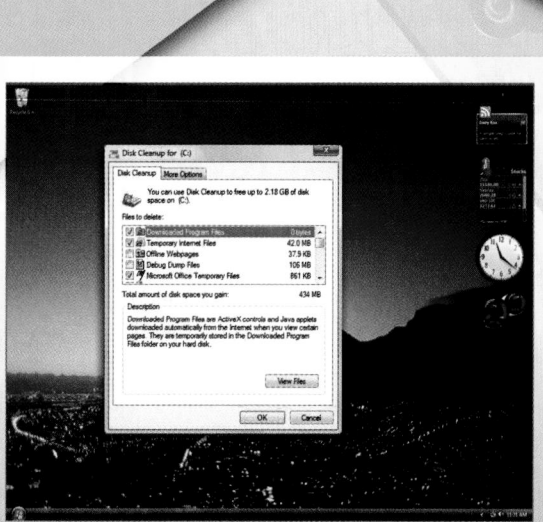

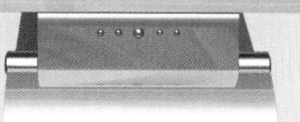

2 To help you clean up your hard disk, Windows Vista offers the Disk Cleanup utility. You use Disk Cleanup to find and delete any and all unused files.

Type of File to Clean Up	Folder Path
Downloaded program files	\Windows\Downloaded Program Files
Temporary Internet files	\users\username\Local Settings\Temporary Internet Files
Offline web pages	\Windows\Offline Web Pages
Recycle Bin	\Recycler
Temporary files	\users\username\Local Settings\Temp

3 Depending on which options you select, Disk Cleanup searches specific directories for different types of files.

4 All files stored in these target directories are then permanently deleted from the hard disk.

5 Since these files are not sent to the Recycle Bin, as deleted files normally are, that disk space is immediately freed up for future use.

How Disk Defragmentation Works

1 When a file is saved to your PC's hard disk, that file is divided into small chunks of data and each chunk is stored on a separate *sector* of your hard disk. Each sector holds exactly 512 bytes of data, so a large file could be stored in hundreds or thousands of separate sectors.

2 When a hard disk is fresh from the factory, all the sectors for a single file can be stored contiguously—that is, all in a row. This makes it easy for the read/write head of the hard disk to access the complete file.

3 As more files are stored to the hard disk, and as older files are erased, contiguous hard disk space might not be available when saving a new file. When this happens, the chunks of the file are stored in whatever sectors are available—even if those sectors are widely separated on the hard disk. When a file is fragmented in this fashion, it takes more time for the hard disk's read/write head to access each of the individual chunks and thus assemble the file for use.

4 You can improve the performance of your hard disk—that is, how long it takes to access a file—by *defragmenting* the disk. This is accomplished by the Disk Defragmenter utility. In Windows Vista, this utility works in the background to continuously defragment your hard disk.

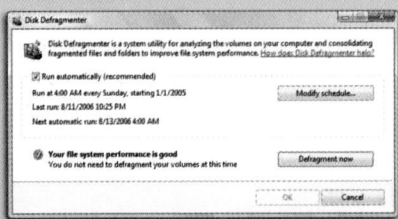

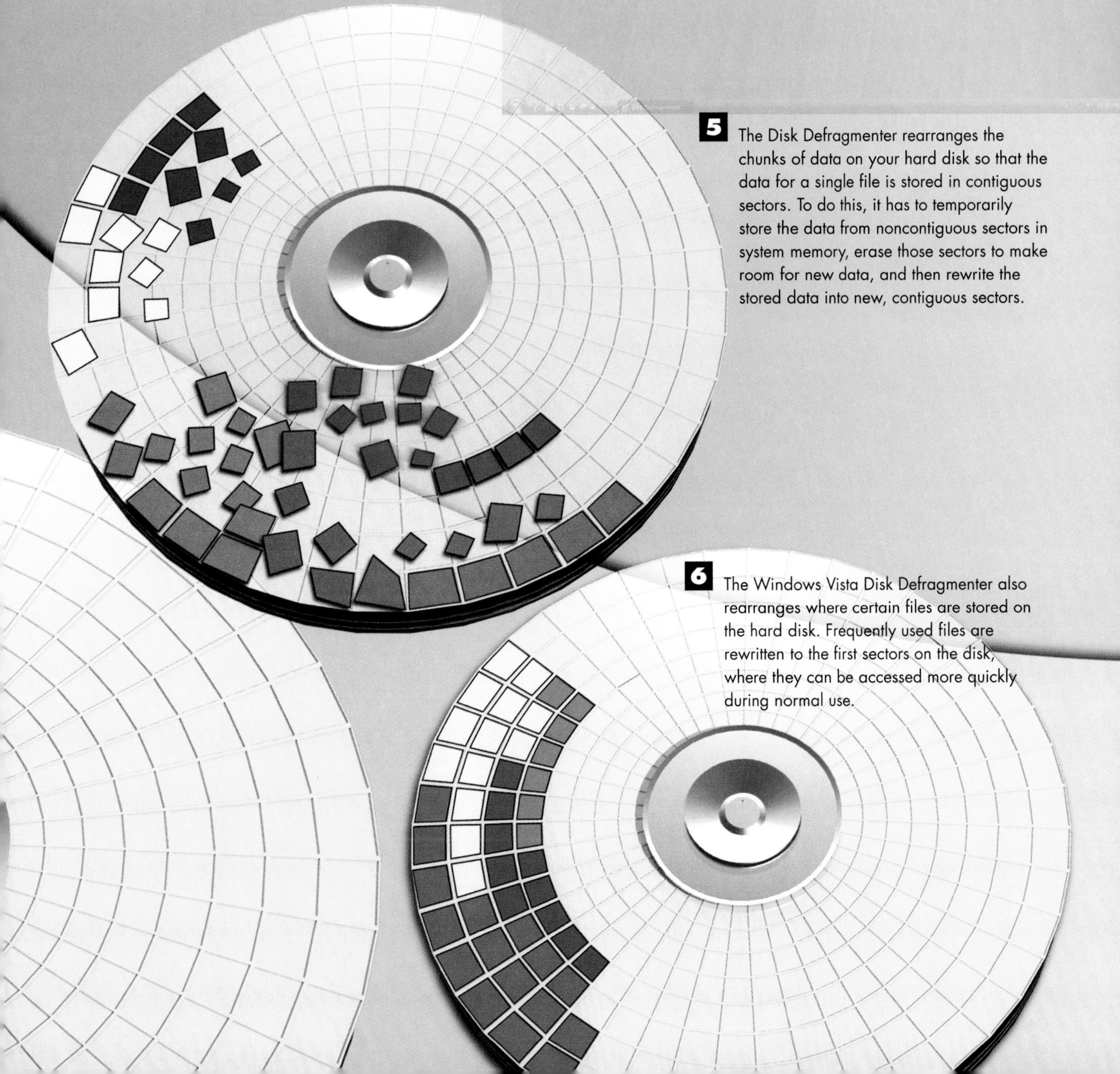

5 The Disk Defragmenter rearranges the chunks of data on your hard disk so that the data for a single file is stored in contiguous sectors. To do this, it has to temporarily store the data from noncontiguous sectors in system memory, erase those sectors to make room for new data, and then rewrite the stored data into new, contiguous sectors.

6 The Windows Vista Disk Defragmenter also rearranges where certain files are stored on the hard disk. Frequently used files are rewritten to the first sectors on the disk, where they can be accessed more quickly during normal use.

How to Back Up Your Data

1 For protection in case of hard disk or computer failure, it's a good idea to make a backup copy of all your important data files. You can back up your data to an external hard disk, a network drive, a tape backup drive, a CD-ROM or DVD, or to an Internet-based backup service.

2 If you have a computer failure, you can restore your data files from the backup copies.

3 In Windows Vista, the backup process is handled by the Windows Backup and Restore utility. Windows Backup and Restore lets you manually back up your data when you choose or schedule automatic backups—either weekly or daily.

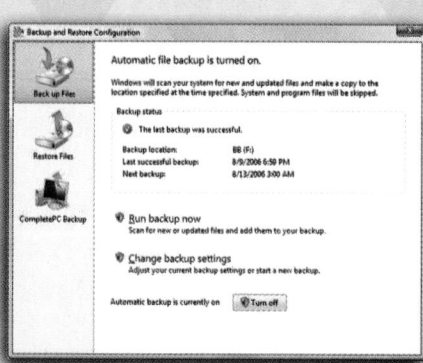

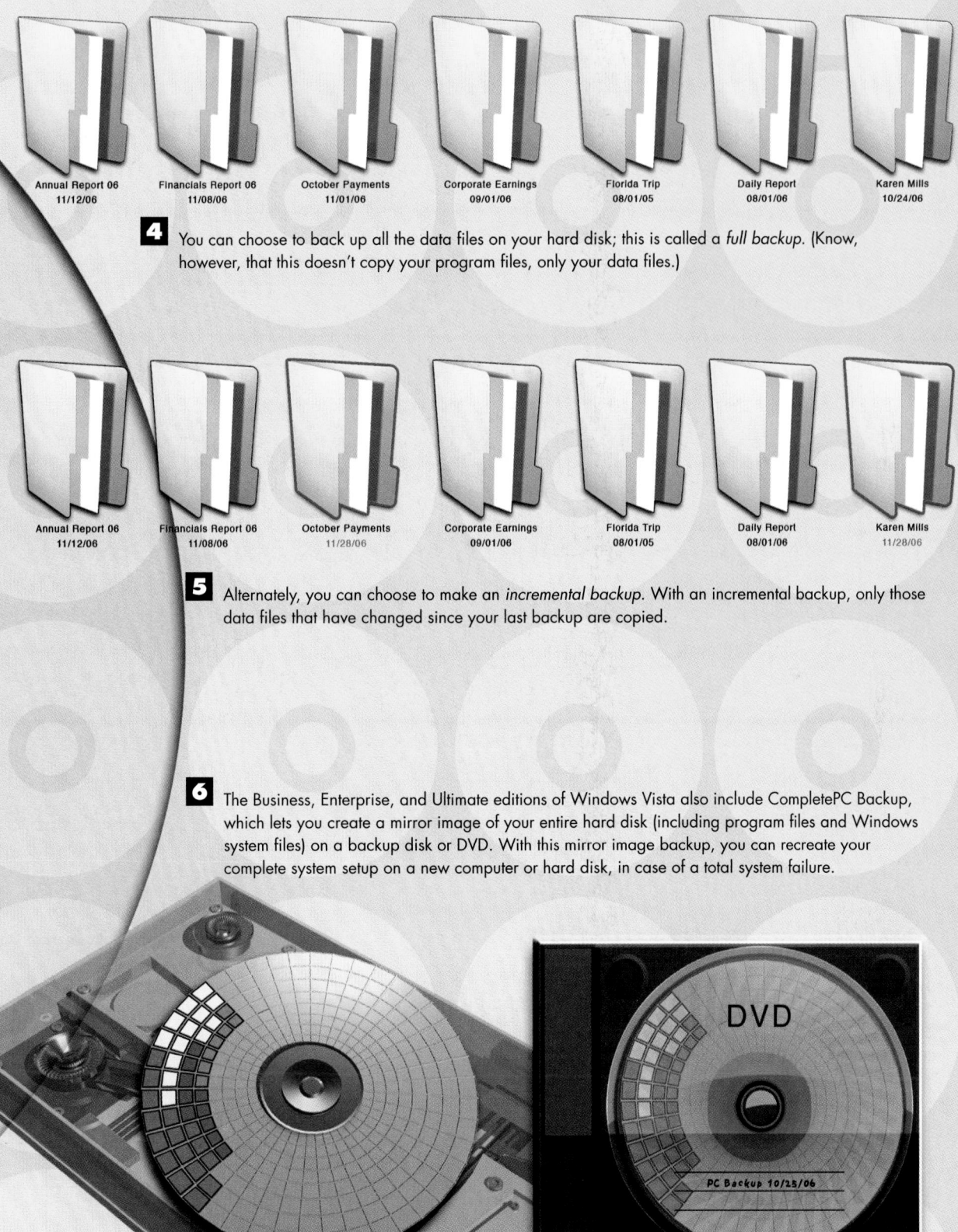

Annual Report 06   Financials Report 06   October Payments   Corporate Earnings   Florida Trip   Daily Report   Karen Mills
11/12/06   11/08/06   11/01/06   09/01/06   08/01/05   08/01/06   10/24/06

4 You can choose to back up all the data files on your hard disk; this is called a *full backup*. (Know, however, that this doesn't copy your program files, only your data files.)

Annual Report 06   Financials Report 06   October Payments   Corporate Earnings   Florida Trip   Daily Report   Karen Mills
11/12/06   11/08/06   11/28/06   09/01/06   08/01/05   08/01/06   11/28/06

5 Alternately, you can choose to make an *incremental backup*. With an incremental backup, only those data files that have changed since your last backup are copied.

6 The Business, Enterprise, and Ultimate editions of Windows Vista also include CompletePC Backup, which lets you create a mirror image of your entire hard disk (including program files and Windows system files) on a backup disk or DVD. With this mirror image backup, you can recreate your complete system setup on a new computer or hard disk, in case of a total system failure.

DVD

PC Backup 10/25/06

How Windows Lets You Return to a Previous Version of a Document

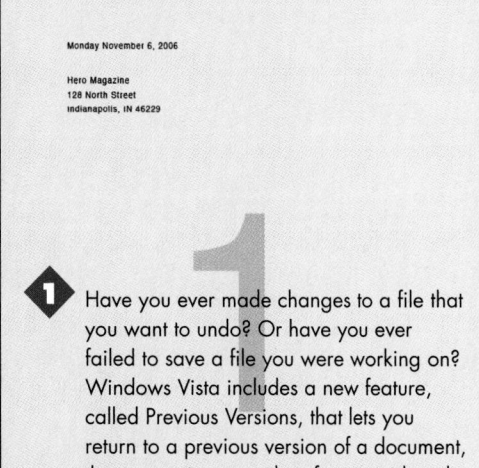

1 Have you ever made changes to a file that you want to undo? Or have you ever failed to save a file you were working on? Windows Vista includes a new feature, called Previous Versions, that lets you return to a previous version of a document, thus protecting your data from accidental change or loss.

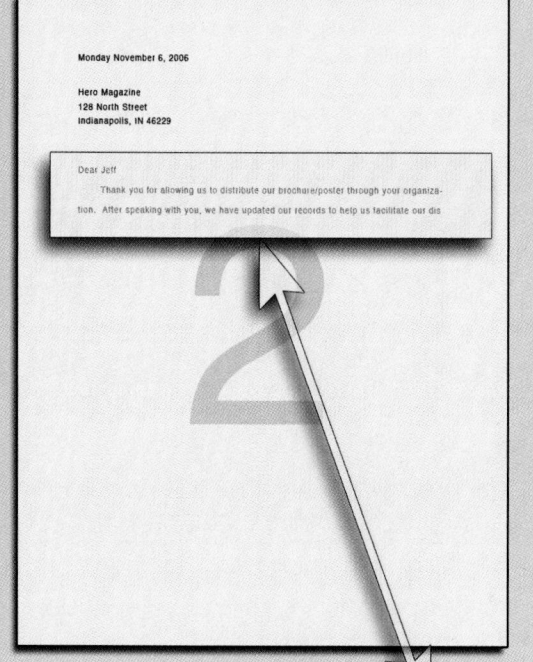

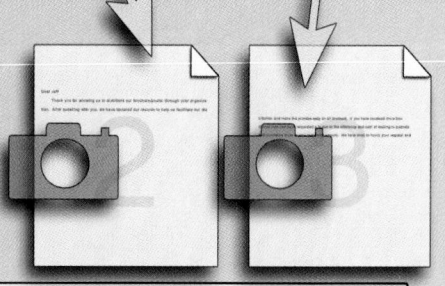

2 Previous Versions uses *volume shadow copy* technology to create a series of restore points for the files you're working on. Each restore point is a "snapshot" of the file as it exists at that point in time—even if you haven't saved the file to hard disk.

3 The restore point for a file doesn't take up as much disk space as the original file because it only captures that part of the file that has changed since the previous restore point. The original file can be constructed by adding the changed data to the previous version of the file.

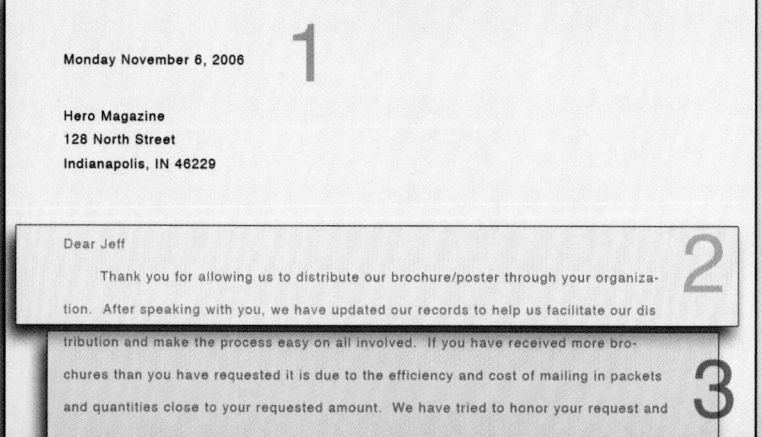

4 A set amount of disk space is used for storing these previous versions. As that disk space is filled, the oldest versions are automatically deleted to make room for newer versions. You can typically access about a month's worth of previous files on your hard disk.

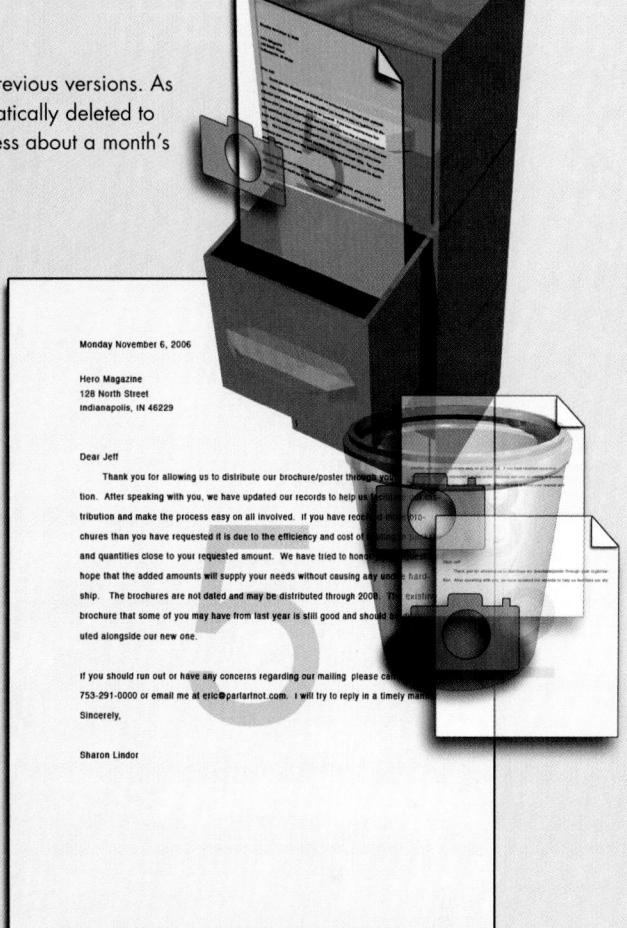

5 To access a previous version of a file, all you have to do is right-click the filename in Windows Explorer, select **Properties**, and then select the **Previous Versions** tab. From there, you can select which version of the file you want to open.

How System Restore Puts Your System Back in Working Condition

1 When you experience problems with your system, Windows lets you restore it to a prior condition, using the System Restore utility. This is a great way to recover from problems caused by the installation of new hardware or software.

2 System Restore works by creating snapshots of key system files, called *restore points*, before major changes are made to your system. These "trigger points" include the installation of new hardware and software, device driver updates, and the installation of automatic Windows updates. Other restore points are automatically created once every 24 hours, and can also be created manually, at the user's command.

3 Each restore point includes copies of the Windows Registry, user profiles, device drivers, and selected dynamic system files. Restore points are stored in a special cache on your system's hard disk.

System Restore Isn't a Backup

System Restore only restores Windows system files and Registry entries. It does not back up or restore documents and other data files—which is why you still need to back up your data files on a regular basis.

4 To restore your system to a prior condition, you use the System Restore utility to pick a specific restore point.

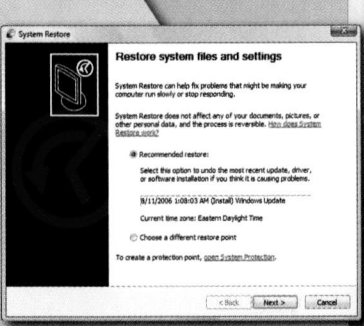

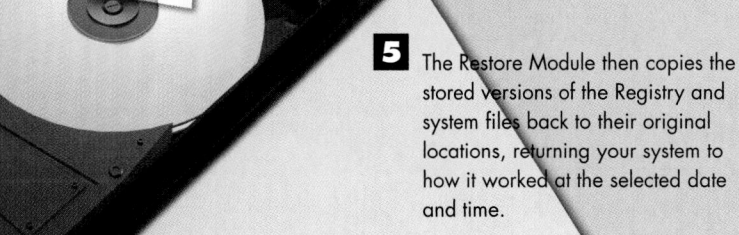

5 The Restore Module then copies the stored versions of the Registry and system files back to their original locations, returning your system to how it worked at the selected date and time.

How Windows Update Keeps Your System Up-to-Date

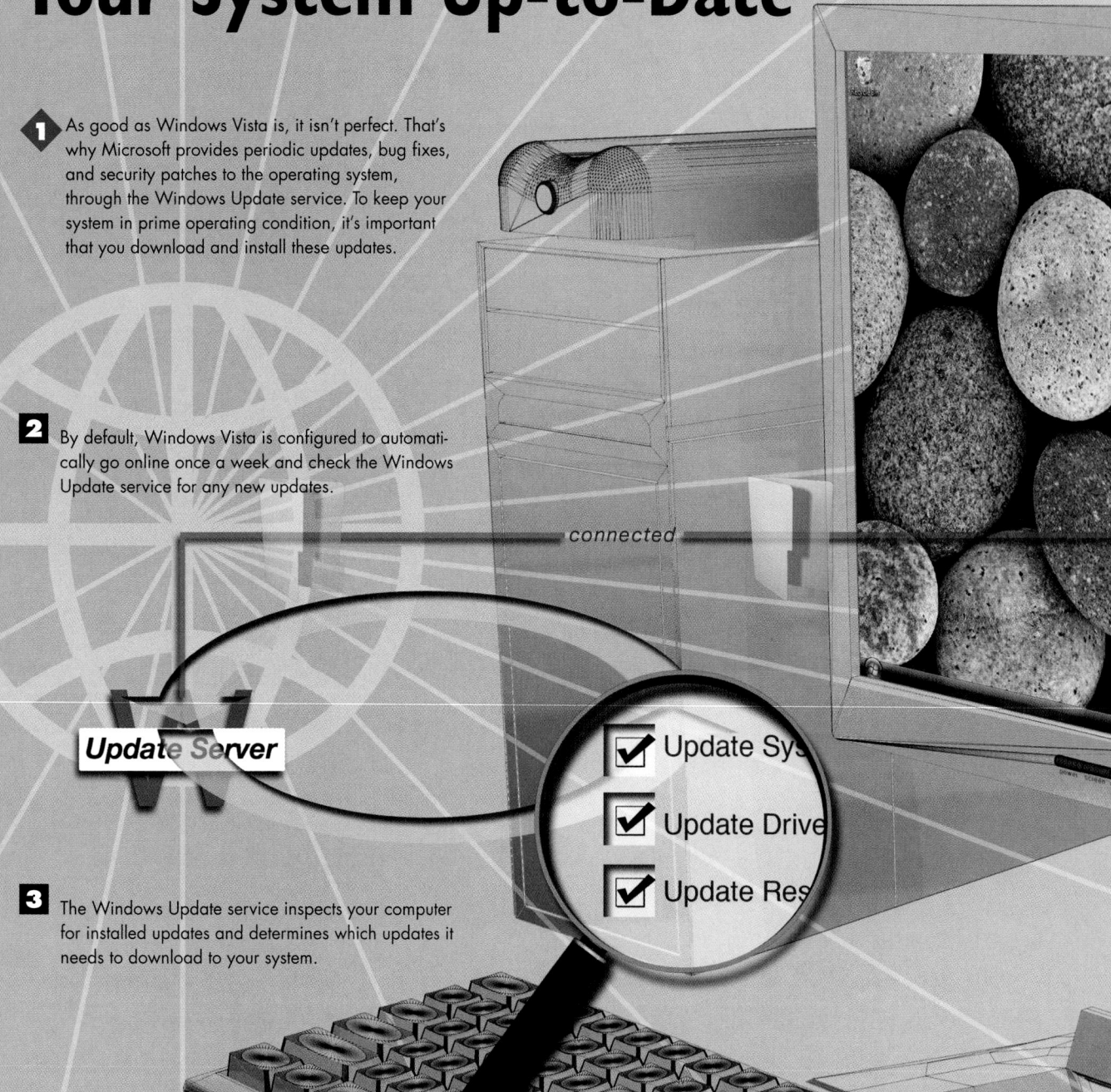

1 As good as Windows Vista is, it isn't perfect. That's why Microsoft provides periodic updates, bug fixes, and security patches to the operating system, through the Windows Update service. To keep your system in prime operating condition, it's important that you download and install these updates.

2 By default, Windows Vista is configured to automatically go online once a week and check the Windows Update service for any new updates.

connected

Update Server

Update Sys

Update Drive

Update Res

3 The Windows Update service inspects your computer for installed updates and determines which updates it needs to download to your system.

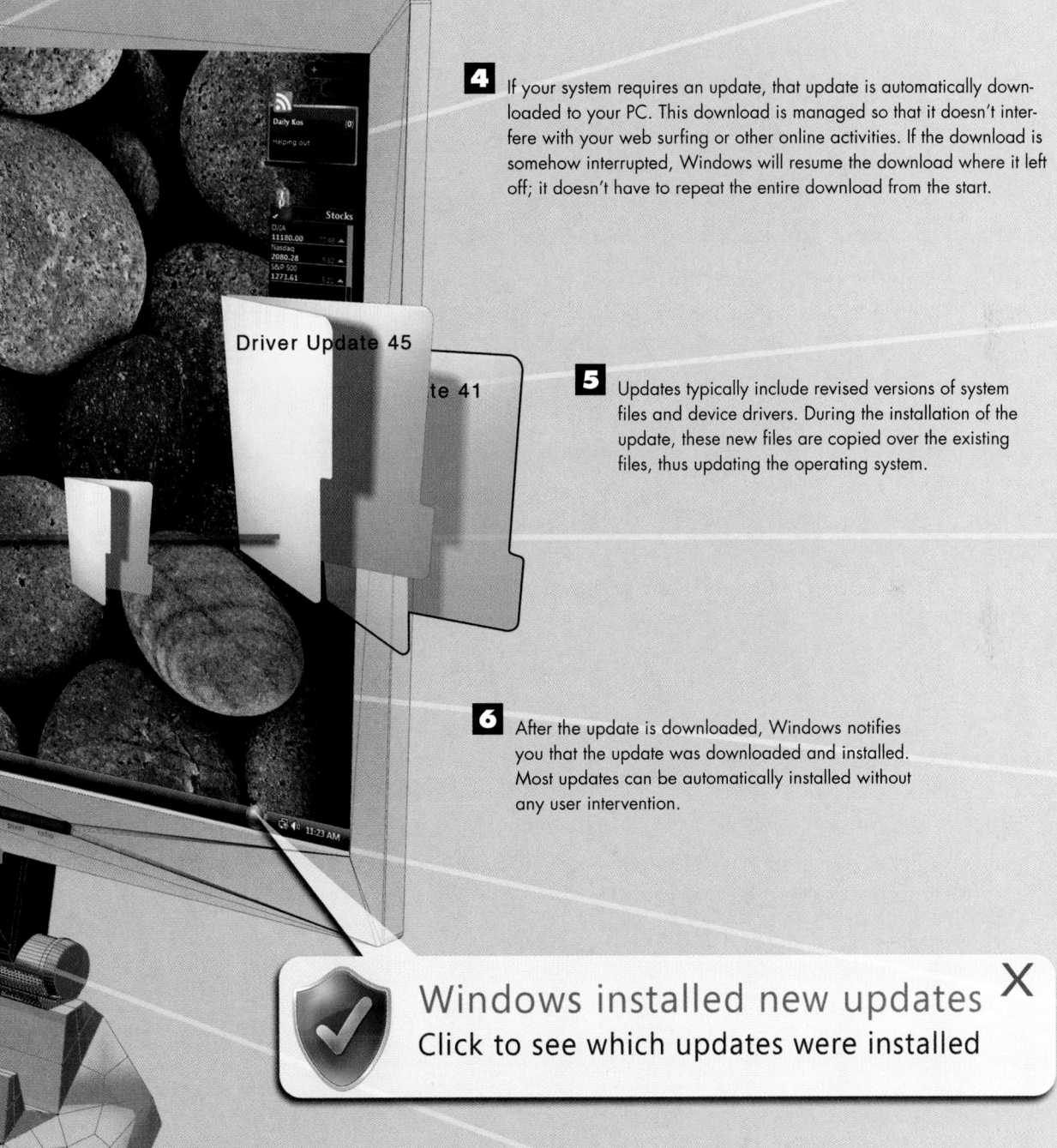

4 If your system requires an update, that update is automatically downloaded to your PC. This download is managed so that it doesn't interfere with your web surfing or other online activities. If the download is somehow interrupted, Windows will resume the download where it left off; it doesn't have to repeat the entire download from the start.

5 Updates typically include revised versions of system files and device drivers. During the installation of the update, these new files are copied over the existing files, thus updating the operating system.

6 After the update is downloaded, Windows notifies you that the update was downloaded and installed. Most updates can be automatically installed without any user intervention.

Driver Update 45

te 41

Windows installed new updates X
Click to see which updates were installed

Glossary

.WDP   Stands for Windows Media Photo; Microsoft's new digital image format.

.XPS   Stands for XML Paper Specification; Microsoft's new portable document format.

.ZIP   The file format for compressed files.

480i   The standard definition format used for traditional analog television broadcasts; it transmits 480 horizontal scan lines with interlaced scanning.

480p   A higher-quality variation on the standard analog broadcast format, transmitting 480 horizontal scan lines with progressive scanning.

720p   One of the two main HDTV formats in use today; it transmits 720 horizontal scan lines with progressive scanning.

1080i   One of the two main HDTV formats in use today; it transmits 1,080 horizontal scan lines with interlaced scanning.

1080p   The highest-resolution HDTV format, used in the next-generation Blu-ray and HD DVD formats; it transmits 1,080 horizontal scan lines with progressive scanning.

A

ADC   See *analog-to-digital converter*.

Aero   The new glass-like interface included with most versions of Windows Vista. Aero includes a three-dimensional look, translucent windows, and sophisticated window animations.

analog-to-digital converter (ADC)   A device that samples analog audio or video at designated intervals and creates a corresponding stream of digital bits.

API   See *Application Programming Interface*

application   A software program.

Application Programming Interface (API)   A set of operating system routines used by an application to request and perform lower-level services.

B

backup   The act of copying or saving data to a different location for safekeeping.

basic input/output system (BIOS)   The built-in software that configures essential devices on a computer system and loads the operating system.

BCD   See *Boot Configuration Data*

BIOS   See *basic input/output system*

bit rate   The rate at which digital data is transmitted or processed, defined in bits per second (bps).

boot   The process of turning on your computer system.

Boot Configuration Data (BCD)   A file that functions as a "data store" for all files and processes used in the PC's boot sequence.

boot sector   The section of a hard disk that stores information about the layout of the disk and the file system structures, and also contains the boot code that launches the Windows operating system on startup.

bootstrap loader   See *Windows Boot Manager*

burn   The act of copying files to a CD or DVD.

C

CableCARD   A removable flash memory card that enables the viewing of digital cable or satellite television on a cable-ready television set, without the need for a set-top decoder box.

central processing unit (CPU)   The group of circuits that directs the entire computer system by (1) interpreting and executing program instruction and (2) coordinating the interaction of input, output, and storage devices.

ClearType   A display technology used to improve the appearance of onscreen text, especially on LCD monitors.

cluster   The smallest amount of hard disk space that can be allocated to a file; a group of sectors on a hard disk.

compressed folder   A folder that holds one or more files compressed in the .ZIP format.

computer   A programmable device that can store, retrieve, and process data.

Control Panel   The Windows utility that centralizes all of the operating system's configuration settings.

CPU   See *central processing unit*

D

DAC   See *digital-to-analog converter*

desktop   The entire screen area on which you display all your computer work. The Windows Vista desktop can contain icons, the taskbar, the Sidebar, and individual application windows.

Desktop Windows Manager (DWM)   The graphics utility in Windows Vista that manages desktop composition.

device   A computer file that represents some object—physical or nonphysical—installed on your system.

Device Manager   The Windows utility that displays key data about all the devices connected to your system—both internally and externally.

digital   A means of transmitting or storing data using "on" and "off" bits (expressed as 1 or 0).

digital rights management (DRM)   Technology used to protect digital products from copyright infringement, typically using some form of content encryption.

digital-to-analog converter (DAC)   A device that re-creates an analog audio or video signal from a stream of digital bits.

Direct3D   A DirectX API used to create three-dimensional vector graphics.

DirectAnimation   A DirectX API used for the display of animation.

DirectDraw   A DirectX API used to create two-dimensional raster graphics.

DirectInput   A DirectX API used to input data from a keyboard, mouse, or game controller.

DirectMusic   A DirectX API used for the playback of music soundtracks.

DirectPlay   A DirectX API used for network gaming.

DirectSetup   A DirectX API used for the installation of other DirectX components.

DirectSound   A DirectX API used for the playback and recording of waveform sound.

DirectX   A collection of APIs used to create and manage high-performance multimedia applications.

DirectX Transform   A DirectX API used to manage interactivity.

disk   A device that stores data in magnetic or optical format.

Disk Cleanup   A Windows utility that identifies and deletes unused files from a hard drive.

Disk Defragmenter   A Windows utility that defragments files on a hard drive.

disk drive   A mechanism for retrieving information stored on a magnetic disk. The drive rotates the disk at high speed and reads the data with a magnetic head similar to those used in tape recorders.

Disk Operating System (DOS)   A character-based predecessor to the Windows operating system, released by Microsoft in 1981.

DLL   See *Dynamic Link Library*

DOS   See *Disk Operating System*

download   A way to transfer files, graphics, or other information from the Internet to your computer.

driver   A support file that tells a program how to interact with a specific hardware device, such as a hard disk controller or video display card.

Driver Store   In Windows Vista, a repository of all installed driver packages for a particular installation of Windows.

DRM   See *digital rights management*

DWM   See *Desktop Windows Manager*

Dynamic Link Library (DLL)   A packet of universal program code that is shared between multiple Windows programs.

E

email   Electronic mail; a means of corresponding with other computer users over the Internet through digital messages.

encryption   A method of encoding files so that only the recipient can read the information.

Ethernet   The most common computer networking protocol; Ethernet is used to network, or hook together, computers so that they can share information.

Extensible Application Markup Language (XAML)   The markup language used to define user interfaces in Windows Vista, via the Windows Presentation Foundation.

F

Fast Boot and Resume   A Windows Vista technology that speeds up the boot process by performing nonessential tasks after the Windows system is loaded.

FAT   See *file allocation table*

FAT 32   The disk file system used by versions of Windows prior to Windows NT and Windows XP.

favorite   A bookmarked site in Internet Explorer.

file   Any group of data treated as a single entity by the computer, such as a word processor document, a program, or a database.

file allocation table   A file system table used by an operating system to track where data is stored on a disk.

file system   The data structure used for organizing files and directories on a hard disk.

firewall   Computer hardware or software with special security features to safeguard a computer connected to a network or to the Internet.

FireWire   A high-speed bus used to connect digital devices, such as digital cameras and video cameras, to a computer system. Also known as iLink and IEEE-1394.

folder   A way to group files on a disk; each folder can contain multiple files or other folders (called *subfolders*).

Function Dispatch Table   A database that tells Windows about each driver installed on the system.

G

gadget   A dedicated mini-application developed for the Windows Vista Sidebar.

GB   See *gigabyte*

gigabyte (GB)   One billion bytes.

GPU   See *graphics processing unit*

graphical user interface (GUI)   A system that uses graphical symbols called icons to represent available functions; these icons are generally manipulated by a mouse and a keyboard. The Windows operating system utilizes a graphical user interface.

graphics   Pictures, photographs, and clip art.

graphics processing unit (GPU)   A special processor dedicated to creating onscreen graphics.

GUI   See *graphical user interface*

H

hard disk   A sealed cartridge containing a magnetic storage disk(s) that holds much more memory than removable disks—up to 500GB or more.

hardware   The physical equipment, as opposed to the programs and procedures, used in computing.

HDTV   See *high-definition television*

high-definition television (HDTV)   A subset of the new digital TV standard that reproduces pictures in either 780p or 1080i resolution, with a 16:9 aspect ratio and Dolby Digital 5.1 surround sound.

hive   A major section of the Windows Registry. There are five hives in the Registry, each stored in its own system file.

hot spot   A public WiFi access point.

HotStart   A technology that enables PC manufacturers to include a special button that launches Windows Media Player for music or movie playback, even if the computer is in sleep mode or powered completely off.

hub   Hardware used to network computers together, usually over an Ethernet connection.

I

icon   A graphic symbol on the display screen that represents a file, peripheral, or some other object or function.

Instant Search   The system search functionality built into Windows Vista.

Internet   The global network of networks that connects millions of computers and other devices around the world.

Internet Explorer   Microsoft's web browser application, used to access web pages on the Internet. The version included with Windows Vista is Internet Explorer 7.

Internet Protocol version 6 (IPv6)   The latest version of the technology that manages a computer's connection to the Internet. The previous version was Internet Protocol version 4 (IPv4).

Internet service provider (ISP)   A company that provides end-user access to the Internet via its central computers and local access lines.

interrupt   A temporary break in a CPU's execution of program instructions, to enable it to handle a request from a peripheral.

IPv6   See *Internet Protocol version 6*

ISP   See *Internet service provider*

K

kilobyte (KB)   A unit of measure for data storage or transmission equivalent to 1,024 bytes; often rounded to 1,000.

L

LAN   See *local area network*

Linux   A competitor to the Windows operating system, based on the older Unix operating system. Not typically used on consumer PCs.

local area network (LAN)   A system that enables users to connect PCs to one another or to minicomputers or mainframes.

lossless compression   A means of reducing file size without removing any essential data from the original file.

lossy compression   A means of reducing file size by removing some data from the original file.

M

Mac OS   The operating system used on Apple Macintosh computers.

malware   Any type of malicious software—includes spyware, viruses, and the like.

Master Boot Record (MBR)   A small program that is executed when a computer powers on; the MBR is located in the first sector of the hard disk and initiates the boot process.

Master File Table (MFT)   A database that contains all the information necessary to locate and retrieve files from a hard disk.

MB   See *megabyte*

MBR   See *Master Boot Record*

Media Center Extender   A device that connects to a Media Center PC over a network to play back digital media.

Media Center PC   A personal computer designed for home theater use, typically running Windows Vista's Media Center interface.

megabyte (MB)   One million bytes.

memory   Temporary electronic storage for data and instructions, via electronic impulses on a chip.

metadata   Data that is used to describe other data. In Windows Vista, metadata is used to describe the contents of various types of files.

MFT   See *Master File Table*

microcomputer   A computer based on a microprocessor chip. Also known as a *personal computer*.

microprocessor   A complete central processing unit assembled on a single silicon chip.

Microsoft Phishing Filter   The anti-phishing technology built into Windows Vista, utilized in both Internet Explorer 7 and Windows Mail.

modem   Short for modulator/demodulator, a device that connects to a computer and transmits and receives data from the Internet.

motherboard   The largest printed circuit board in a computer, housing the CPU chip and controlling circuitry.

multitasking   The ability to run multiple processes at virtually the same time.

N

NAP   See *Network Access Protection*

network   An interconnected group of computers.

Network Access Protection (NAP)   Technology in Windows Vista that monitors all the computers connected to a network, looking for those that are most susceptible to viruses and other malware.

NMI   See *non-maskable interrupt*

non-maskable interrupt (NMI)   A special type of interrupt that cannot be ignored by the processor.

NT File System (NTFS)   The disk file system used by Microsoft operating systems from Windows NT to Windows Vista.

NTFS   See *NT File System*

O

open source software   Free software, developed and distributed in the public domain.

operating system (OS)   A sequence of programming codes that instructs a computer about its various parts and peripherals and how to operate them. Operating systems, such as Windows Vista, deal only with the workings of the hardware and are separate from software programs.

OS   See *operating system*

OS/2   A graphical operating system designed for use on IBM's PS/2 line of personal computers. No longer in use.

Outlook Express   The email client included with previous versions of Windows.

P

Parental Controls   A set of user controls in Windows Vista that lets parents monitor and control their children's online activities.

path   The collection of folders and subfolders (listed in order of hierarchy) that hold a particular file.

PCB   See *process control block*

peripheral   A device connected to the computer that provides communication or auxiliary functions.

phishing   The act of tricking someone into giving up confidential information, typically by the use of fraudulent email messages or websites.

pixel   The individual picture elements that combine to create a video image.

pixel shader   A function on a graphics card that calculates visual effects on a per-pixel basis.

playlist   A list of individual songs, assembled from any album or artist.

pop-up   A small browser window, typically without menus or other navigational elements, that opens seemingly of its own accord when you visit or leave another website.

Pop-up Blocker   The technology in Internet Explorer that blocks the automatic display of pop-up windows.

port   An interface on a computer to which you can connect a device, either internally or externally.

POST   See *power-on self test*

power-on self test (POST)   The computer's pre-boot sequence.

printer   The piece of computer hardware that creates hard copy printouts of documents.

Previous Versions   A Windows Vista technology that restores a previous version of a document, even versions that were not formally saved.

process control block (PCB)   A data structure in the Windows kernel that tracks the state of a given process.

Protected Mode   An Internet Explorer operating mode that keeps applications separate from each other, for security purposes.

R

RAM   See *random access memory*

random access memory (RAM)   A temporary storage space in which data can be held on a chip rather than being stored on disk or tape. The contents of RAM can be accessed or altered at any time during a session but will be lost when the computer is turned off.

raster graphics   A type of graphics file that stores images as a collection of pixels. Also known as bitmapped graphics.

read-only memory (ROM)   A type of chip memory, the contents of which have been permanently recorded in a computer by the manufacturer and cannot be altered by the user.

Real Simple Syndication (RSS)   Technology used to syndicate, or distribute, content from blogs, news sites, and other websites with constantly updated content.

REGEDIT   See *Registry Editor*

Registry Editor   The utility used to edit settings in the Windows Registry. Also known as REGEDIT.

resolution   The degree of clarity an image displays, typically expressed by the number of horizontal and vertical pixels or the number of dots per inch (dpi).

restore point   A snapshot of system settings, as stored by the System Restore utility.

rip   The act of copying music from a CD to a computer's hard disk.

ROM   See *read-only memory*

root   The main directory or folder on a disk.

router   A piece of hardware or software that handles the connection between two or more networks.

RSS   See *Real Simple Syndication*

S

Safe mode   A special mode of operation that loads Windows in a minimal configuration, with a low-resolution display and without any unnecessary device drivers or software.

server   The central computer in a network, providing a service or data access to client computers on the network.

Service Set Identifier (SSID)   The technical name of a wireless network.

Sleep mode   A special Windows Vista hibernation mode that halts all running processes without turning off the PC.

software   The programs and procedures, as opposed to the physical equipment, used in computing.

spyware   Software used to surreptitiously monitor computer use (that is, spy on other users).

SSID   See *Service Set Identifier*

Start menu   The main menu in the Windows operating system, accessible from the Start button at the lower left corner of the screen. The Start menu is where all programs and utilities are accessed, as well as where the system is shut down or put to sleep.

SuperFetch   A Windows Vista technology that automatically preloads frequently used applications into system memory.

System Configuration Utility   A utility used to manage the applications and processes that load when Windows launches. Also known as MSCONFIG.

System Information   The Windows utility that displays key information about all aspects of your computer system.

System Restore   A Windows utility that restores an entire system to a previous working condition, in the event of some sort of system problem.

system unit   The part of your computer system that looks like a big beige or black box. The system unit typically contains the microprocessor, system memory, hard disk drive, floppy disk drives, and various cards.

T

TCP/IP   See *Transmission Control Protocol/Internet Protocol*

theme   A combination of desktop wallpaper, window colors, screensaver, and similar desktop features.

TPM   See *Trusted Platform Module*

Transmission Control Protocol/Internet Protocol (TCP/IP)   The core technology behind both networking and internetworking connections.

Trusted Platform Module (TPM)   A type of microcontroller that contains secured information. In Windows Vista, used to implement BitLocker Drive Encryption.

U

UAC   See *User Account Control*

uniform resource locator (URL)   The address that identifies a web page to a browser. Also known as a *web address*.

universal serial bus (USB)   An external bus standard that supports data transfer rates of 12Mbps and that can connect up to 127 peripheral devices, such as keyboards, modems, and mice.

UNIX   A competing operating system to Microsoft Windows, developed in the 1960s and 1970s by AT&T. Not typically used on consumer PCs.

upgrade   To add a new or improved peripheral or part to your system hardware. Also to install a newer version of an existing piece of software.

upload   The act of copying a file from a personal computer to a website or Internet server. The opposite of *download*.

URL   See *uniform resource locator*

USB   See *universal serial bus*

User Account Control (UAC)   A means of improving security in Windows Vista. Operates by not assigning administration privileges to users and programs.

V

vector graphics   A type of graphics file that uses mathematical formulas to define scalable lines, curves, and other shapes.

virtual folder   An ad hoc folder that doesn't contain any physical files per se, but rather contains pointers to actual files that are stored in other locations.

virus   A computer program segment or string of code that can attach itself to another program or file, reproduce itself, and spread from one computer to another. Viruses can destroy or change data and in other ways sabotage computer systems.

W

WBM   *See Windows Boot Manager*

WDDM   *See Windows Display Driver Model*

web page   An HTML file, containing text, graphics, and/or mini-applications, viewed with a web browser.

website   An organized, linked collection of web pages stored on an Internet server and read using a web browser. The opening page of a site is called a *home page*.

WEP   See *Wireless Equivalent Privacy*

Wi-Fi   The radio frequency (RF)-based technology used for home and small business wireless networks, and for most public wireless Internet connections. It operates at either 11Mbps (802.11b) or 54Mbps (802.11g). Short for "wireless fidelity."

Wi-Fi Protected Access (WPA)   A form of wireless security that uses a constantly changing network key.

Windows   The generic name for all versions of Microsoft's graphical operating system.

Windows 1.0   The very first version of the Microsoft Windows operating system, released in 1985.

Windows 2.0   A prior version of Microsoft Windows, released in 1987.

Windows 2000   An older version of Microsoft Windows, designed for the corporate environment, released in 2000.

Windows 3.0   The first commercially successful version of the Microsoft Windows operating system, released in 1990.

Windows 95   A prior version of the Microsoft Windows consumer operating system, released in 1995.

Windows 98   A prior version of the Microsoft Windows consumer operating system, released in 1998.

Windows Backup and Restore   The data backup utility included with Windows Vista.

Windows BitLocker Drive Encryption   A means of encrypting the data on a hard disk drive to protect the data from theft.

Windows Boot Manager (WBM)   The first system file loaded during a computer's boot process; it tells your system to launch other Windows pre-boot applications.

Windows Calendar   The calendaring/scheduling application included with Windows Vista.

Windows DVD Maker   The DVD authoring utility included with Windows Vista.

Windows Defender   The anti-spyware utility included with Windows Vista.

Windows Display Driver Model (WDDM)   The new graphics driver model for video cards running under Windows Vista.

Windows Explorer   The interface used in Windows Vista to browse files and folders on a computer system.

Windows Firewall   The firewall utility included with Windows Vista.

Windows Flip   The onscreen task switcher in Windows Vista. You activate Windows Flip by pressing Alt+Tab.

Windows Flip 3D   An expansion of Vista's task switching, which displays a three-dimensional stack of all open windows. You activate Flip3D by pressing Start+Tab.

Windows for Workgroups   The first multiuser version of the Microsoft Windows operating system, based on Windows 3.0, released in 1992.

Windows Kernel   The central part of the Windows operating system, responsible for managing the system's resources and the communication between hardware and software components.

Windows Mail   The email client included with Windows Vista; based on the older Outlook Express program.

Windows Me   A prior version of the Microsoft Windows consumer operating system, released in 2000.

Windows Media Center   A "ten-foot interface" that runs on top of Windows Vista and lets you use your PC to manage digital media in a living-room home entertainment system.

Windows Media Photo   Also known as WMPhoto, Microsoft's new digital image file format. The extension for WMPhoto files is .WDP.

Windows Media Player   Microsoft's digital music and movie player. The version included with Windows Vista is Windows Media Player 11.

Windows Meeting Space   The group collaboration utility included with Windows Vista.

Windows Mobility Center   A utility in Windows Vista that centralizes many of the settings used in mobile computing. Found only on notebook PCs.

Windows Movie Maker   The digital movie editing application included with Windows Vista.

Windows Movie Maker HD   A version of Windows Movie Maker that can edit high-definition video files.

Windows NT   The first corporate version of the Microsoft Windows operating system, released in 1993.

Windows Photo Gallery   The photo management and editing application included with Windows Vista.

Windows Presentation Foundation (WPF)   The new three-dimensional graphical subsystem included in Windows Vista.

Windows ReadyBoost   A Windows Vista technology that lets you improve system performance by using a removable flash memory device as temporary memory.

Windows Registry   A database that contains configuration data about the hardware and environment of your PC, the Windows operating system, and many Windows applications.

Windows Security Center   The panel in Windows Vista that centralizes all security-related utilities.

Windows Service Hardening   A Windows Vista technology that prevents critical Windows services from being misused in the file system, in the Windows registry, or over a network.

Windows Sidebar   A pane on the side of the desktop that displays gadget mini-applications.

Windows SideShow   A small exterior display on notebook computers and other portable devices that can control specific Windows operations.

Windows Update   A utility that automatically downloads regular updates to the Windows Vista operating system as necessary.

Windows Vista   The latest version of the Microsoft Window operating system, released in 2007.

Windows Vista Business   The version of Windows Vista designed for small business use.

Windows Vista Enterprise   The version of Windows Vista designed for use in large organizations.

Windows Vista Home Basic   The most basic version of Windows Vista, designed for home use.

Windows Vista Home Premium   A more full-featured version of Windows Vista, designed for home use.

Windows Vista Ultimate   A fully featured version of Windows Vista, designed for homes, small businesses, and power users.

Windows XP   The previous version of the Microsoft Windows operating system, released in 2001.

Wireless Equivalent Privacy (WEP)   A type of wireless security that uses either a 40-character (WEP-64 bit) or 104-character (WEP-128 bit) network key.

wireless security   Technology used to secure a wireless network from intrusion. The four primary wireless security protocols in use today are WEP-64, WEP-128, WPA, and WPA2.

WPA   See *Wi-Fi Protected Access*

X

XAML   See *Extensible Application Markup Language*

Xbox 360   Microsoft's popular videogame system.

Index

How can we make this index more useful? Email us at indexes@quepublishing.com

J–L

JPEG format, 167

kernel, 52
kernel space, 52

laptop computers. *See* notebook computers
Lempel, Abraham, 88
Linux, history of, 11
live thumbnails, 19
lossless compression, 89, 153, 168
lossy compression, 153, 168
LZW algorithm, 88-89

M

Mac OS, history of, 11
maintenance. *See* system utilities
malware, 231
masking interrupts, 57
Master File Table (MFT), 58
Media Center. *See* Windows Media Center
Media Center Extenders, 135, 148-149
memory, multitasking, 98-99
memory management, 28, 52-53, 60-61
memory requirements, 16
Message Integrity Code (MIC), wireless
    security, 215
metadata, 84, 154
MFT (Master File Table), 58
MIC (Message Integrity Code), wireless
    security, 215
microprocessors. *See* processor management
Microsoft Phishing Filter, 22, 191, 232-233
monitoring system performance, 68-69
movies. *See* video
moving files, 82
multitasking, 50, 98-99
music
    Windows Media Center, 138-139
    Windows Media Player, 151
        digital audio overview, 152-153
        HotStart, 164-165
        playing digital music, 156-157
        playlists, 158-159
        ripping CDs, 162-163
        storing digital music, 154-155
        synchronizing with portable music players,
            160-161
Music Explorer, 69

My Computer. *See* Computer Explorer
My Documents, Documents Explorer, 69
My Music, Music Explorer, 69
My Pictures, Pictures Explorer, 69

N

NAP (Network Access Protection), 205,
    210-211
navigating with Windows Explorers, 80-81
Navigation Pane (Windows Explorers), 80
Network Access Protection (NAP), 205,
    210-211
Network Interface Layer (TCP/IP), 188
network keys, wireless security, 214
networking, 21, 205-207
    file sharing, 216-217
    NAP (Network Access Protection), 210-211
    TCP/IP, 187-189, 205
    Wi-Fi hotspots, connecting to, 212-213
    Windows Meeting Space, 218-219
    wireless networks
        security, 214-215
        setting up, 208-209
Next Generation TCP/IP stack, 187, 205
NMIs (non-maskable interrupts), 57
nonce-value, wireless security, 215
notebook computers
    BitLocker Drive Encryption, 225, 236-237
    Windows SideShow, 128-129
NTFS, 58-59, 77

O

open source software, 11
OpenSearch, 198
operating systems
    list of, 10-11
    purpose of, 27
OS/2, history of, 10
Outlook Express. *See* Windows Mail

P

page tables, 53
Pairwise Master Key (PMK), wireless
    security, 215
Pairwise Transient Key (PTK), wireless
    security, 215
Parental Controls, 22, 74-75
payloads (data packets), 189

THIS BOOK IS SAFARI ENABLED

INCLUDES FREE 45-DAY ACCESS TO THE ONLINE EDITION

The Safari® Enabled icon on the cover of your favorite technology book means the book is available through Safari Bookshelf. When you buy this book, you get free access to the online edition for 45 days.

Safari Bookshelf is an electronic reference library that lets you easily search thousands of technical books, find code samples, download chapters, and access technical information whenever and wherever you need it.

TO GAIN 45-DAY SAFARI ENABLED ACCESS TO THIS BOOK:

- Go to **http://www.quepublishing.com/safarienabled**
- Complete the brief registration form
- Enter the coupon code found in the front of this book on the "Copyright" page

If you have difficulty registering on Safari Bookshelf or accessing the online edition, please e-mail customer-service@safaribooksonline.com.

NATIONAL BESTSELLER
MORE THAN 2 MILLION COPIES SOLD

HOW IT WORKS

The How It Works series offers a unique, visual, four-color approach designed to educate curious readers. From machine code to hard-drive design to wireless communication, the How It Works series offers a clear and concise approach to understanding technology—a perfect source for those who prefer to learn visually. Check out other books in this best-selling series by Que:

How Computers Work, Eighth Edition
ISBN: 0-7897-3424-9

How Computers Work, Eighth Edition offers a unique and detailed look at the inner workings of your computer. From keyboards to virtual reality helmets, this book covers it all.

How the Internet Works, Eighth Edition
ISBN: 0-7897-3626-8

How the Internet Works, Eighth Edition clearly explains how the Internet works and gives you behind-the-scenes information. Find out what actually happens when you send an email or purchase goods over the Web.

How Networks Work, Seventh Edition
ISBN: 0-7897-3232-7

How Networks Work, Sixth Edition visually demonstrates how the components of a network function together. With this book, you will learn how an electric signal is transmitted, how firewalls block unwanted traffic, and how everything in between works.

How Home Theater and HDTV Work
ISBN: 0-7897-3445-1

How Home Theater and HDTV Work digs deep into all aspects of high-definition television and home theater systems. It takes the same illustrative approach of the best-selling *How Computers Work* and *How the Internet Works* to explain today's hottest consumer electronics technologies.

www.quepublishing.com